Life Improvement Guides®

Money Savvy

How to Live Rich on Any Income

Edited by Stephen C. George,
Senior Editor, Men's Health Books

Reviewed by Malcolm A. Makin, a certified financial planner and president of Professional Planning Group, a financial planning and registered investment advisory firm located in Westerly, Rhode Island

Rodale Press, Inc.
Emmaus, Pennsylvania

Notice

The information contained in this book is based upon information obtained from contributors, interviews, and a wide range of authoritative sources. It is intended for use as an approach to dealing with the day-to-day decisions we all make regarding the wise use of our money. It is not in any way intended for investment purposes, nor as a substitute for advice from legal, financial, or other professionals. Rodale Press, Inc., assumes no responsibility for any injuries suffered or damages or losses incurred as a result of following this information.

Printed in the United States of America on acid-free ∞, recycled paper ♻

Other titles in the *Men's Health Life Improvement Guides* series:

Command Respect	*Food Smart*	*Powerfully Fit*	*Stronger Faster*
Death Defiers	*Good Loving*	*Sex Secrets*	*Symptom Solver*
Fight Fat	*Maximum Style*	*Stress Blasters*	*Vitamin Vitality*

Library of Congress Cataloging-in-Publication Data

Money savvy : how to live rich on any income / edited by Stephen C. George.
p. cm. — (Men's health life improvement guides)
Includes index.
ISBN 0–87596–505–9 paperback
1. Finance, Personal. I. George, Stephen C. II. Series.
HG179.M5969 1998
332.024—dc21 98–28020

Distributed to the book trade by St. Martin's Press

2 4 6 8 10 9 7 5 3 1 paperback

OUR PURPOSE

"We inspire and enable people to improve their lives and the world around them."

Money Savvy Staff

Editor: **Neil Wertheimer**

Managing Editor: **Jack Croft**

Senior Editor: **Stephen C. George**

Writers: **Ronald Campbell, Don Crinklaw, Thomas M. Kostigen, Terry McManus, Barbara Tannenbaum**

Contributing Writers: **Jennifer A. Barefoot, Bridget Doherty, Doug Hill, Brian Paul Kaufman, Mary Kittel, Deanna Moyer, Lorna S. Sapp**

Associate Research Manager: **Jane Unger Hahn**

Lead Researcher: **Lorna S. Sapp**

Editorial Researchers: **Jennifer Fiske, Paula Rasich**

Copy Editor: **Kathryn A. Cressman**

Associate Art Director: **Charles Beasley**

Cover Designer and Series Art Director: **Tanja Lipinski-Cole**

Series Designer: **John Herr**

Cover Photographer: **Mitch Mandel**

Part Opener Illustrator: **Bryon Thompson**

Chapter Opener Illustrator: **Alan Baseden**

Layout Artist: **Donna G. Rossi**

Manufacturing Coordinator: **Melinda B. Rizzo**

Office Manager: **Roberta Mulliner**

Office Staff: **Julie Kehs, Mary Lou Stephen**

Rodale Health and Fitness Books

Vice President and Editorial Director: **Debora T. Yost**

Executive Editor: **Neil Wertheimer**

Design and Production Director: **Michael Ward**

Marketing Manager: **Sharon Lawler-Sudell**

Research Manager: **Ann Gossy Yermish**

Copy Manager: **Lisa D. Andruscavage**

Production Manager: **Robert V. Anderson Jr.**

Associate Studio Manager: **Thomas P. Aczel**

Manufacturing Manager: **Mark Krahforst**

Photo Credits

Page 148: **James Rudnick**

Page 150: **Courtesy of Nick Lowery**

Page 152: **Marko Shark/Corbis-Bettmann**

Page 154: **Courtesy of Tribune Media Services**

Back flap: **Alex Gotfryd-Peter C. Jones/Corbis-Bettmann**

Contents

Introduction vi

Part One
The Money Mindset

Mastering Your Money 2
The Necessary Tools 5
Getting Organized 8
Using Your Computer 10
Your Money Habits 14
Measuring Your Worth 18
Setting Financial Goals 22
Setting Up a Budget 24
Choosing Allies 28

Part Two
Tactics for Daily Living

Electronic Banking 34
Financial Institutions 36
Credit Cards 38
Bill Paying 42
Wallet Strategies 46
Tightwad Strategies 48
Shopping 54
Sales Tax 58
Negotiating 60

Part Three
Tactics for Smart Investing

Safety Net 64
Balance 68
Timing 72
Choices 74
Reading Prospectuses 80
Buying Investments 82
Keeping Up 84

Part Four
The Big-Ticket Issues

Income Taxes 88
Mortgages 92
Home Ownership 96
Property Insurance 100
Health Insurance 105
Life Insurance 110
College Planning 112
Car Buying 116
Mounting Debt 121
Bankruptcy 124

Part Five
Retirement Planning

Strategies 128
Social Security 130
Pension Plans 132
Making the Most of Your 401(k) 136
Individual Retirement Accounts 141
Withdrawals 144

Part Six
Real-Life Scenarios

Quest for the Best

Andrew Tobias, Financial Expert and Best-Selling Author 148

Nick Lowery, Veteran NFL Kicker 150

Ron Popeil, Entrepreneur and TV Pitchman 152

Humberto Cruz, Nationally Syndicated Financial Columnist 154

You Can Do It!

Progressive Parsimony Brad Lemley, Topsham, Maine 156

It's Never Too Late to Save Gordon M. Bennett, Long Beach, California 158

Financial Fixer-Upper John Shmilenko, Portland, Oregon 160

Building with Trust Peter Simon, Chilmark, Massachusetts 162

Credits 164

Index 165

Introduction

Make Yourself Comfortable

Right about now, you're probably wondering, "What the heck is *Men's Health* doing publishing a financial advice book?" Maybe you thought we changed our name to *Men's Wealth* when you weren't looking. After all, what's money got to do with a guy's fitness level? Who ever gave us the idea that a man's financial situation had any bearing on his health and well-being?

Why, you did.

Every now and then we like to check in with our readers, find out what's going on in their lives, learn what they're interested in, see what keeps them up at night. In focus groups and surveys that we conduct across the country, the message comes through loud and clear: You're worried about money. You want to make more of it, sure (who doesn't?). But more than that, you want to make the most of what you have. You want to know that your family is set if anything happens to you; that your kids won't have to worry about where the college money is coming from; that you'll be able to retire when you want, secure in the knowledge that a cushy nest egg is just waiting for you to turn 59½. You don't have to be rich; you just want to be comfortable.

In our estimation, that makes money a mighty big worry and a major cause of stress. And that kind of stress can't be good for your health. That's where we come in. When it comes to gathering advice that's going to help you enjoy a healthy, worry-free life, no one does it better than *Men's Health*. Whether we're talking about workout strategies or investment strategies, our mission is the same: to give you the best, no-nonsense advice from the top experts in the field. To give you the tools you need to enrich your life, physically and fiscally. To make you more comfortable.

That's exactly what you'll find in *Money Savvy*. If you want to disaster-proof your retirement, you'll learn how here. If you want to learn the investment basics that will have you buying and selling like a pro, we have the plan for you. If you've had your eye on the newest digital whatsit, we'll tell you not only how to save for it but also how to negotiate for the best price on it. We'll even tell you how to make sure that you'll never be stuck penniless on some forlorn roadside. The smart-money secrets packed in this volume represent the distillation of wisdom from dozens of business and personal-finance experts. And you won't need an M.B.A. to figure this stuff out, we promise. The men and women who gathered this information for you have many dozens of years of full-time business writing and editing experience. They know how to cut through the mumbo jumbo and get at the useful information you need to make the most of your hard-earned dough.

We can't guarantee that you'll become a millionaire overnight, but we can make this promise: When you're finished reading this book, you will come away believing—knowing—that you can master your money and that you'll always be able to live comfortably.

If that's not a healthy attitude, I don't know what is.

Stephen C. George
Senior Editor

Part One

The Money Mindset

Mastering Your Money

You Can Get There from Here

In old Westerns, masked desperadoes terrorized their victims with the words "Your money or your life!" These days, it's hard to tell the two apart. Whether it's money or life, we'd like it to last forever. We always want to have more of it. But as often as not, we have a vague uneasiness that someday, when we let down our guards, our money will fail us, or worse, we will fail our money.

Welcome to the club.

The fact is that almost all of us worry about money, whether we are rich, poor, or part of what former Labor Secretary Robert Reich dubbed "the anxious middle class." Even people within striking distance of the "Forbes 400" list of the wealthiest Americans sometimes wake up in a cold sweat, worrying about money.

Sound improbable? James D. Schwartz, a retired fee-only financial planner in Englewood, Colorado, and author of *Enough: A Guide to Reclaiming Your Financial Dream,* would beg to differ. He made his money advising well-heeled clients, and even the richest of them worried about losing what money they had.

Even financial planners have blind spots when it comes to their own money, says Rennie Gabriel, a certified financial planner in Encino, California, and president of the Financial Coach consulting firm. "We're in the same boat as the rest of the population," he says. Case in point: One of his clients was a fellow financial planner who was bringing home $130,000 a year—and spending $150,000. "This has occurred time and time again," Gabriel says. "I've had several certified public accountants file for bankruptcy."

Making Up Your Mindset

This anxiety about finances is not a healthy state of affairs, for many reasons. We won't give you the "money doesn't buy happiness" rap. What role money plays in your life, well, that's up to you.

It's this worrying that's bothersome. You see, a man only worries about things he can't control. Which brings us to a couple of simple but crucial points.

1. Managing money is far easier than you think.
2. Once you start doing it, you will probably enjoy it.
3. Once you start enjoying it, you are much more likely to achieve your goals.

To be money savvy, you don't have to buy into any Wall Street hype, and you don't need a master's degree in business administration (nor need you hire someone who has one). All you need are simple items: a middle-school–level knowledge of arithmetic, basic literacy skills, and a little bit of time. Beyond that, you'll need a money-friendly attitude. There are three components to such a mindset.

A financial plan. No matter how much money you make, without a solid money plan you won't live as well as you could. That requires tapping the huge pipeline of financial information—everything from your checkbook register to stock tips and insurance quotes—and taking just what you need to build a better life for yourself. Trust us, planning pays.

A February 1997 poll commissioned by NationsBank and the Consumer Federation of America found that planners were far more confident than nonplanners that they had made the right financial choices. They also felt more comfortable about money and more in control of their financial situations. Planners save dramatically more than nonplanners, according to the survey. Remarkably, this is true at every income level.

Having a plan is more important than being financially sophisticated. Many nonplanners correctly answered the pollsters' questions about financial basics, such as the type of investment with the best long-term yield and highest risk (stocks), the cost of a four-year education at a state college ($30,000), and the minimum percentage of annual income they should set aside for retirement (10 percent). But knowing these things didn't mean people acted on them. "Having a comprehensive plan," the survey concluded, "is more important than having a good grasp of basic savings and investment concepts."

Awareness. With the proper awareness, you can banish needless worries, and you can focus your attention on the real problems in your financial life.

But there's a stumbling block. Talk with financial planners, and most will tell you that the institutions that should be spreading financial know-how—the family, the schools, the media—are doing a lousy job. Sure, financial information is available in overwhelming amounts. But financial awareness—the knowledge of how to use information wisely—is scarce.

Gabriel has talked with thousands of people about financial awareness. One-tenth of them learned it from their parents or school. Another tenth picked it up on their own. "Eight out of 10 didn't get the information, didn't seek it out, and don't have it," he says. Don't be one of those eight.

Personal values. Managing your finances is like constructing a home. The walls and roof, the stuff everyone can see, are your financial plan. Underneath, holding things in place like the frame, is the financial awareness you've created. And below that, forming the foundation for everything, are your personal values.

Don't discount the value of values in forming the proper money mindset. When making your financial goals, observes Delia Fernandez, a fee-only personal financial planner in Los Alamitos, California, "you add in the numbers after the real groundwork has been done, and the real groundwork is figuring out who you are and what you want to be in life."

Don't confuse the emphasis on personal values with a feel-good approach; understanding your values before you make financial plans is an exercise in hard-core realism. Fernandez says that if she tries to write a financial plan without first identifying her client's values, she's "just running numbers for people who won't implement the plan."

Mind over Money

It's all well and good to identify these three components, but how do you put them together so you can pull off that early retirement or buy the sports car or never have to worry about money again? It can take some time—a lifetime, in fact—but there are things you can do today, right now, to get you on the right track and to solidify the mindset that will have you worrying less about your money and enjoying more of your life. Here's how.

Make an inventory. To build the foundation of a mindset you can live with, ask some basic questions of yourself. For example, "Do you value security or the thrill of the hunt?" asks Judith Lau, a certified financial planner; president of Lau and Associates, a financial consulting firm in Wilmington, Delaware; and chairperson of the Institute of Certified Financial Planners, based in Denver. How important are material comforts, career advancement, family time, and leisure activities? Do you like to be part of a team or do you prize independence? These questions all get at the central issue—who you really are—and they all carry big financial implications.

Write a mission statement. Make your personal version of the corporate craze that has launched a thousand *Dilbert* cartoons. Corporate statements are often wordy, airy documents, written by committee. Yours, by contrast, should be simple and straightforward. Focus on what you really want, not the means for getting there. Look beyond purely economic issues to the things you treasure. Early retirement is a means; volunteering full-time for your church or satisfying your lifelong wanderlust is an end. Owning a business is a means; flourishing on your own is an end. A financial planner cannot write your mission statement for the same reason that he can't live your life. "You have to take control," Schwartz says, and "make your own mission statement."

Define your goals clearly. With your values in mind, it's time to write financial goals that express those values. Don't settle for catchphrases. Financial independence may rank high on your list, but you need to describe what that means to you: enough money to quit your job and travel, or something more basic? "If financial independence means never living in your kid's back bedroom," Lau says, "that's more important than just getting more money."

Hope for the best. Goal-setting should be an optimistic exercise. This isn't the time to say that a particular goal is impossible. "I try to get the client to envision the best case of what they want in their lives," Fernandez says. Maybe you want to retire to a condo in Florida or buy a vacation house in the mountains three years form now or earn enough money that your wife can be a stay-at-home mom. "You can have anything you want in the world," Fernandez says. "You just can't have everything."

Tie your goals to specific steps. "You can write down 'save enough money for retirement,' and it doesn't really matter," Lau says. You could tell yourself that's your goal, but then turn around and blow $500 in a single Saturday night. Good intentions aren't good enough. In order to achieve your goals, you need to put your money where your mouth is. That may mean staying at home and renting a video most weekends instead of going to dinner and a movie, or putting the maximum allowable percentage of your pay in your 401(k). If you are not prepared to accept that a goal carries a financial cost, perhaps a significant cost, that goal doesn't belong on your list.

Make choices between goals. So you want to save enough money to start your own business in two years, and you want to take a family vacation to Italy this summer, and you want to buy a big new home. You have to choose. "Smart people suffer over choice," Schwartz says. "You have to have focus."

Recognize conflicts among your goals. Even after you have whittled down your list of goals to the handful that are most important, conflicts still are likely. You may want to retire early and to send your kids to college. It might be possible to do both, but it could require you to tighten your belt in other areas. Spotting the conflict early will help you plan effectively.

Pick meaningful goals. For most of us, owning a shiny red convertible is a nice dream. But it isn't a goal that would motivate most of us to take bologna sandwiches to work every day, put in lots of overtime, and return home to repair our sinks and mow our lawns ourselves. The more important a goal is to you, the more likely you will make achieving it a high priority. Accumulating more for its own sake is a losing game. Goal-setting is not about acquiring more of everything. It is about acquiring enough to satisfy your needs while honoring your values.

The Necessary Tools

Your Arsenal for Accounting

The art of personal finance is like cooking. For every weekend chef with a kitchen full of cooking gadgets, there is someone who makes great meals with nothing more than a few simple utensils and a lot of determination. When it comes to managing money, you could have a computer with all the latest math coprocessors and accounting software, a calculator with 500 buttons, a stack of impressive ledgers, a shelf of accounting-made-easy books, and a little green visor to wear on your head. Or you can be a credit to the human race and use simple, frugal, easy tools to manage your cash.

Tool Time

If you're determined, you can manage your money well with tools readily at hand and easy to understand. "A calculator is good enough," says Rennie Gabriel, president of the Financial Coach consulting firm. "A piece of paper is good enough." The important thing, he and other experts say, is to use tools and resources that you understand and that are comfortable for you. Buy something that you don't quite understand or need, and what you've purchased is not a helpful tool, but an obstacle you'll have to wrestle with every time you sit down to get your affairs in order—or an excuse to put it off that much longer.

Here, we'll look at some of the tools, accessories, and informational resources that experts suggest using if you want to keep a good accounting of yourself.

A Designated Space

One of the most important tools in your personal finance kit is a place to watch your money. "You can put everything you need on a month-to-month basis in a pretty small space," says Laura Tarbox, a certified financial planner and president of Tarbox Equity in Newport Beach, California. But you do need that space.

Consciously set aside a location for managing your finances. It doesn't have to be an office with a desk and personal computer, although that's the ideal. In a pinch, a kitchen table will do. But if you use the kitchen table, Ron Hulnick, Ph.D., and Mary Hulnick, Ph.D., authors of *Financial Freedom in Eight Minutes a Day*, suggest keeping all your equipment in a cardboard storage box close by so that you can pack and unpack your tools as needed.

A calculator: While a basic calculator will certainly serve you in good stead, the Hulnicks recommend getting a calculator that can print—that way you'll have a paper record showing all your calculations.

If you want to get really serious about it, a programmable calculator can be a valuable pocket tool for keeping tabs on your money, says Tarbox. These handheld computers, which can run from $75 to $200, have built-in business and statistical functions that can amortize (calculate monthly loan payments), do interest conversions, calculate depreciation, and countless other functions for which you thought you'd need a certified public accountant. But beware: If you aren't a math whiz, the learning curve could be steep. Go to your local office superstore and test-drive one before you buy it.

A computer: If you have a home computer, don't just use it to surf the supermodel Web sites or keep the kids entertained—put it to work as a powerful money-management tool. As it is, most computers on the market are already sold with preloaded management tools and record-keeping functions. For more details about making the most of your computer as a money-management tool, see Using Your Computer on page 10.

Amortization and inflation tables: Available in library reference sections, these tables can help pencil-and-paper planners anticipate the push-pull effects of interest and inflation. For example, the tables will tell you that $1,000 invested today at 5 percent interest will be worth $2,527 in 20 years; but if inflation runs at a modest 2 percent annually, that $2,527 will be worth only $1,721.

Office supplies: You'll need some basic desktop staples to do your work. The need for most of these items will be obvious, and we'll tell you when to use them in the next chapter, Getting Organized, which begins on page 8. The experts recommend having the following on hand.

Words to Live By

Dozens of magazines and other publications can help keep you up to speed on financial issues. Here are some of the biggest and best.

- ***Barron's National Business and Financial Weekly*: Dow Jones and Company's weekly publication focuses more on the issues affecting the nation's financial community. Each week's installment highlights particular stocks of interest and identifies and examines trends in the market. A must-read for the serious investor.**

- ***Consumer Reports*: Published by the nonprofit Consumers Union of U.S., this monthly does unbiased reviews and tests of every product from toasters to sport utility vehicles, plus pricey services such as life insurance.**

- ***Forbes*: A brash and breezy read—just what you'd expect in a magazine that calls itself a capitalist tool. Besides its bread-and-butter corporate and investment coverage, *Forbes* covers the pleasures money buys with real verve. Published biweekly by Forbes Publishing.**

- ***Fortune*: Personal finance is a sideline in this Time Incorporated Ventures financial magazine. This is the one to pick if, in addition to coverage of investments, you want thoughtful, thorough reporting about the big issues in business. *Fortune* is published every two weeks.**

- ***Inc.*: It may seem an odd choice for a list of personal finance magazines, but the publication is filled with financial advice for would-be entrepreneurs. The Goldhirsh Group publishes this periodical 18 times a year.**

- Blue pen (ink is much more visible when you have to make copies, and blue ink can help distinguish an original from a copy)
- Basic office supplies (envelopes, eraser, pencils, rubber bands, stamps, stapler and staples, and wastebasket)
- Color-coded files (for storing different types of bills or records)
- Tray for bills to be paid
- Tray for outgoing mail
- 12 file folders or a 12-month divided accordion file (for storing the current year's bills and expenses)
- 12-month calendar, preferably one that you can hang on your wall right over your desk
- 2 filing cabinets/storage boxes

Your Touch-Tone Tool

With the aid of a Touch-Tone phone and the rise of automated telephone systems, you

• *Kiplinger's Personal Finance Magazine*: **Published by the Kiplinger Washington Editors, this monthly magazine is the most sober of the bunch. No celebrities here but plenty of detailed financial advice for people with a variety of goals.**

• *Money*: **Published monthly, *Money* is filled with a mix of stories about real people plus opposing viewpoints from financial gurus. *Money* is to personal finance what *People Weekly* is to current events—no surprise since both are published by mighty Time Incorporated Ventures.**

• *SmartMoney*: **The *Wall Street Journal*'s personal finance monthly is published by Hearst Magazines Corporation. It features financial profiles of B-list celebrities but otherwise takes a down-to-earth tone. For example, after publishing model stock and bond portfolios, it routinely updates readers on how well those portfolios are doing.**

• *The Wall Street Journal*: **The nation's most-respected financial newspaper and among the world's best papers of any kind. Famous for its well-written coverage of business, the financial markets, and personal finance, it's published Mondays through Fridays by Dow Jones and Company.**

• *Worth*: **Published by Capital Publishing 10 times a year, this magazine offers well-written articles for investors and those concerned about their own financial well-being. One feature is a list of the "Best Financial Advisors" in America, which can assist consumers in identifying what to look for and look out for when seeking professional help.**

can push-button your way to better money management, without ever leaving the comfort of your armchair. "The phone is probably the most convenient tool that the American consumer has," says Don Owen, senior vice president of Bank of America's California call center, based in Glendale. "You can literally be in your car, you can be at work, whatever, and you can access information about your account. There's almost nothing that you can't do over the phone," he says. Except maybe cash a check.

With each call you have to punch in your account number, an identification code such as your Social Security number, and several numbered instructions. Keep those in a secure place, and always have a blank paper handy to record the confirmation numbers of your transactions.

Here are just some of the ways that you can make the best use of that handset to handle your finances.

Manage bank and investment accounts. Most big banks, mutual funds, and brokerage firms will let you check your account balances and shift money between accounts by phone. This is the most basic form of money-by-phone management, and it's worth taking a couple minutes some night to learn how your bank's system works. Is this safe? "Absolutely," says Owen. In fact, automated systems may be even more safe and efficient than a human bank teller, who is prone to the same mistakes we all make.

Caution: Talk isn't always cheap. Some banks have begun billing their customers for routine phone inquiries. Ask about fees before you proceed.

Pay bills. Most large banks and many smaller ones offer this service. Prices vary widely, but you can expect to save a bundle on postage. You call the bank, enter your account number, a number to identify the bill you wish to pay (for example, the "1" button for your mortgage or the "2" button for your car loan), and the payment amounts.

Buy insurance and stocks. Banks and discount brokerages such as Charles Schwab and Company have seized on the telephone as the great equalizer in their attempt to take business from traditional insurance companies and brokerages. But you have to be willing to take charge. Remember that you are buying sophisticated financial products without the aid of an informed professional. You're on your own.

Getting Organized

Bedrock for Your Bucks

Big businesses call it "process engineering." For the business of running your family, you can just call it "the way I do stuff." It's your routine, your day-to-day method for managing your finances. The goal is simple: to be sufficiently organized that you can find information immediately and make decisions quickly.

Setting Yourself Up

Before you can get organized financially, you have to get organized physically. Of course, you'll want to organize according to the space you've allotted for yourself, but as a general blueprint, here's how experts suggest setting up your home office.

On your desk: Your computer or calculator live here, along with a pad of scratch paper and a pencil cup holding assorted pencils and blue pens. Have a phone here, too, so you can check bank balances and do telephone transactions if needed. Make sure this phone has a speakerphone feature so you won't have to kill your neck cradling the handset between your head and shoulder while you write. Keep your notebook here with all of the numbers that you usually call to perform transactions. Have a stackable set of in-out boxes for mail and other current papers. On the wall above the desk, hang a plastic rack for current bills and your 12-month calendar so you can see important dates at a glance.

In the desk: Stow all your other office supplies where they'll be close at hand. Keep a roll of stamps on hand, as well as your preprinted name and address stickers for the return-address spot on envelopes.

Near the desk: You need two receptacles close by: a filing cabinet for storing all ongoing financial matters, such as mortgage-payment receipts, bills, investment records, and the proverbial "circular filing cabinet" where you will store your refuse until you haul it to the curb.

Not far away: In a closet, you need a second filing cabinet. This one contains long-term, nondaily papers: old taxes, owner's manuals to everything you buy, home/auto-purchase documents. Off-site (read: at your bank), it's a good idea to have a safety deposit box that holds crucial pieces of paper for you and your family: your home's first trust deed, titles to your cars, birth certificates, passports—anything that you deem irreplaceable or awfully hard to duplicate.

The Paper Chase

As you go along, you'll accumulate a lot of paper: old bills, account statements, insurance policies, and warranties. Don't let it all ferment in a pile, says Cyndi Torres, a professional organizer with Streamline Organizing Company in Pomona, California.

Sort the real mail. Sort those incoming envelopes into four piles. The categories are "to pay," "to read," "to do," and "to file."

Take special care of that "to pay" stack. Torres says to set aside bills in that plastic rack on the wall. If you prefer, it can be an accordion file or a tray you've set aside just for bills. The key here is to stow them regularly in a prominent place.

Junk the junk mail. If it's something that you don't have the least bit of interest in, don't put it on your "to-do" pile.

If it didn't grab your attention in the first 30 seconds of being in the house, it's likely not something you want or need. "Dump it in a trash can or recycling bin," Torres says.

Toss recent mutual fund statements. You only need to keep the end-of-year statement for last year and the most recent statement for this year. Everything else is just taking up space, says Laura Tarbox, president of Tarbox Equity in Newport Beach, California.

Purge most records every year. After you pay your taxes is a good time to do a little spring cleaning of your papers. With the special exceptions of tax records and unexpired warranties, older documents are just taking up space.

Keep your tax records . . . forever. An important, perhaps obvious note that does bear repeating: don't throw out your tax records. The Internal Revenue Service only looks back three years for unpaid taxes. Unless, of course, it thinks you committed fraud, in which case it can go back as long as it wants. Paranoia is the best policy, says Tarbox.

Keep auto repair records. If you plan to sell your car, keep service and repair records for it, says Delia Fernandez, a fee-only personal financial planner in Los Alamitos, California. Sure, you've babied that car. You can show prospective buyers all the receipts for all that preventive maintenance you've done.

Keep a year's worth of utility bills. If you ever plan to sell your home, this documentation can come in handy for prospective buyers, Fernandez says. It will help answer their questions about the cost of heating and lighting your palace. Keep this in your second file drawer, too.

Keep records of securities. For whatever you've purchased, keep a paper trail showing how much you paid. This will establish for tax purposes how much you made or lost on a given investment, says Tarbox.

Keep your will where family will find it. Yes, we know. You plan to die at age 100, surrounded by your great-grandchildren. But if you get hit by a bus while reading this book, will your relatives know where to find your will and funeral plans? Put them someplace where your family will think to look, says Fernandez.

Never Forget a Bill Again

Here are three approaches—high-tech, low-tech, and middle of the road—to ensure you never miss a bill. Pick the approach that suits you.

High-tech: Bill scheduling. **One of the simplest and most useful features of financial software such as Quicken and Microsoft Money is a built-in calendar. Record dates, payees, and amounts owed, and the software will prompt you to pay your bills. But remember: This system works only if you diligently record bills as they arrive, points out personal financial planner Delia Fernandez.**

Middle ground: The accordion file. **Any size will do, even the little coupon-sized files. Label one pocket "Due 1st–10th," another "Due 11th–20th," and a third "Due 21st–31st." Label other pockets "Next month," "Two months," "Three months," and so forth. As bills arrive, put them in the appropriate pockets, suggests Cyndi Torres of Streamline Organizing Company.**

Low-tech: Mark the calendar, label the envelopes. **As each bill arrives, open it, throw away the "special offers" and notices, write the date and amount due on the outer envelope, and stuff the contents back inside. Keep the bills in one place, advises Laura Tarbox of Tarbox Equity. Or simply go through your 12-month calendar and mark the dates that your bills are due. Hey, who needs a computer?**

Using Your Computer

Digital Dollar Dealing

Since the beginning of the digital age, personal computers and personal finance have gone hand in hand, or mouse in hand, as the case may be. After all, the very first software that took personal computers from garages into offices two decades ago was a spreadsheet program. Today, thanks to a generation of technological innovation, you can do a lot more than just record your assets and liabilities. With the advent of personal finance software and interactive online services, you can run a sophisticated financial empire—pay bills, shop for the best prices and products, make investments, track performance, and much more—through the computer sitting on the desk in your home office.

So what's stopping you? Usually, it's two different types of fear. First is fear that these programs or online services are complicated, over your head, or more effort than they're worth. Well, forget that. With each day that goes by, these programs and services get easier. They use conversational language, simple step-by-step procedures, and a certain delight factor to keep you engaged. As for speed, we guarantee that you can't get useful information or conduct a transaction any faster than through your computer, whether it's finding a price for that camera you've been eyeing or shifting money between two mutual funds.

Second is your concern about security. It seems inevitable to worry about hackers and computer criminals when you think about moving your money around online. It's a natural enough fear, but a largely unfounded one. Fact is, your bank transactions are probably safer, and certainly more private, online than they ever were in line at a bank teller or an automated teller machine (ATM). Virtually every online bank encrypts transactions using a long string of numbers as the key. This method is so hard to break that bankers and the computer industry had to fight government code-breakers for the right to use it. It's a lot safer than putting something on paper where five or six people may see it, says Jim Shelton, executive director of the Online Banking Association, based in Corte Madera, California.

Virtual Reality

Personal financial software, which often comes preloaded on the computers you can buy today, takes a lot of the drudgery out of money management. This software—the two most popular programs are Quicken and Microsoft Money—keeps your checkbook, balances it without asking you to do the math, monitors your budget, and tracks your progress toward long-term goals such as building a retirement nest egg. Specialized programs can help you do your taxes, handle legal concerns like your will, or make financial investments.

But no matter how much you might use it, remember that a computer is just a tool, not an organizational cure-all. It can't write your budget or hold you to it. Only you can do that. "The computer is not relevant to the habit of managing money properly," says Rennie Gabriel, president of the Financial Coach consulting firm. "It doesn't change anything unless there's a corresponding change of attitude."

That said, the computer itself can change your attitude about managing money. Once people become computer-literate, many find that it's actually fun to manage their finances on the computer, according to Malcolm A. Makin, a certified financial planner and president of Professional Planning Group in Westerly, Rhode Island.

If you have a computer or are thinking of buying one in the near future, we think it's worth investing a little time to make the attitude change that will allow you to use that computer to make your money planning easier. All you need to do is remember a few basics.

Play around. When you first sit down at the keyboard, don't try to chart the financial course of the rest of your life. Your goal for the first couple sessions at the computer is simply to noodle with the equipment and get a feel for how it works. Don't worry, you're not going to break anything. Before you run that financial software package, check for a tutorial program and run that—it'll tell you so much you need to know, you probably won't even have to open the instruction book. The goal is to get comfortable with this new form of money management so when it comes time to start tracking things electronically, you'll be a pro.

Focus on one function. With today's software packages, it's a given that your financial software will have about 12 more features or functions than you're ever going to use in this lifetime. While it's nice to think you're getting a lot of byte for your buck, don't be overwhelmed by the idea that you have to master all these whiz-bang features to get your money's worth out of the program. Sure, it's cool to learn how to make pie charts denoting all your expenses, or to teach the software to play a trumpet fanfare every time a bill is due, but try to stay focused on learning one main function at a time. For starters, just

Software Size-Up: Quicken versus Money

If you're looking for a bank, a mutual fund, or a financial planner, you have thousands of choices. If you're looking for checkbook and bill-paying software to organize your finances, as far as the experts are concerned, you have just two choices: Quicken by Intuit and Microsoft Money by Microsoft.

The two products have a great deal in common, including price. An upgrade to the latest version of each sells for around $35, including manufacturer's rebate. New users pay around $55 for Microsoft Money and roughly $60 for Quicken. Each product will keep and balance your checkbook, print checks, and pay bills electronically while tracking your investments, taxes, credit cards, and budget. Each also will link you with up-to-date financial information on the World Wide Web.

Don't be deceived by claims that one product or the other has far more or far better features. Intuit and Microsoft constantly add features to match or beat the other. The competition helps explain the sheer bulk of each program: 20 megabytes for the most basic features.

There's one important difference between the two products. Quicken and Money each taps its own Web site. While both sites provide stock quotes and news, each has a distinct look and feel as well as some unique content. To decide which one is best for you, check out both Web sites before you buy the software.

learn to use it as a digital checkbook. Once you've spent a few weeks mastering that, then move on to the other features. Try to learn everything about your computer software at once, and you'll more likely get frustrated and give up.

Back up. Need we remind you about Murphy's Law? Computers break. Fires, thieves, and small children with open soda cans all threaten your computer and the financial records inside it. Protect yourself. Copy your financial data to a diskette frequently—once a week or even daily—and keep that copy in a safe place, away from the computer and errant soda cans. Better yet, get in the habit of backing up every time you write a check or input data.

Beyond ATMs: Online Banking

Online banking offers the ultimate convenience: a virtual banker in every home. Since 1997, when the online boom began in earnest, hundreds of banks nationwide have been handling transactions online.

For example, you can set it up for your bank to automatically send your mortgage company a payment on the twenty-fifth of every month, or to pay your monthly utility bills, taking the money from a specified account. No stamps, no handwritten checks, no fuss or thought. Or, if the checking account is running a bit low, you can transfer money over from your savings account by dialing into the bank's computers, at any time, without another human ever getting involved.

Eventually, all banks will provide that service, says Shelton. "Our theory is, get online or get left behind." Make sure that when online banking arrives in your home, it comes on your terms.

Shop around first. Fees for online banking are "just all over the board," Shelton says. That shouldn't be a surprise. Fees for traditional bank services vary widely too. A July 1997 survey by the U.S. Public Interest Research Group found that big banks charged customers an average of $218 annually for regular checking accounts, more than double the $108 charged by credit unions. Consumer groups haven't looked closely at online banking fees yet. But you can research them yourself on each bank's Web site. If your bank's online fees are too high, see if they'll negotiate. It never hurts to ask.

Take advantage of free trials. Some banks such as San Francisco-based Wells Fargo and Company, an online pioneer, let their online customers check account balances, review statements, and transfer money between accounts for free. Gee, sounds just like ATMs a few years ago, before banks started drubbing you with $1 or $2 transaction fees. "Things that are free now may not be free in the future," says Gail Hillebrand, senior attorney for the West Coast regional office of Consumers Union of U.S., based in San Francisco.

Before you sign up for free online banking, ask the bank if or when they plan to charge a fee. Make a note of the date on your calendar. Then enjoy the free test drive. As you get closer to the date it stops being free, decide whether you use the service enough to justify paying for it. If you're not getting all you thought you would from the service, you can always cancel before you start paying.

Research Your Investments

The World Wide Web is the new frontier for investors. A lucky few have reaped fortunes from Web-based companies such as Yahoo! and Netscape by investing in their stock when it first became available on the market. But for most investors, the real payoff is information. While the Web is a mercurial beast, with information and addresses changing every day, there are some reliable resources you'll be able to use. Here's what our experts suggest—some driver's ed tips for the information superhighway.

Start your engine. When you use the Internet, get to know how to use the search engines available on the Web. Just hit the "Search" button inevitably found at the top of any Web browser's menu. From there, you can type in terms and names you'll want to research (including the terms and names you'll see mentioned throughout this book).

Educate yourself about investments. If you subscribe to online services like CompuServe or America Online, you'll discover an amazing wealth of investment information that is continually being upgraded, plus links to many of the best financial Web sites. A good example: Morningstar, the Siskel and Ebert of the mutual-fund world, uses a five-star rating system to rank the world's funds and provides detailed evaluations of each and every one. Snippets from its reviews are available on the Morningstar Web site, along with the star ratings and lots of articles and background. The Motley Fool Web site preaches that you are the best person to manage your money, provided that you do the homework. You can start that homework right here.

Go to the source. Any major investment provider likely has a Web site of its own. Have you heard some good things about a particular mutual fund at Fat Cat Investments? Go to Fat Cat's Web site to read all about it, even order a prospectus. (Hint: Then go to the Morningstar site for some independent analysis.)

Conduct transactions. Some discount brokerage houses, like Charles Schwab and Company, let you do your stock, bond, and mutual fund trading right online. Be sure to check fees, but generally, they are relatively cheap and give you the power to adjust your portfolio at any time without having to go through a live broker.

Research companies. The mother lode of information for serious investors is EDGAR. Short for Electronic Data Gathering Analysis and Retrieval, EDGAR is an online database created by the U.S. Securities and Exchange Commission (SEC). After a phase-in period ending in May 1996, some 10,000 public companies have been filing SEC-required reports electronically, according to Rick Heroux, EDGAR administrator. On an average day, the SEC site (http://www.sec.gov) gets 500,000 visitors, "and it just seems to keep growing," says Heroux. EDGAR can give you a lot of information that somehow never makes it into public companies' cheery annual reports. Among the most important: management's view of the business and key competitors, quarterly financial results, and major changes that could help or hurt the stock.

Subscribe to a service. Several online companies sell "value-added" services to make EDGAR easier to use. Examples include "watch lists" (which alert you via e-mail when a particular company files an SEC report), indexed EDGAR reports (letting you instantly find the few pages you need in a massive report), and analytics (which compare EDGAR filings for competitors).

Check out your broker. If you have a stockbroker, you've entrusted him with thousands of your hard-earned dollars. Do you know if he has ever been convicted of a crime or fined for cheating clients? NASD Regulation knows. It's the enforcement arm of the National Association of Securities Dealers, which regulates the nation's 500,000 brokers. You can ask for your broker's disciplinary record, or find it yourself if he's been sanctioned since 1995, at NASD Regulation's Web site (http://www.nasdr.com). You can also file a complaint if you suspect wrongdoing.

Don't get sick. In addition to whatever financial software you have on your computer, make sure that your PC has an antivirus program, which you can buy at any computer or office supply store. For less than $100, you can get a program that will automatically scan any files you download off the Web, screening out malicious computer code that could turn all your electronic bookkeeping into so much gobbledygook. Consider it one of the wisest computer-related investments you'll ever make.

Your Money Habits

Get a Handle on the Way You Spend

One thing about money management is that it's predictable. The paycheck comes every Thursday. The mail comes every day but Sunday. The bills come once a month. The financial statements come every quarter. The tax man comes every April.

This begs the question: Why are so many people harried by money? A big part of the answer is bad habits. We get in the pattern of hitting the automated teller machine (ATM) wherever and whenever, of dealing with bills whenever the feeling hits, of choosing television over an hour spent shopping for a better credit card.

What's the solution? Good habits, of course. Get into some healthy routines—simple stuff, like scheduling time for paying bills or managing your wallet cash smartly—and money management becomes worlds easier.

Assessing Your Spending Habits

Where does the money go? If you have to ask, then you need to do the following exercise. Here's a simple and smart program for getting your spending habits under control.

Step one: Think about your spending. Just from memory, try to fill in your budget. Doing this purely from recollection will help you to later identify blind spots (places where you're spending more money than you believe you are) once you've compared your memory budget to your actual budget. "The process of comparing perception with reality can be very revealing," says Malcolm A. Makin, a certified financial planner and president of Professional Planning Group in Westerly, Rhode Island.

Step two: Track your spending. Go back a year if you can, or at least a few months. Write down every check, every credit card purchase, every ATM slip, including the date, amount, and purpose, says Delia Fernandez, a fee-only personal financial planner in Los Alamitos, California.

Step three: Categorize your spending. Organize all spending into three types. Some expenditures, such as your rent or mortgage, are *fixed*. They don't vary from month to month. Others, like insurance and car repair, are intermittent or *variable*. Still others, like entertainment costs, are *discretionary*. Recognizing which is which will help you predict your monthly expenditures and pinpoint areas where you can make painless cuts, says Fernandez.

Then, divide your spending into 10 major and about two dozen minor categories (household, mortgage, food, clothing, etc.), suggests Kitty O'Keefe, vice president of Drake Capital Securities in Santa Monica, California. The information you collect here will be the framework for the spending plan you'll build in the budget chapters of this book. Don't leave any big expenses out. The worksheet in this chapter will give you a starting point.

Step four: Track your cash. Once you've categorized all your spending, you'll probably find a chunk you can't explain. A big chunk. All in cash. Take a notebook with you every day for a couple of weeks and carefully note how you spend your cash. If you're married, ask your wife to do the same. Then sit down with the notebook and see where your cash is going, says Fernandez.

If you'd prefer a root canal to counting nickels and dimes, Fernandez suggests this alternative: Put $50 in your wallet on Monday morning. On Friday afternoon, check to see how much is left. Then put $50 more in your wallet for the weekend and see how much is left Sunday night. This experiment will tell you how much "walking-around" money you spend during each part of the week. When the time comes to write a spending plan, you'll simply give yourself what your parents gave you a few decades ago: an allowance. "Just the process of tracking one's money in this way is a deterrent to foolish spending," says Makin.

Times to Remember

Part of a healthy money habit is staying informed. The world is filled with financial and economic data, far too much to follow regularly. So we've boiled down the essential information into four categories (add a fifth if you actively trade stocks). Get in the habit of staying current about the following measures of economic health, and you'll be a far savvier money manager.

Daily stock indexes. The investor has so many indicators available that the major problem is settling on one or two to watch. The venerable Dow Jones Industrial Average tracks the daily movement of 30 blue-chip stocks. That helps explain its fame and also its occasional blind spots. For example, the index's keepers dropped International Business Machines Corporation (IBM) in 1939 and didn't bring it back until 1974, long after IBM had become one of the biggest and most influential companies in the world. Another daily index, the Standard and Poor's 500, gives a broader read on the nation's major companies. The daily NASDAQ (National Association of Securities Dealers Automated Quotation System) index generally covers newer firms, including some giants such as Microsoft. In addition, larger newspapers publish daily specialized indexes for industries such as technology.

Interest rates. These percentages heavily influence what you'll pay for your next home or car. If indicators point to rising interest rates, you'll want to sign loan papers before the next meeting of the Federal Open Market Committee. The committee, an arm of the Federal Reserve System, helps set the direction of interest rates at its eight meetings each year. The meetings usually occur on Tuesdays within 7 to 10 days of the following dates: February 1, April 1, May 20, July 1, August 20, September 20, November 20, and December 20.

Generally, the Fed raises interest rates when it sniffs inflation and lowers rates when it fears a recession or wants to increase the supply of money to individuals and businesses. You can gauge which way rates are going by watching for these reports.

The Producer Price Index and the Consumer Price Index. The first index measures changes in the cost of producing goods, while the second measures changes in the cost of living. A big increase in either index, say more than a few percentage points a year, will raise inflation alarms—and maybe interest rates. The government publishes the preceding month's indexes in the middle of each month.

Unemployment rates. The government reports the previous month's national unemployment rate in the first 10 days of the month. Rising unemployment could signal a recession—and a drop in interest rates. If you're thinking of changing your job or moving to a different part of the state or country, watch for the state and metro-area unemployment reports. The government publishes them five to six weeks after the end of the month.

Earning report releases. Serious investors who follow a few companies closely should ask those companies for the dates when they'll issue their quarterly earnings reports. Institutional investors frequently buy and sell the stock in anticipation of the big day. If the earnings are disappointing, they may punish the company by selling its stock. If enough large investors do this, the price of the stock will go down providing a buying opportunity if you have a strong stomach. Smaller, more volatile companies are especially susceptible to "earnings disappointment."

Where the Money Went

This worksheet will help you track down your money. Start by determining the monthly amount you spend or pay in each category. Then break that number down into the "Fixed," "Variable," and "Discretionary" categories. *Note:* Use these columns only if applicable. For example, while many of your household expenses might be fixed or variable, only a few or none may fall in the discretionary category. Conversely, most of your entertainment expenses will likely be discretionary. Finally, determine expenses for the entire year in the "Annual Total" column. Use your best judgment and be honest with yourself; it's the best way to keep track of your funds.

Expenses	Monthly Average	Fixed	Variable	Discretionary	Annual Total
Household					
• Mortgage/rent					
• Food					
• Clothing					
• Child care or support					
• Utilities					
• Maintenance					
• Supplies (cleaning items, toiletries, etc.)					
• Other					
TOTAL					
Entertainment					
• Dues, membership fees, etc.					
• Dining					
• Dates and excursions					
• Vacations					
• Videos, CDs, etc.					
• Parties					
• Gifts					
• Other					
TOTAL					

Expenses	Monthly Average	Fixed	Variable	Discretionary	Annual Total
Transportation					
• Car payments					
• Repairs					
• Gas and oil					
• Parking and tolls					
• Other					
TOTAL					
Insurance					
• Life					
• Property					
• Liability					
• Medical					
• Dental					
• Disability					
• Other					
TOTAL					
Taxes					
• Federal					
• FICA, SDI, etc.					
• State					
• Property					
• Other					
TOTAL					
Loan Payments*					
• Medical care					
• Charity					
• Cash/Miscellaneous					
TOTAL					

*Includes credit card payments, overdraft charges, and personal loans

Measuring Your Worth

Casting Your Net

Net worth is a simple concept; ultimately, it's just a single number. Add up all your investments, possessions, and money due from deadbeat brothers; subtract all the money you owe to banks, credit cards, mortgage companies, and rich uncles; and you have your net worth. Hopefully, it is greater than zero. It could be less.

Measuring your net worth can be scary business the first time you do it. It requires you to take a good, hard, honest look at what you've made for yourself in this life to date. The answers you get may not be pretty—who wants to look at the bottom line and see that their net worth is a negative number?—but financial experts say that your net worth is perhaps the single most important number you need to know and keep track of. It's the only way you to know for sure whether you're making progress or not.

Before you finish this chapter, you're going to know everything you need to know about figuring out your net worth. And you'll likely want to fill out the net worth worksheet we've provided (see page 20). But first, you need to review your assets and liabilities—what you have and what you owe. Here's where our experts suggest you start.

1. Distinguish between invested and use assets. Knowing the difference between an invested and a use asset will make it easy for you to distinguish between the things that you want to own for personal use or that you need in order to live, and the assets that you could sell in an emergency or reinvest for better returns, says Judith Lau, a certified financial planner in Wilmington, Delaware. Invested assets are held to make money. They can be converted relatively easily into other types of assets. Cash is the ultimate invested asset. Use assets are things that fill a need, and that you're not likely to sell because you need them—utensils for preparing and serving food, for example.

2. Don't count on your house. As you look at your assets, remember that your home is not an investment. You can list it as an asset, of course, but as a use asset, not as an investment. Shelter is a basic, inescapable human need; stocks and bonds are not, says Lau.

3. Find your market value. When you're ascribing value to your invested assets, try to use the market price for those assets, says Delia Fernandez, a fee-only personal financial planner in Los Alamitos, California. Sure, it's useful for tax purposes to know how much you paid for these assets. But the market value tells you what they'd be worth right now if you needed or wanted to sell them. In many cases, it's easy to determine market value. Banks that hold liquid assets like checking accounts and money markets routinely report account balances. The current values of thousands of stocks, bonds, and mutual funds are reported in the business sections of most daily newspapers and on the Internet.

4. Include your insurance. In your figuring, be sure to include the cash value portion, if any, of your insurance policies, but don't count the death benefit. If you have a whole life policy or universal life policy, it includes a cash value component that increases with time. This is a great source of emergency cash. Be sure, however, to account for any loans you've taken against your policy and to include any charges the insurer would levy if you surrendered the policy for cash. You'll find the net cash value on a recent statement, says Fernandez. (For more information on these policies, see Life Insurance on page 110.)

5. Don't list what you won't sell. Yes, your great-grandfather's World War I uniform may be valuable to a collector. So is Aunt Sally's tea set. But despite their enormous value to you and your family, they aren't really assets. When her clients list collectibles as assets, Lau asks, "When do you plan to sell it?" If the answer is never, then she doesn't mark the value as an asset. For the purposes of your net worth, if you're never going to convert it to cash, it has no cash value.

6. Mind your own business. If you own your own business, be conservative in trying to determine its value. An appraiser can help you figure out how much your business is worth. But beware: The more your business depends on you—on your ideas, your salesmanship, your energy—the less valuable it may be to someone else. "Maybe if you're not there, it's not worth a plugged nickel," Lau says.

7. List the full amounts for debts. When you figure your liabilities into your net worth, don't list only the monthly payments on your credit cards—list the whole amount, says Kitty O'Keefe, vice president of Drake Capital Securities in Santa Monica, California. This part of the net worth statement will tell you two things: How much you owe in total and the cards on which you've run up the biggest tabs.

8. Take an interest in interest. When you figure your worth, also list the interest rates for each credit card on which you owe money. You don't need this information to calculate your net worth, but it will help you see where your financial life might be hemorrhaging. How? Compare the balance outstanding with the interest rates. Large credit card balances are always a problem, but large balances on double-digit interest-rate cards are a financial cancer and a sign to start shopping for credit cards with lower interest rates, says Lau. The most telling aspect of credit card debt is the average monthly balance that you maintain on all of your cards, combined.

If you have large balances on high-rate cards, you have plenty of company, says Stephen Brobeck, executive director of the Consumer Federation of America. Brobeck estimates that nearly 60 million American families owe an average of $6,000 each on their credit cards. They pay an average of $1,000 in interest annually. For some, the cost is far higher—bankruptcy. Brobeck says credit card debt is largely to blame for the record-shattering one million personal bankruptcies filed in 1996.

9. List your mortgage as a liability. Note both the final due date and the interest rate. A mortgage, of course, is a long-term debt. The debt probably far outweighs what you owe on credit cards, but you have years to pay it, and it's offset by the value of your home. The difference between your home's market value and the mortgage is your equity, and it's probably one of the biggest pieces of your net worth, says O'Keefe.

10. List loans as liabilities. Be sure to note the purpose of each loan as well as the interest rate and date due, says O'Keefe. And for each liability, list the monthly payment. While this is not part of the net worth calculation, the total monthly payment will tell you at a glance how much of your income goes to pay debt. As a general rule, financial planners say that revolving debt such as credit cards should not consume more than 15 percent of your income.

11. Do the math. Now, subtract liabilities from assets to determine net worth. Here is the state of your financial health in one number. It may simply confirm your feelings that you're well-off or buried in debt. In either case, it strips away uncertainty and demands realism. As Lau notes, $10,000 in savings is worth exactly nothing if you have $10,000 in debts. Comparisons like that are what make net worth statements a powerful planning tool.

Your True Worth

The bottom line on net worth is simple: assets minus liabilities. Getting to that point, however, may take a little time. This worksheet is designed to help you find the right numbers.

Assets	Amount/Value	Int. Rate	Notes
Investable Assets			
Liquid			
• Checking accounts			
• Savings accounts			
• Money markets			
• Life insurance cash value			
TOTAL			
Fixed			
• Bonds			
• Bond and fixed-income mutual funds			
• CDs			
TOTAL			
Equities			
• Common stock			
• Stock mutual funds			
• Your employer's stock			
• Restricted stocks and options			
TOTAL			
Real estate investments			
• Real property			
• Equity real estate investments			
TOTAL			
Gold/commodities			
• Gold			
• Other commodities			
TOTAL			
Use Assets			
Personal real estate			
• Primary home			
• Vacation homes			
TOTAL			

Assets	Amount/Value	Int. Rate	Notes
Other assets			
• Business holdings			
• Collectibles			
• Household furnishings			
• Miscellaneous personal property			
• Notes receivable			
• Partnerships			
• Trusts and estates			
• Vehicles			
TOTAL			
Retirement savings			
• 401(k) plans			
• IRA/Keogh			
• Company pensions (vested)			
TOTAL			
TOTAL ASSETS			

Liabilities	Total Owed	Int. Rate	Notes
Residences			
• Mortgage (primary home)			
• Mortgage (second home)			
• Total – mortgage principal			
Investments/partnerships			
Investment property mortgages			
Credit cards			
• Card 1			
• Card 2			
• Card 3			
TOTAL			
Loans			
• Student loans			
• Car loans			
• Personal loans			
• 401(k) loans			
• Other debts (overdue payments/interest on bills, utilities, etc.)			
TOTAL			
TOTAL LIABILITIES			
NET WORTH (ASSETS – LIABILITIES)			

Setting Financial Goals

How to Get Your Priorities Straight

All right. You now have a nicely organized desk. Powerful financial software loaded in your computer. A file cabinet with a basic sense of order. You are ready to create a brilliant financial empire for yourself. What do you do next?

Step one: Completely forget about money. Completely. Think about life instead. As in, what is important to me? What do I really want, materially speaking, and when do I want it? How are my folks' health, and will I need to aid them in their final years? How important is my dream of Harvard for my children? What truly gives me the deepest pleasure, and how can I maximize that?

Setting the Right Goals

See, having lots of money is not an end unto itself. Money is a tool—just one tool, but an important one—for achieving the life you want. Always let your life goals shape your financial goals, and not the other way around. In many ways, this is the hardest and most important part of financial planning.

Once you make explicit your personal goals, your financial goals become obvious. And putting together a smart financial program to achieve those goals flows naturally, like a carpet unrolling. You reassess your spending habits. Create a budget. Establish the appropriate accounts. And keep an eye on things. It's pretty much that simple. Here's how to get started.

Be specific. Goals should be definable, measurable, specific. Don't just say, "Retire early." That doesn't spell out your financial expectations, and it won't help you write a budget. Instead, you should set a price tag for each goal, says Kitty O'Keefe, vice president of Drake Capital Securities in Santa Monica, California. For example, instead of saying "retire early," you might say, "Have $5,000 a month in spending power in today's dollars by the time I'm 45, for the rest of my life." Now that's a goal. The more concrete you can be, the more you can reduce your budgetary goals to dollars and cents, and the more successful you'll be.

Agree on your goals. Even if you live alone, there is an inescapable tension between your short-term wants and your long-term goals. Those tensions compound themselves if you have a spouse and a family. In many families, one spouse is a saver, the other a spender. A blowup is inevitable unless the saver and spender in your home agree on how to balance the now and the later, says Judith Lau, a certified financial planner in Wilmington, Delaware. "You have to get everyone on the same page," she says.

Determine your "gottas," "oughtas," and "nicetas." And recognize the difference between the three. For example, you "gotta" have shelter for your family, says James D. Schwartz, author of *Enough: A Guide to Reclaiming Your Financial Dream.* You "oughta" have a home instead of an apartment. It would be "niceta" have a vacation home, too. You easily can set rough spending priorities by deciding into which category a particular expenditure falls. It would be "niceta" have a new sports car, but you won't buy it as long as there are unfulfilled "gottas" and "oughtas" on your list. Once you have defined your "gottas," "oughtas," and "nicetas," put a price tag on each.

Knowing When to Quit

You're bound to hit a few speed bumps along the way to your financial goals. But here are some ways to make sure the bumps don't spoil the journey.

Abandon goals that cause family strife. **If you're so intent on saving money that you don't notice the holes in your kids' shoes, it's time to scale back your goals, says certified financial planner Judith Lau.**

Balance your goals. **Avoid an all-or-nothing approach, says Lau. Sure you want the best for your kids. But that doesn't mean you have to put them in private school, pay for after-school tutoring, and save for college tuition. It may make more sense to look at your overall goals—in this case giving your children good educations—and decide to pay for private school now and let them compete for college scholarships later.**

Ditch impossible goals. **When you track your progress each year, be sure to ask whether your goals still are realistic. You are doing yourself and your family no favors by devoting money to an unreachable goal. The whole point of financial planning, says Laura Tarbox, president of Tarbox Equity in Newport Beach, California, is to recognize that "you usually have competing goals. The thing that creates the anxiety is not knowing where you stand."**

Honing Your Financial Goals

Now that you have your big-picture goals established, you need to flesh out financial goals that will help you achieve them. Here are some key considerations to help you get started.

Pay yourself first. Your long-term goals are more important than any short-term financial demand, and far more important than casual expenditures, says Delia Fernandez, a fee-only personal financial planner in Los Alamitos, California. So put money aside for your goals first. Pay your bills next. Live on whatever is left.

Pay off debt quickly. Manage your debt smartly, and carry as little of it as you can. In particular, avoid carrying balances on your credit cards. Credit card debt is horribly expensive—while interest rates on cards have fallen, they are still far, far greater than investment rates. This is one case where paying money is much healthier than saving money, says Lau. After all, what good is saving money at 5 percent interest, when at the exact same time you are paying 17 percent on a credit card debt?

Make time your ally. By delaying or modifying long-term goals, you can make their achievement cheaper and surer, says Lau. Maybe you'll send your children to an inexpensive junior college for two years before you have to break open the college fund. Perhaps you can delay your retirement from age 55 to age 60. In both cases, you're giving yourself more time to save while reducing your expenses.

Make compound interest work for you. Over the long term, 5 to 10 years or more, compound interest works magic, says Schwartz. The earlier you start saving for goals such as retirement the easier compounding will make it for you.

Adjust for inflation. Huge inflation can make a mockery of your plans. For example, if you figure that a year of state college costs $7,000 now, and if college costs inflate 8 percent annually, your very bright 3-year-old will need $22,200 for her freshman year in college.

Setting Up a Budget

Secrets to a Solid Spending Plan

Budgets have a bad reputation—just ask anyone in the federal government who has ever tried to balance one. So every time you encounter the dreaded "B word" in this book, feel free to replace it with the more soothing phrase "spending plan." By either name, the fact remains the same: If you want to take control of your hard-earned money, this is the single most powerful tool that you could ever wield. And it's a tool that you can custom build. We'll show you how.

Budgeting Basics

In the preceding chapters, our experts have shown you how to do the prep work—calculating your net worth, tracking your spending habits, and setting financial goals. Once you've assembled that information, you're down to the nitty-gritty: the actual setting of your own personal budget, using the worksheet in this chapter. But before you take pencil in hand, here are a few basic rules to writing a budget and a few simple tools to turn that spending plan into a reality you can live with.

Be realistic about your income. List the income you really get, not the income you'd like to get. Your budget is not the place to fantasize about the big sales bonus you hope you'll get, if you somehow land a particular deal, and if your boss somehow recognizes that you made it all possible. If you aren't reasonably sure you'll get the money, don't put it in your budget.

Cut variable and discretionary expenses first. With occasional exceptions, these are usually the softest part of the family budget: things like out-of-the-office lunches that add up quickly without really adding anything of value. That makes them relatively easy to cut. Big-ticket items like your mortgage or insurance premiums also can be cut, but seldom quickly and never without a lot of research first.

Treat savings like a bill. You remembered to pay the phone bill last month, didn't you? Handle your savings the same way. Mark it on your calendar and send a check to savings routinely, say Victoria Felton-Collins, Ph.D., and Suzanne Blair Brown in their book *Couples and Money.*

Use payroll or automatic deduction whenever possible. Don't send a check to savings if your boss will do it for you, says Delia Fernandez, a fee-only financial planner in Los Alamitos, California. Don't make a mortgage payment if your bank will deduct it automatically from your account. This is a simple way to remove clutter from your financial life and to ensure that you've covered some of your most basic goals before you even open up your checkbook.

Go on a cash diet. Try to live with 5 percent or 10 percent less cash than you currently do. Try taking the money and stashing it in an account where you can't get to it easily, suggests Fernandez. This stratagem plays off perception: If you don't think you have the money (or if you've forced yourself to forget you had it), you'll probably find that you won't need it.

Give everybody allowances. The above notwithstanding, everyone—you, your spouse, your kids—should have a little money that they don't have to account for. This will prevent arguments that could destroy the budget, and family harmony along with it.

Boycott Madison Avenue. Your budget should tell you what you need and what you ought to spend for it. Unfortunately, paying attention to your budget won't be easy. A major American industry—advertising—exists largely to persuade you that you need something you didn't know you needed (or often don't really need at all). When it comes to budgeting, "Madison Avenue is no ally," says Rennie Gabriel, president of the Financial Coach consulting firm. When you see commercials, when you feel the overwhelming urge to buy, always try to ask yourself: Do I really *need* this, or do I just *want* it?

Keep targets flexible. Don't try to account for every penny you spend. The Senate Subcommittee on Lunches and Foolish Expenditures won't call a hearing if you slip and only brown-bag it three days instead of four this week. If you overspend in one category, you often can make it up elsewhere.

Extras and Essentials

Whatever goals you've set for yourself, however much money you may have allocated for the various lines in your budget, once you've established a basic budget for yourself, there are changes you'll want to—*have to*—make. There are extras you'll want to build into your core spending plan, additions that may one day become essential to your financial well-being. Here are some of the ways in which you may need to revise your budget.

Set up an emergency reserve. As a general rule, you should have sufficient money set aside to cover at least three months of expenses, says Judith Lau, a certified financial planner in Wilmington, Delaware. Put money in your savings account every month until you reach that magic number, until your reserve is full. But don't touch it unless it's absolutely necessary.

Reserve for retirement. We can expect, if anything, longer retirements than our parents'. The traditional benchmark has been to set aside 10 percent of your gross income for retirement. That goal may be too conservative, says Lau. She advises stashing 20 percent of gross income for retirement if possible. And, the closer you are to retirement, the more you may need to invest. But, she warns, don't go into debt to do it. (*Note*: In the chart on page 26, be sure to list monthly contributions to your retirement accounts; don't just list the totals you currently have in each account.)

Save for intermittent expenses. These are bills that come due every few months or that can vary widely, such as insurance, taxes, or car repair. But these bills don't fit into monthly budgets, and they're so large that they can disrupt your normal cash flow. The answer is to stick some money in a savings or money market account and "earn interest while waiting to pay," says James D. Schwartz, author of *Enough: A Guide to Reclaiming Your Financial Dream.*

Bank your bonus. As your income begins to grow, stick with your old budget, says Lau. Put bonuses and pay raises into savings and investments. Dedicate each raise to a particular goal.

Plan for contingencies. Everyone over 40 has heard horror stories about someone's mother or father who exhausted a lifetime of assets to pay for a year or two of long-term nursing care. "Whether you're rich, poor, or in-between," Schwartz says, there's a risk you will have to deal with long-term care. The potential financial risk is particularly great for baby boomers who waited until their thirties to have children. Many of them will have to help their parents pay for nursing care at the same time that they themselves are approaching retirement and their children are enrolling in college.

Budgeting Your Money

Category	Current Monthly Amount	Adjustments	New Monthly Amount
Income (Pretax)			
Your job			
Your spouse's job			
Part-time job			
Rental income			
Interest income			
Investment income			
• Bonds			
• Mutual funds			
• Real estate			
• Stocks			
Miscellaneous income			
TOTAL INCOME			
Savings			
Retirement savings			
• 401(k) plans			
• IRA/Keogh			
• Company pensions (vested)			
Life insurance cash value			
Other long-term savings			
Emergency reserve			
Money market			
Other short-term savings			
Total savings			
DISPOSABLE INCOME (INCOME – SAVINGS)			
Expenses			
Household			
• Mortgage/rent			
• Food			
• Clothing			
• Child care or support			
• Utilities			
• Maintenance			
• Supplies (cleaning items, toiletries, etc.)			
TOTAL			

Category	Current Monthly Amount	Adjustments	New Monthly Amount
Transportation			
• Car payments			
• Repairs			
• Gas and oil			
• Parking and tolls			
• Miscellaneous			
TOTAL			
Entertainment			
• Dues, membership fees, etc.			
• Dining			
• Dates and excursions			
• Vacations			
• Videos, CDs, etc.			
• Parties			
• Gifts			
TOTAL			
Insurance			
• Life			
• Property			
• Liability			
• Medical			
• Dental			
• Disability			
TOTAL			
Taxes			
• Federal			
• FICA, SDI, etc.			
• State			
• Property			
• Other			
TOTAL			
Loan payments*			
Medical care			
Charity			
Cash/Miscellaneous			
• You			
• Your spouse			
• Your children			
TOTAL			
TOTAL EXPENSES			

*Includes credit card payments, overdraft charges, and personal loans

Choosing Allies

Finding a Financial Friend

Few things are more personal, more proprietary, to a man than those digits on his paycheck, or on his bank statement. Although we know we shouldn't, although we know there's more to life than dollars, the truth is that we have a deep, close relationship with our money. And so we hold our financial information close to our vests; a personal truth too intimate to share with anyone but the closest friend or family member.

Sorry to tread on a deeply held conviction, but that mind-set is exactly what keeps many men from realizing their true financial potential—because they don't trust someone else with their money. By "someone else," we mean a professional. A financial ally.

It's easy to lose perspective about oneself, says Rennie Gabriel, president of the Financial Coach consulting firm. That's why most of us talk with friends about our parents, our jobs, even our sex lives. That's also why men with money concerns should talk to an advisor—to get an outside perspective on their finances.

Asking for Help

Now, for the most part, you can get along fine on your own. Unless you're *really* bad at organizing your life, you don't need a financial advisor to help you balance your checkbook, for example, says Delia Fernandez, a fee-only personal financial planner in Los Alamitos, California. But there are going to be key situations when you'll truly benefit from the wisdom of a professional who makes his money by making money. When, then, is a good time to call in the experts?

To solve a difficult financial problem. Examples include caring for an aging relative or building a college fund for the kids. Any time you're facing a big-ticket expenditure that demands a thorough understanding of inflation and the tax laws, that's the time to pick up the phone.

To manage a complicated legal and/or financial issue. Let's say you have enough money that you want to do something fairly complex, such as establishing a living trust for your children or grandchildren. You'll definitely need help for that one—specifically, an attorney specializing in such financial issues. You'll need legal help if you have minor children. In that case, you have to ensure that, if you and your spouse die, someone you trust will become your children's guardian. And you have to provide the guardian with sufficient assets (including insurance) to care for your children, says Fernandez.

To manage large assets. If you've gained a big windfall, or you find yourself sitting on large amounts of cash that you haven't put anywhere except your savings and checking, seek professional help. And don't tell yourself you'll do the investing yourself when you have more time. That was the excuse of one tax analyst who was a client of Laura Tarbox, president of Tarbox Equity in Newport Beach, California. The analyst was so busy working 80-hour weeks, telling other people what to do with their money, that she didn't have time to invest her own. She kept it all in cash for two years before hiring Tarbox to manage it. Don't make her mistake.

To evaluate your own money plan. Once you've written your own financial plan, a pro can tell you quickly whether you've covered all the bases, says Fernandez. At best, the pro charges you a few hundred dollars to give you a pat on the back. At worst, the pro finds some major flaws, and you have to spend hours rethinking your strategy. Either way, you win.

Planner Precautions

Fact: Few of the people offering financial advice actually make most of their money doing so, according to the Consumer Federation of America (CFA). "The majority," CFA says, "earn some or all of their income selling mutual funds, annuities, insurance, and other financial products."

That poses a big conflict for advisors, who must choose between their own pocketbooks and their clients' best interests. It also raises a big mystery for clients: Whose side is my advisor really on?

Now, by and large, most financial planners are a reputable, reliable bunch. Just the same, you can and should look after your own interests. Here's what our experts—many of them financial advisors and planners themselves—recommend as possible ways to ensure that you get your money's worth.

Insist on up-front disclosure. Compensation can take many forms. Ask about fees and commissions, of course, but also ask about the more subtle ways an advisor can make money on your account. Examples include "surrender charges" or "back-end fees" (charged when you pull out of an insurance policy or investment early), contingency fees, prizes, bonuses, and "soft-dollar benefits" (such as payment for training or office expenses). If an

Alphabet Soup

Thousands of people—financial advisors and planners, insurance agents, accountants, and lawyers—will help other people handle their money for a fee. According to the experts, here's how to tell them apart.

- ***Financial planners*** **help clients achieve short- and long-term financial goals. Anybody can call himself a financial planner, and not all financial planners are registered with the Securities and Exchange Commission (SEC). Generally, registration is required if the advice pertains to investments in specific securities. Registration may also be required of a financial planner who merely advises on securities investments (as opposed to other types of investments). Many financial planners are licensed as investment advisors, certified financial planners, accountants, insurance salespersons, and securities brokers.**
- ***Certified financial planners*** **(CFPs) are members of the Institute of Certified Financial Planners. They must pass an exam, complete 30 hours of continuing education every two years, and abide by the institute's ethical standards.**
- ***Personal financial specialists*** **(PFSs) are certified public accountants who hold this special designation. In addition to their CPA credentials (which subject them to regulation by all 50 states and the SEC), they must take 72 hours of continuing education and engage in 750 hours of financial planning every three years.**
- ***Professional financial planners*** **(PFPs) are just that, professional financial planners who have trained in the field at accredited universities.**
- ***Chartered financial consultants*** **(CFCs) and chartered life underwriters (CLUs) are both insurance specialists.**
- ***Registered investment advisors*** **(RIAs or IAs) number at about 24,000 nationwide. Most of them are individuals. A few are institutions such as American Express, which employs hundreds of advisors under its license. RIAs managing $25 million or more register with the SEC. Others generally register with state securities regulators. Standards vary from state to state; no training is required for SEC registration.**

advisor won't disclose compensation or won't put it in writing, leave, says James D. Schwartz, author of *Enough: A Guide to Reclaiming Your Financial Dream.* Some professionals, including investment advisors regulated by the Securities and Exchange Commission (SEC), are legally required to disclose their fees—and even to tell you if their fees are unusually high. Others belong to professional organizations whose ethical codes mandate disclosure. Don't settle for less.

Watch for conflicts in compensation. There's a potential conflict anytime the planner can influence you to put more money in his pocket. For example, take planners who charge a "fee-offset." They might charge you a fee to prepare a plan and then reduce that fee based on commissions they earn from selling you investments. It sounds great. But as the Consumer Federation of America points out, if a planner offsets $2,000 in fees against $10,000 in commissions, your "free" plan has just earned the planner $8,000.

"There are serious conflicts," says Bob Plaze, associate director of the SEC's division of investment management, "but those conflicts can be resolved through disclosure."

Trust, but verify. There are thousands of reputable planners and advisors who will work hard for your money, says Plaze. But don't expect state, federal, or industry watchdogs to weed out the bad apples. Although investment advisors collectively manage $8 trillion in assets, most state and federal overseers check up on an advisor only when there's a complaint. The SEC has just 50 people to keep watch over 7,300 investment advisors—one inspector for every 146 firms, Plaze says. That means you will have to watch out for yourself by insisting on frequent, prompt, and thorough reports from the people who manage your money. Don't be bashful about insisting on those updates—that's your hard-earned cash, remember.

How to Select an Advisor

A financial advisor could help you achieve your dreams or saddle you with nightmares. Here are some tips suggested by James D. Schwartz, author of *Enough: A Guide to Reclaiming Your Financial Dream*, for selecting a potential advisor.

First, interview each candidate in person. When you do, discuss the following.

- **Ask about his business philosophy and areas of specialization.**
- **Request information about his experience and qualifications: education—including continuing education—and number of years in the business. Remember, anyone can call himself a financial planner.**
- **Make sure that you know what you want the planner to do for you. Remember, also, that most planners will be interviewing you at the same time you are interviewing them. Planners like to work with enjoyable clients and will try to avoid the demanding, dissatisfied "client from hell."**
- **Ask how he develops his recommendations. Look for someone who will pay close attention to your current circumstances, your goals, and your willingness to take risks.**
- **Ask if he will have control of any of your money. Many investment advisors actively manage clients' funds, buying or selling at their own discretion. These advisors can react quickly to changing market conditions. But they also can put clients' money at greater risk or make excessive trades to generate commissions, a practice known as "churning." The vast majority of discretionary managers work on a fee-only basis. Don't pay on a com-**

mission basis with a discretionary account, says Malcolm A. Makin, a certified financial planner and president of Profession Planning Group in Westerly, Rhode Island. The conflicts of interest are too great.

- **Ask if he is regulated by any state or federal agency. If he is a registered investment advisor, ask for his Securities and Exchange Commission (SEC) Form ADV or the state equivalent. It will contain a lot of background on the advisor's experience and business practices.**
- **Ask if he has a disciplinary history. Federally regulated investment advisors must disclose any legal or disciplinary events that are material to their integrity or could affect their ability to deliver on financial commitments to you.**
- **Ask for at least three references. They should be clients with circumstances similar to your own who have been with the advisor for at least three years. Be aware that some planners will not divulge the names of any of their clients, believing that such information is of a strict confidential nature.**
- **Check him out with regulators. Yes, you asked him directly; but make sure he told you the truth. Look for state securities-and-insurance regulators in the blue pages of the phone book, and ask them for the Central Registration Depository files on your advisor. (If you can't find the right listing, contact the North American Securities Administrators in Washington, D.C., to get the name and phone number of your state's regulator.) You can also check federally registered advisors with the SEC (again, turn to the government pages of your phone book). Be particularly wary of advisors cited for offenses such as churning or selling unsuitable investments.**

Consulting the Specialists

Although financial planners and investment advisors are probably your most critical allies in making the most of your money, there are other professionals or venues that could be helpful—and one that isn't. Here's the rundown.

Investment clubs. Unless you're billionaire investor Warren Buffett or mutual fund superstar Peter Lynch, there's a lot about investing you don't know. So swap ideas and share research chores with co-workers or neighbors. It's one of the easiest ways to get investment information. But take what advice you get with a grain of salt—after all, these are your friends, and not necessarily financial experts, says Fernandez. If things go well, celebrate together. If things go poorly, you'll have plenty of company to help you weather the bad news. Self-help can take you far in financial planning, and a little help from friends can take you farther.

Credit agencies. This is one of the easiest, cheapest forms of financial information. If you're planning a major purchase, for example, you'd do well to order a copy of your report from one of the major credit-rating agencies. If you find an error or outdated information, ask the agencies for a correction. The three big agencies are Experian (P. O. Box 949, Allen, TX 75013-0949), Equifax Incorporated (P. O. Box 740241, Atlanta, GA 30374-0241) and Trans Union Corporation (Consumer Disclosure Center, P. O. Box 390, Springfield, PA 19064-0390). They generally charge $10 or less for a copy of your report. You're entitled to a free copy if you've been denied credit in the past 30 days because of information on your report.

Discount brokers. If you're not satisfied with mutual funds and want to invest in individual stocks, there are plenty of low-cost brokers to help you do it. You don't need a full-service broker, provided you are willing to do your own research. With full-service brokers, says Tarbox, "you pay a lot in commissions for nonobjective advice." Be sure the broker has sufficient insurance. The Securities Insurance Protection Corporation protects investors when a brokerage goes bust. The minimum coverage it provides is $500,000 per investor—$100,000 for cash accounts and $400,000 for all other accounts, including stocks, bonds, and money markets. If you expect to exceed these limits, make sure your broker has supplemental insurance.

Debt counselors. Filing bankruptcy is easy, but the long-term cost could be severe, especially if you plan to borrow money anytime soon. A bankruptcy can remain on your credit report for up to 10 years. Nonprofit credit counselors can help. For the nearest office of the Consumer Credit Counseling Service, check the yellow pages under "credit and debt counseling." Largely funded by credit-card issuers to discourage bankruptcy, the service can help you prepare a budget and, if necessary, arrange a debt-repayment plan with your creditors.

Credit repairmen? Here's one ally you don't need: the wiseguy who tells you he can "repair" a bad credit report. If the report is true, and the information is no more than 7 years old for unpaid bills or 10 years old for bankruptcies, neither you nor the credit-repair operators can do a thing about it. But if you decide to hire a credit-repair outfit anyway, remember that federal law gives you three days to change your mind and bars the business from charging you a penny before it has done its job.

People Worth Watching

Thousands of self-proclaimed "experts" offer the public advice about their finances and their investments. Here are a handful who may be worth your attention.

Humberto Cruz. **Syndicated columnist Cruz is refreshingly down to earth. He writes like the guy next door, but better-informed.**

Peter Lynch. **Although he retired in May 1990 as portfolio manager for Fidelity's Magellan Fund, Lynch still authors money books and is a regular contributor to *Worth* magazine. Lynch preaches an optimistic gospel: An average person with average diligence can invest his money better than the pros can.**

Stephen M. Pollan. **The personal finance commentator for CNBC/FNN and a frequent guest on the network morning shows, Pollan mixes lots of personal anecdotes with bite-size advice on financial questions.**

Jane Bryant Quinn. **A book author and a columnist for *Newsweek* and other magazines, Quinn combines a thorough knowledge of finance with a commonsense approach. Unlike too many personal finance writers, she writes with grace and wit.**

Louis Rukeyser. **Host of PBS's *Wall Street Week with Louis Rukeyser* since 1970, Rukeyser has helped open the mysterious world of Wall Street to Everyman. But beware: If you're seeking guidance on your overall finances, you won't find it here.**

Allan Sloan. **Lots of people will tell you to stick your last dime in the stock market. Sloan, a columnist for *Newsweek*, isn't one of them. If you want to learn how to cut through the hype surrounding investments, make Sloan a habit. He can find the warts hidden in the best-looking stocks.**

Part Two

Tactics for Daily Living

Electronic Banking

The New Way to Manage Your Money Flow

Imagine this scenario, offered by Lee Naas, a certified financial planner with Prudential Securities in St. Louis: You get the bill from, say, the gas company. You go to your phone and dial your bank's toll-free number. When you get an answer, you punch in a series of passwords and account numbers that, in seconds, instructs your bank to pay the exact amount of the gas bill—on the exact day you want to pay it.

Wake up, amigo. This is hardly science fiction; it's available *now.* It's just one example of the types of bill-paying services offered by many brokerage houses, banks, and credit unions. It costs a few bucks a month (some banks offer it free) and pays an unlimited number of bills.

Even better, with a little front-end paperwork, that gas bill could be paid directly and automatically—without your ever having to pick up the phone.

Digital Dealing

The brave new world of electronic money management is not something in the future, like the colonization of outer space. It's here, it's immensely sophisticated, and it offers on Wednesday things that were unheard of on Monday.

Right now, a computerized account can pay your bills, distribute cash among your investments, prepare tallies for the tax man, and post interest on your savings account—while you sit like a sultan in your den, punching keys, issuing commands, and never stepping inside a bank. Here are just a few ways you can use technology to manage your money so it doesn't manage you.

Perform a wire act. The most basic of cash management services is direct deposit. Your employer may, at your request, wire your paycheck right into any accounts you dictate, says Christine Moriarty, president of Moriarty Financial Services, which has offices in Needham, Massachusetts, and South Burlington, Vermont. That wire system can have your money sitting there earning interest in seconds. You couldn't drive it across town that fast, and if you mailed it in, you'd lose three or four days interest.

The benefits don't end there. Some financial institutions will offer lower interest rates on loans if you take advantage of direct deposit. That makes it easier for the bank to get its money, so the bank makes it cheaper for you to take out a loan.

Just plain bill. Automatic bill paying is the next step. "When you open a checking account, you can instruct the financial institution to automatically pay the bills you designate: gas bill, light bill, phone bill, and any others," says Sunny Harris, a professional trader, financial expert, and president of Sunny Harris and Associates, the Carlsbad, California, publisher of the *Traders' Catalog and Resource Guide.* When these bills come due, the creditors will signal your account, prompting your bank to write and mail a check. There's a slight fee, perhaps 15 cents per check. Or for those who aren't particular about having a paper trail, some banks simply transfer the money to your creditor's account electronically.

Don't lose interest. If you want your money to make the absolute most interest for you, watchfulness is the key. First, ask yourself when your paycheck is deposited into your account and when you want the bills paid. If the paycheck arrives on, say, the first day of the month, you might instruct your bank to schedule a mass bill paying on the fifteenth. That will earn you two weeks of interest on your interest-bearing checking account.

If the fifteenth of the month—or whenever it is your money goes out—falls on a Saturday or Sunday, make sure the bill is paid the Monday after and not the Friday before, adds Moriarty. No point in throwing away that interest.

Give yourself a line of credit. If the unthinkable happens and through absolutely no fault of yours a—gulp!—bad check gets written, be sure your financial institution offers overdraft protection, sometimes called reserve credit or a line of credit. That means the bank will cover the check—for up to thousands of dollars, depending on the amount you qualify for. The downside is, you'll pay for this insurance—some banks charge you a daily fee of 1 percent of the amount they advance you to cover the check, or up to 25 percent annually. But if you can cover that check right away, it's still cheaper than a bounced-check charge. Some banks will hold a check for 10 days before they consider it written on rubber; some will give you only a day's grace.

Manage your 'Net assets. If you have a personal computer at home, give computerized banking a try. "Every bank has its own software just for that purpose," says Harris. "Sometimes they'll give you a diskette along with instructions for using it; other times you can download the software from the Web site." You'll have a password and an account number, and you'll pull up a page that actually looks like a check. You can write in the information, specify where you want the check sent, and push a button. It will create a check and put it in the mail for you.

Doin' It the Old-Fashioned Way

So you're not quite ready to trust your hard-earned money to the ether of cyberspace? Relax. You're not alone. In fact, some money managers say there's plenty of reason for people to manage their funds the old-fashioned way—by hand.

"Remember that the banks came up with this electronic stuff to make it easier for them, not for you," says Moriarty Financial Services president Christine Moriarty. "I still believe in the emotional side of money, and I believe people are not behaving responsibly about their money unless they sit down with it and manage it themselves. I'm finding more people are doing that because they've been burned by their emotional attachment to an electronic system. It led them to act like they were wealthier than they were. They never sat down and put their hands on their money."

What's more, there's a certain ritual to handling your finances without the aid of computer or Touch-Tone phone. "Rituals are a way of connecting people to their lives," notes Constance Barber, a certified financial planner and president of Barber Financial in Needham, Massachusetts. "For many people, there's a ritual in opening the bills, seeing the bills, having time to talk about them with a spouse." There's also a ritual in handling the paper kind of money, whether it's cash or checks, "and there aren't very many rituals left in life," Barber notes.

But that doesn't mean that you should be any less organized about your finances, says Moriarty. "I'm meeting more people who are going back to the old envelope system. After the paycheck is cashed, so much money is put in an envelope labeled 'Rent,' so much in an envelope marked 'Groceries.'"

Financial Institutions

The Most Bank for Your Bucks

Banks used to offer you gifts to get your money. Open an account, get free dishes, encyclopedias, toasters. That was then. Today, you *pay* for the privilege of giving them your money—especially if you're trying to open a checking account. You pay monthly fees if you don't maintain a minimum balance. Ever-rising check-printing fees. Automated teller machine (ATM) fees. And to top it all off, the bank pays you either a low rate of interest for the use of your money or no interest at all. It adds up.

Can you negotiate these matters? Of course. We'll show you how you can bypass some of these rigid banking rules with a little time, patience, and study. Or if you can't bypass them, how to make them work in your favor.

Where to Go

When is a bank not a bank? It sounds a bit like a riddle, but the fact is, there are places to bank your money that aren't, in the strictest legal sense, banks at all. Here's a brief scorecard of the different types of places where you can stow your money.

Banks. The traditional banks are doing their best to lose their pinstripe-and-flint image by offering more services, such as computerized bill paying or investment help. Federal regulation limits what businesses a bank can be in, however. It's a point of constant debate in Washington. And understand that banks make more money by serving businesses than they do individuals.

Credit unions. Some of these are mom-and-pop operations staffed by inexperienced help; others are sophisticated services attached to well-heeled organizations. They lend at a lower rate of interest than banks, pay you interest at a higher rate, "and some will do direct deposit and automatic bill paying," says Sunny Harris, president of Sunny Harris and Associates, in Carlsbad, California.

"Credit unions are among the leading purveyors of checking accounts now," says Lee Naas, a financial planner with Prudential Securities in St. Louis. Ostensibly, unions are not for profit, because they are owned by their members. The members then charge themselves lower interest rates on loans than they could get from a bank. Unions also waive a lot of fees that most banks charge on accounts.

What's the drawback? Credit unions don't let just anyone join. If you have a friend or a relative who works for a company with an attractive credit union, you may be eligible. Teachers' credit unions admit students. Some credit unions are open to members of religious congregations, while others require only residence in a certain ZIP code. Check with your company to see if it has a relationship with a credit union; membership may be as easy as filling out a form.

Brokerage houses. Known mostly for managing stock and bond accounts for clients, these firms offer automated banking features, and they can connect your checking account to a broader range of vehicles like money market funds, which pay better interest rates than banks.

The catch? Many of the banklike features offered by brokerage houses are what are known as enhanced services, designed to lure you into sampling their investments.

What You Need to Know

Once you've narrowed down the choices of where to bank, you'll want to look carefully at the features and charges your institution of choice offers. Here are a few suggestions that our experts recommend.

Choose what service you need. Yes, a bank is a very safe place to invest. The federal government guarantees bank savings accounts for up to $100,000. Plus, a bank is a good option for fulfilling your short-term cash-flow needs, such as checking, access to ATMs, and a central account through which your money flows in and out. But the interest rates they pay on your savings are among the lowest around. So if you're looking for a place to park cash safely and get a slightly better return, choose a money market account.

Be calculating. Get literature from each institution and look for the schedule of fees. Tally up all of the fees charged for various services and features, and weigh them against the options you'll get, says Andrew Tobias, financial expert and author of *My Vast Fortune* and other books. Then see how much money you have to keep in the bank in order to waive those fees. You should always maintain "the balance a bank requires to avoid all fees," Tobias advises. Let's say this amount is $2,000 in a noninterest-bearing account. Sound self-defeating? Let him explain.

"If you figure that, at 4 percent interest, the after-tax value return you could earn on $2,000 is $80, then it has cost you $80 in a year's time to avoid all those fees." Bank maintenance fees on these accounts average $10 a month, or $120 a year. By parking that two grand, you've saved yourself $40 in fees.

Bundle up. Banks won't negotiate checking account interest rates, but they will "bundle" the checking with another service. That means they'll take a fraction of a percent of interest off your mortgage or car loan or other personal loan rate if you keep your check business with them. Ask for at least one-eighth of a percent. The hook: If you are late with a loan payment, the bank may feel free to withdraw the payment from your checking account.

Checklist for Checking Accounts

When you go shopping for a checking account, sit down with a customer service representative and ask this list of questions suggested by our experts.

Do you have limits on check writing? **Some accounts restrict you to a certain number of checks per month; write more and the extra will cost you.**

Do you have restrictions on deposits? **Yes, some banks decree that if you make more than a certain number of deposits, you may be charged per deposit.**

Do you have an online service and a Web site? **If the answer is yes, you can start doing transactions electronically. Also, it's a good indicator that the firm is trying to stay current with the latest trends. You don't really want a bank that's behind the curve, do you?**

Will I have access to an automated teller machine (ATM)? **And if you use another bank's ATM, will that cost extra? If so, how much?**

How much "face time" can I expect to have with a cashier? **If you have a lot of cash deposits, you may prefer to go inside and talk to a cashier. Unbelievably, many banks now charge you a buck or two to do a transaction inside the bank; they want you to use the slots outside and not bother the tellers. These charges, though, are negotiable, depending on how much money you have in your account and how much other business you do with the bank.**

Credit Cards

Don't Get Spastic with Plastic

Those little oblong plastic cards fit snugly into the pockets of your wallet, just as if they belong there. And they do. We move a little closer to a cashless society each day, and even now there are businesses that don't want your money; they want that row of numbers raised like braille on the front of that card. Try renting a car without a credit card. Or applying for a car loan or a mortgage. No credit history? Sorry.

Credit cards are not only access to the marketplace, they are part of it. Like fire was to early man, credit has become a dangerous but indispensable tool in our daily lives. Treat it with respect and you'll reap manifold benefits. But turn your back on it, take it for granted, and it'll snuff out on you. Or worse, it'll flare up, consuming everything you've worked for, and burn you but good.

In 1996, a year when unemployment was low and the Wall Street bull market was charging to record heights, the U.S. Bankruptcy Court system also was setting records. A million people filed personal bankruptcy, a 27 percent increase over 1995 and the biggest total since the 1981–82 recession.

Credit card debt appears to be the major reason why more people are going bust during boom times. A Purdue University study of personal bankruptcy filings in 13 cities showed that debtors had average incomes of $19,800—and average credit card debts of $17,544.

With the encouragement of credit card issuers, consumers are piling ever-larger debts on their plastic, typically at interest rates of 15 percent and higher. Revolving debt reached $463 billion at the end of 1996. It grew 11.8 percent during the year, three times faster than personal income.

What's in the Cards?

Chances are good that this very day, you received a solicitation in the mail for a new credit card. But not all cards are created equal. In fact, some of the cards we often think of as credit cards really aren't. Here's a quick rundown of the different card types available.

Credit cards. These cards permit you to carry an unpaid balance from month to month—and pay interest on it. "A credit card is something that allows you to lend yourself money at a specified interest rate," says Sunny Harris, president of Sunny Harris and Associates in Carlsbad, California. Examples are MasterCard, Visa, and most department store and gas station cards. Because you can pay a little bit off every month and then immediately borrow back an amount equal to that payment, these cards are known as revolving debt cards. The interest rate on credit cards is compounded monthly. It is usually 15 to 18 percent, though some will hit you with up to 24 percent, the highest lending rate the law allows. Often, another point or so is tacked on for cash transactions, like a visit to an automated teller machine (ATM). If you're not using your bank's ATM, they will probably get you for another buck or so just to process the transaction. Finally, there can be a yearly fee added to your statement—usually around $25.

Charge cards. With these cards, you have to pay the balance in full each month. American Express is the best-known example, Harris says. They will advance you money with no interest charge, "but you only get it for 30 days, then you have to pay it back." The fees start at about $55 a year and range to up to $300 for a "platinum" card, for those with exceptional financial resources.

Secured credit cards. This is a growing option for people with bad credit or no credit rating. Essentially, it's a prepaid credit card—you put money, perhaps as little as $100, into the sponsoring bank's account. Now your card is secured, and you can "charge" as much as you have in the card's account. Secured cards may be especially useful in helping people establish good credit histories—or rebuild bad ones.

Debit cards. Also offered by banks, these cards are an interesting extension of the checkless society. You can buy your groceries without charging them or writing a check by presenting this card, which reaches right into your checking account and pulls out the money instantaneously. A "walletectomy," the humorists call it. There's no lag time, which has made it the preferred method of payment among vendors now. There are a couple of drawbacks. For one thing, with a normal credit card, if you go over the limit, the card issuer usually rejects the charge. When the money's drawn off a bank account, it's the same as bouncing a check—with all attendant penalties exacted on you. What's more, if your debit card is stolen, a thief could wipe out your entire account in minutes. When a regular credit card is stolen, you generally have a greater level of protection.

Single-company cards. These are credit cards offered by a single retail chain (say, a department store or gasoline company) and good only at stores owned by that company. They rarely have annual fees, but their interest rates are often high and the grace periods are minimal. In return, they often provide discounts on company merchandise and special services.

Giving Yourself Some Credit

If you want to manage your credit cards and use them wisely, you need to know that all the details, rates, fees, and perks can be manipulated to your advantage. With a little scrutiny of the fine print and a willingness to work the phones, you can turn these high-interest monsters into a valuable resource and a source of the cheapest loans available anywhere. Here's how to do it.

Avoid carrying debt from month to month. Pay off your credit cards each month. If you can't, don't carry cards. Nothing will ruin your finances more than large credit card balances. Why? Credit card interest rates are exorbitant. As a rule of thumb, $6,000 in credit card debt will cost you $1,000 a year in interest. The best stock market players would love that kind of guaranteed return. Here's another way of looking at it: If you buy your family a dinner in a restaurant and revolve it for a year, you'll pay the bank more than what you tipped the waiter.

Pay no fees. Many credit cards charge an annual fee of $25 to $50. But many don't. And those that do will often waive it if you ask. In fact, they should offer to waive it forever if you charge a certain amount to your card each year. It's usually around $2,000. Bottom line: Never pay an annual fee for a credit card.

Watch the clock. When does the interest meter start ticking on your credit card purchases? Does the issuer start charging you interest the moment you buy something? That is unacceptable. You want a credit card that will begin charging after the due date on the statement. That is, if you get a bill in mid-October for your September charges, you should have at least 10 interest-free days from the time the bill was generated to get a check in. When you get a solicitation for a new credit card, look in the fine print under "grace period" and read carefully. If there is not a window in which to pay off your bill without interest, forget that card.

Avoid large credit lines. Financial experts generally believe it's dangerous for a consumer to owe more than 15 to 20 percent of his income in revolving debt. Don't fall into the trap of thinking that credit card issuers won't give you more credit than that. Get enough credit cards and you'll have a credit line greater than your *entire* annual income. If you feel you are not disciplined enough to guard your credit card spending, then don't let your total credit line from all cards exceed 20 percent of your income.

Be underrated. Yes, the goal is never to pay credit card interest. But sometimes, you have no choice. Understand that there are many credit cards out there that charge you considerably less than 18 percent interest, says Lee Naas, a certified financial planner with Prudential Securities in St. Louis. Competition for your business is fierce, and the banks and the credit card companies are constantly manipulating rates to pull you in. You can begin your investigation, if you have the resources, by typing "credit cards" into your computer's search engine. Or you can visit each national bank's Web site. There's a good chance, though, that you won't have to go looking for lower-interest cards—if you have a mailbox or a telephone, they'll come looking for you.

Get credit for a shortcut. If you have an existing credit card with a high interest rate and you have been accepted by one with a lower interest rate, call your existing credit card company, advises Robin Bullard Carter, a financial educator and counselor and owner of MoneySense in Newbury, Massachusetts. Tell them, "I've been offered *this* higher credit limit at *this* lower interest rate. Before I move my money, I wanted to see if you could match it." This approach works some of the time.

Try a switch. "People who are credit worthy will normally be inundated with solicitations," says Naas. "Introductory offers of a 9.5 percent interest rate are common, and some go as low as 4.7 percent." You can move the balance on your current high-charging card to the new card, often by simply filling out a "check" the new card company provides. "Introductory" means that the low rate is only in effect for six

Company Cards

Credit cards, usually MasterCard or Visa, are available from airlines now, offering free airline miles for every dollar charged on them. People who love to fly—or have to—put every charge they can on the card, and pay the balance in full every month. That gives them a nice bonus: if they charge $20,000 a year, at the end of each year they have 20,000 miles worth of tickets to wherever that airline flies.

A gasoline company offers a credit card imprinted with the company name. When you use the card at the company's station, the merchant benefits, the card company benefits, and even you benefit, getting perhaps a 1 percent discount on everything you buy.

The major automakers have their own MasterCards or Visas, which will allow you to accumulate credit toward the purchase of a new car.

In the world of consumer credit, these are known as affinity cards, a marketing maneuver designed to keep those credit cards active by attaching them to premiums—or freebies—that are of some use to you. The ones mentioned above are commonplace; what is not generally known is their pervasiveness in nearly all areas of commerce. Are they worth it?

"You will benefit with these affinity cards only if you can pay the account in full every month," says Don Williams, president of Club Technology Corporation, a Dallas-based company that processes credit card charges.

"If you have to revolve your airline card, you could *buy* a trip for less than what it's costing you in interest. If your goal is to get miles to take a trip, get and use *just* that one card. Don't get another card for gas and a card from General Motors to buy a car. If you do, you'll never get anything, because you won't use any one of them enough to get any benefits."

Cobranding is another credit card marketing strategy, rather like affinity cards. It is a MasterCard or Visa offered by a club or an organization, which hopes to get some assured business—and a bit of the action—by offering a perk or two to members.

When you join, say, the country club or tennis club, you would get a 5 percent discount on your annual membership fee by getting a credit card cobranded by the club. The club automatically puts the fee charge on the card. You get a discount, and the club is able to make sure that anybody who joins up is jolly well going to pay his dues on time.

If you're out to join a gym or health club, you might ask if they issue their own credit cards. Is there a benefit, like the 5 percent discount mentioned above? Some clubs, with or without a cobranded card, will offer you reduced rates if you charge your membership each month, because they can get the money directly from your credit card or checking account without the hassle of sending you an invoice, says financial educator and counselor Robin Bullard Carter.

months or a year; then it clicks back up to the dreaded 18 percent. But that's okay: by that time, you'll have collected a swarm of new low-rate introductory offers, and you'll be ready to switch again. And again. Just be sure to cancel the old credit cards promptly; having lots of credit card accounts makes you more susceptible to overspending, not to mention having a card get stolen.

Heed the cautions of counselors. Every financial planner and credit counselor we interviewed insisted that a warning be included: credit cards can be dangerous.

"Credit cards are a major nemesis of young people, both emotionally and financially," says Carter. She sees no difference between the way banks market these cards to young people and the way the tobacco companies market cigarettes to them. "Young people are most at risk. And both credit cards and cigarettes are addictive."

"Understand that when you get into the world of credit, you can spend the early years of your young life paying nothing but interest on debt," adds Don Williams, president of a company that processes credit card charges.

Carter advises having no more than one credit card. That way, you're going to stay focused on how much you're running up.

"Put your credit card in your checkbook cover, along with the check register," Harris advises. "Every time you use your credit card, write down the date, time, place, and amount, just as if you were writing a check. When you get home, you know just how much you're going to have to pay."

If you are in trouble, seek help quickly. Nonprofit consumer credit counseling services in most cities can help you work out a debt repayment plan. They also can intercede on your behalf with angry creditors. If you get in a credit hole, don't wait; get help.

Bill Paying

The Story of Owe

You might think this should be a very short chapter. A bill arrives. You groan. You put it in a pile. At the end of the month, you write a check. You mail it. End of story.

But as with all things money, applying some thought and strategy to your bill paying techniques will benefit you in surprising ways. Like freeing up time, putting a few dollars back in your pocket, relieving you of unneeded stress, and making you look like a champ in the eyes of the lenders (no small thing for anyone who plans to get a loan someday). Here are some thoughts and tips to maximize your bill paying practices.

The Science of Timing

Most people do one of two things when it comes to bill paying: write the check the day it arrives so they don't have to think about it; or wait until the end of the month to pay all bills at the same time. Neither is optimal in purely financial terms. But bill payers who think solely of maximizing every penny are sentencing themselves to a fair bit of agony.

"Keep it simple," says Constance Barber, president of Barber Financial in Needham, Massachusetts. "You can nickel-and-dime yourself to death figuring out the exact day to pay each bill. You can have so much clutter in your mind trying to keep track that it's not worth it for the few pennies here and there that you're going to save."

As part of the simplicity approach, consider going to automatic bill paying, that is, arranging to have your bank automatically pay certain bills on the same day each month. But only do this for bills that stay stable each month. (For more on automatic deductions, see Electronic Banking on page 34.)

Bills that will vary from month to month fall into a handful of categories: credit cards, big-ticket loans, utilities, and billed purchases. As you will see below, some of these you should pay off quickly. Others you can comfortably sit on until the end of the month. Our recommendation is to do a short financial sit-down every two weeks. Pay off the crucial bills fast, put the rest in the "end of month" pile, and balance the checkbook (remember to write in those bills that were paid automatically by the bank). Total time: a half-hour. Smart and easy. Here is some advice to make this process go even more smoothly.

Pay credit off fastest. The bills that are most deserving of prompt attention are those "that would cost you the most money (in interest or late fees) or grief (in embarrassment or hassle) if you left them unpaid," says Andrew Tobias, author of *My Vast Fortune.*

That's a good definition of credit cards, which "have an unusual way of charging interest," says Shel Horowitz, a consumer writer based in Northampton, Massachusetts, and author of *The Penny-Pinching Hedonist.* "If you don't pay the entire balance, they charge interest on the part you paid as well as the part you didn't pay, starting from the time you made the purchase until your payment was received. So while you think you're paying 6 to 18 percent interest, you're often paying double that."

The message: Pay credit card bills in full and on time. A good time to mail a bill is 7 to 10 days before it is due. That way, you've given the postal service a fair bit of time to deliver, and you've gotten the maximum usage of the money without paying interest.

Pay off loans faster. Pay off your big-ticket loans as early in the month as you can, and when possible, in amounts greater than what is due. Here's why. A mortgage on a house has an unusual interest structure in that your payments pay the interest off first, says Horowitz. As the life of the mortgage goes on, the payments begin to reduce the amount of principal. (This may hold true for some car and student loans as well.)

"Let's say your monthly payment is $1,000," he says. "If you pay $1,200 instead, the $200 is applied to principal." Depending on how often you this (and how much you send when you do it), Horowitz says, you can save up to half the total cost of the house. You need to make sure that your bank allows this and that your bank is properly crediting your payments. Check in with them every few months to make sure the money is credited to your account and applied.

Another option is to make a mortgage payment every two weeks, suggests Sunny Harris, president of Sunny Harris and Associates, the Carlsbad, California, publisher of the *Traders' Catalog and Resource Guide.* But don't make a full payment each time. Pay half of the monthly payment. By the end of the year, you'll have made 13 monthly payments, not the usual 12. "You'll pay your house off sooner, and there'll be substantially less interest over the long run." (For more information, see Mortgages on page 92.)

Be diligent with utilities. Hey, these guys control your water, your electricity, your ESPN. You want them to be friends. Don't jerk them around much. That said, utilities can be somewhat flexible. If the bill arrives a week or two late, hey, they'll deal with it.

Some utilities are fond of an alternative billing program that they usually speak of as a budget plan. It permits you to pay the same amount each month, and that way you pay a bit more during periods of low usage to avoid getting slugged during periods of high usage. The message here is that it isn't worth it . . . except when it's worth it.

The utilities have found a way to work budget plans to their benefit, claims Ken Cooper, a management consultant based in St. Louis and author of *Always Bear Left: And Other Ways to Get Things Done Faster and Easier.* "The fixed monthly amount is calculated by taking the total yearly anticipated bill and dividing it by 11, not 12," he notes. "What's good for the utility is that you are actually prepaying your bill by a small amount each month." Multiplied by hundreds of thousands of customers, the prepayments add up to a sizable chunk of your money that the utility is earning interest on instead of you. Who could possibly want that?

Well, maybe you. If it's hard for you to come up with the cash for a staggering electric bill in August or a sky-high heating bill in February, the plan is a good option, says Horowitz. Or if you want to automate payment of your utilities through your bank, life gets easier when the payment is the same size each month.

Be a good customer. You probably have bills for things you bought directly from a company, such as magazine subscriptions, mail-order clothes, or plumbing work. The repercussions of paying these late are small at first—lots of angry, pleading letters notifying you of past-due bills. At some point, the companies will turn over the bills to collection agencies. But you know what? Regardless of whether there will be serious consequences of not paying these bills promptly, you should pay every one off at the end of the month. Likely, you'll be doing business with these people again. They have memories. And if they served you well, you should pay them without hassle. This is called integrity.

Dirty Debtor Tricks

A little uncivil disobedience used to be possible in dealing with the Man. Orneriness wasn't just a great deal of fun, it was actually rewarded. Well, sometimes. One fellow who was proud of his exceedingly fanciful tax returns used to brag about his technique of avoiding IRS scrutiny. "When the return is all filled out and signed," he'd say, "I throw it on the floor. Stomp on it. Dance on it. Kick it around. When it's all soiled and wrinkled, I send it in. I figure those clerks will approve it just to avoid handling it."

If that ploy ever worked, it doesn't anymore; an audit or two managed to take the spark right out of the game. Creditors have also caught on to the following classic cons.

Putting the gas company's check in the electric company's envelope. **And vice versa. By the time the honest mistake had been caught and it was pony-up time, the bills had been stalled for at least a week. Now those humorless power companies just add the balance to the next set of bills. With penalties yet.**

"Forgetting" to sign the check. **Innocent mistake, anybody could make it, and days go by while it's straightened out. No longer. The bank may cash it anyway. Or it could be returned to sender, penalty attached.**

Understanding Float

Perhaps the most aggressive strategy for maximizing your bill paying is, to use financial jargon, "playing the float." At it's most basic, the float is the period of time elapsing between the moment you write a check to pay for something and the moment the money is actually withdrawn from your account. It's an enchanted period, because you have actually paid for the item—it's yours—yet you are still earning interest on the money.

You can take advantage of this in a modest way with credit card purchases, particularly substantial ones, like refrigerators and other appliances. First, get to know the closing date on your credit card—that is, the last day of your billing period each month, after which additional charges will not appear until the following month's bill. You can find out what this date is with a call to your card's customer service department. Then buy the big item the day after the closing date. It won't appear on this month's bill. It will turn up on next month's bill. And that bill will have a "pay by" date by which you must make your payment in order to avoid any more finance charges—but that date may be as many as 25 days away.

For instance, if the closing date is the first of the month, buy that behemoth stereo you've been wanting on the second of the month. The bill won't turn up until a month later. Send the check a week before the pay by date. Considering that it will take a few more days for the check to get to the bank, that money will be earning interest for nearly two months after you bought the stereo. You would have lost that interest if you'd paid cash.

The same theory goes for other big bills. Let's say you've had your kitchen redone and you owe the contractor $10,000. Delaying pay-

Messing with the computer. **If the bill is paper rather than a card, chances are it's being read by an OCR (Optical Character Recognition) reader. Some artful dodgers, being careful to use the same color ink, minimally altered certain numbers along the bottom of the bills with felt-tip pens. The OCR rejected them, thus stalling payment. Lately, though, the utilities have been coming after the little inkers who pulled this one.**

Mailing the bill without a stamp. **The utility would pay for the stamp and the sender, who neglected to fill in his return address in the upper left corner, was six whole cents richer—that's what stamps cost back when this routine worked. Now, the utility slits the envelope open, reads the sender's address, and sends it back. Then the payment is considered late, and there is a late fee.**

In a similar move, sometimes a trickster would make out the envelope so that the utility's address was in the upper left hand corner, where the return address goes, and the customer's address was in the center. No stamp. That way when the utility would attempt to return the envelope to the sender, it would just end up being sent back to the utility again anyway. That doesn't work anymore either. It's also mail fraud. A federal offense. Most people conclude that it's not worth going to jail for a free stamp.

ment until the twenty-ninth day means you've had $10,000 to invest for a month. Of course, that means the contractor has had to dip into his own pocket to pay off subcontractors—or delayed their payments until the twenty-ninth day—and, well, you get the point. Again, let integrity, not greed, guide you.

When (and How) to Juggle

Okay, it just might happen someday. Your cash flow, through absolutely no fault of you own, hits a logjam, and your creditors must wait around while you figure out how to rob Peter to pay Paul.

First, take a moment to savor your bank balance while you still have it, and then, "pay the bills that are going to be the most critical to you first," offers Harris. Each month, you must pay the electric bill, the phone bill, and the rent. Everything else can wait. But what if you have to prioritize beyond that? Here's your order. Follow it only in case of emergency, please.

1. If you have only enough to pay two out of three bills, pay the electric bill first. If your electricity is turned off, you'll have a tough time keeping perishables cold and you'll have to read this book by candlelight.
2. Then pay the phone bill. A disconnection means you'll be charged a fee to get reconnected.
3. Let the rent wait. In most circumstances, it takes a landlord at least 30 days to kick you out. If you know the money's coming, holding back a week or so on the rent won't hurt.
4. If a bill has to wait, be sure to let the creditor know that you are aware of it and that you plan to pay it shortly. Creditors don't delight in chasing you or giving you a hard time. In fact, many are willing to work something out with you. Ultimately, they just want to get paid.

Wallet Strategies

Organizing Your Back-Pocket Office

Such are the passages of man. In your adolescence, your wallet contained a school lunch card, maybe a laminated four-leaf clover, and your Boy Scout ID. In your college years, there was a condom, a college ID, a driver's license, and scraps of beer-soaked napkins bearing phone numbers.

Today, you carry a man's wallet. You keep the pants pocket button above it buttoned because you aren't as trusting as you used to be. If you work at the type of job that requires you to wear a tie every day, you probably carry your wallet in your suit jacket pocket. And no matter what the experts tell you about credit card discipline, you carry two of those devil's instruments.

So much for what you do carry; let's examine what you should have in your wallet. A man's wallet must be prepared the way a medieval knight was prepared with shield and lance and plume—for both practical and ritualistic reasons. You really need all the stuff crammed in that folded bit of cowhide. And you're going to look rather feckless if you don't have all of it.

The Cards You Carry

First, you need your cards, the bits of plastic that link you to your place in the world. Always carry the following.

- Your driver's license
- Your credit cards
- Your automated teller machine (ATM) card (but not your PIN number—memorize it, already)

- Your motor club, American Automobile Association (AAA), or roadside emergency card
- Your health insurance or HMO membership card

There is one card that you need but that you shouldn't carry with you: your long-distance phone card. "Memorize the numbers and leave that card at home. If you lose your wallet, bad guys can do more damage with a phone card than with a credit card," says Sunny Harris, president of Sunny Harris and Associates in Carlsbad, California.

The Cash You Carry

No wallet is complete without the legal tender that makes the world go round. Here's what you need in the way of money.

Stash a C-note. "Hide $100 in cash from yourself," Harris suggests. "This is for emergencies." If your car breaks down by the side of the road, and the guy with the tow truck sneers at your motor club card, you'll have the money to get the car towed. And you won't be looking for an ATM in the middle of the night.

Give yourself an allowance. Keep another $100 on hand, Harris recommends, "most of it in twenties, with a few ones in case you need tips."

"Determine how much allowance you're going to give yourself to live on each week," suggests Robin Bullard Carter, a financial educator and counselor in Newbury, Massachusetts. This is the money that will pay for lunch, gasoline, a cup of coffee or a soda. It might range from $15 up to $150; not too many people, Carter says, need more than that. Soon, you'll observe, "Hey, the money is gone. Must be a new week." If you begin to notice you have too much week left at the end of the money, you'll have to either adjust your dollar amount—give yourself a raise—or pay closer attention to what you're doing with your money.

The Extras

Then there are all the little other things that make a man's wallet complete. Here are some examples.

Do discount cards. You get them everywhere—at the bagel store, the photo kiosk, the video store. They're the membership/discount cards that reward you with freebies. Keep the ones from the stores you actually frequent regularly, not the one you never have a hope of taking advantage of.

Keep a photo or two. It is still quite acceptable to carry a photograph of your wife in your wallet. And your kids. And your dog, if you want. In fact, it's a good idea. Then, anyone who asks about your family deserves what happens to him.

"The downside is that photographs do make your wallet fat," says Carter. "So carry one family photo. A group shot."

Stash a few business cards. You never know when business may break out. Always have a few cards available for giving away to potential clients.

Have space for receipts. Don't leave your ATM receipts hanging out of the machine. Fold them up and stash them in your wallet, along with your restaurant receipts and credit card slips. Once a week or so, transfer these to your desk at home, making sure all purchases are recorded. Save them to check against your monthly statements.

Thoughts for Your Penny

Metal money is a nuisance. It can dirty up your pants pockets. In fact, it can make holes in them. It can spill out and get lost when you sit down. And, thanks to inflation, none of it under a quarter is worth much of anything. But you have to deal with it because it's handed back to you in change during nearly every exchange. So where should you stash your silver?

"Carry what you can stand to lug around," says financial educator and counselor Robin Bullard Carter. A coin purse is a possibility, but it's bulky and weighs you down on one side. Of course, if you have a hefty set of keys in the other pocket, that'll balance you out. But then you'll need suspenders.

To deal with all those pennies and nickels accumulating on the dresser, follow these steps.

1. Get lots of empty coin rolls from the bank. Most provide them for free.
2. Write your checking account number on the rolls *before* filling.
3. Pay your kid or the neighbor's kid to roll them for you—offer 5 to 10 percent of the total take. In other words, if he rolls $100 worth, give him $5 to $10. Or buy one of those inexpensive machines that roll coins.
4. Count the coins in the first roll of each denomination to make sure it's correctly done. Then check the others by putting them side by side with the first one. You'll easily see if one is, say, 49 or 51 coins rather than 50.
5. Put the rolls in a box, not a bag (the rolls could split open more easily), and take them to the bank for deposit in your checking account. Tell the teller you have measured each roll for accuracy. Be pleasant when dealing with the teller. He hates coin deposits.

Tightwad Strategies

Learning the Value of Thrift

You can always afford luxuries. It's the necessities that keep you broke.

There is a solution: The more carefully you budget for everyday things, the more money you have for the nice stuff. There's no real need to be a penny-pincher or to take perverse pleasure in denying yourself. But inside every man is a watchful fellow forever toting up balances. Let him have his say sometimes; let him whittle down the cost of things. It won't mean sacrificing the pleasant touches that allow you to enjoy your day, but it will mean having a little dough left over to spend or save as you wish.

Developing a Tightwad Mindset

To truly turn that inner bean counter into a force that will save you money, you'll need to develop the skills that are found in the thriftiest of men. Fair warning: The more prepared you are to do all or most of these, the better the strategies here will serve you.

Do it for fun. Thriftiness is like exercise—if you don't enjoy it, after a few weeks you'll slide back into old habits. There's a certain pleasure to be derived from frugality. You outsmart retailers. You test your wits. You become a better cook. You watch your money accrue. Don't be embarrassed about being frugal; make it a pleasurable pursuit. Set goals and relish the challenge.

Be willing to walk. Bein a true tightwad requires that you be willing to walk the extra mile—yes, sometimes literally—for the best deal. It means doing the legwork necessary to seek out the absolute lowest price, the least expensive way to accomplish a goal. You have to be dogged in your determination.

Always ask. Sometimes, getting a break on a price requires only that you open your mouth. In the world of the thrifty, the most truly economical thing you can do is spend the energy required to ask, "Is there going to be a sale on this soon?" or "Do you accept competitors' coupons?" or "Is this the best you can do?" Remember that asking costs nothing.

Look for freebies. Whether it's the coupon bin at the front of the store or the offers in your local paper, a true bargain gourmand cultivates a palate for the giveaway. He develops a radar for discount days, two-for-one sales, and kids-under-12-stay-free offers. All it takes is the readiness to put your ear to the ground.

Know what time it is. Happy hour is when drinks and food are half-price. Late afternoon is when farmers' markets cut prices in half to move unsold produce. The last day of the month is when car dealers are desperate to make a few extra sales. Spring is the best time of year to buy a winter coat. The frugal guy knows how to time his purchases for maximum discount.

Buy in bulk. When the price is finally right, take advantage of it. Buy a lot. Toilet paper by the case. Six-packs of deodorant. Keep daily essentials stockpiled at home so you never have to make a fast purchase at full retail price.

Do it yourself. A homemade meal is almost always cheaper than a restaurant meal. A homemade bookshelf is cheaper than a store-bought one. The truly frugal enjoy growing their own herbs and vegetables, making things for their houses, or cooking up chili for several days' worth of lunches.

Never confuse thrift with being a cheapskate. A man of thrift knows when to scrimp but also when to splurge. He knows that when the kids need new shoes for school, it's not the time to go down to Goodwill and find shoes that somebody else's kids broke in. Quality always matters. He will not drive his family crazy with crosstown comparison-shopping marathons every weekend. He knows when to be frugal even with his own sense of frugality. Otherwise, he could find himself in all sorts of expensive messes. Divorce court, for example.

Every Store a Thrift Store

Here are some examples of common situations in which you can pull a tightwad tactic or two. Saving money is fun. See how you like it.

In the Men's Department

Start at the top. Clothes shopping should begin "with visits to the top stores in your city," says Andrew Kozinn, president of Saint Laurie Merchant Tailors in New York City. "Learn what the best looks like: suits that cost more than $1,000, shirts over $150, ties above $50, shoes over $200. Handle them. Try them on. Talk to salespeople. A lot of men are intimidated by expensive stores, but you have to know the best to get real bargains later."

Watch the time. When you're buying off-the-rack clothing (and what penny-pincher wouldn't?), bear in mind that "the better ready-made brands all go on sale between Thanksgiving and January," says Lydia Cherniakova, ed-

Write Your Own Discount

You're sore as hell and you don't want to take it anymore? So write a letter. You're just as pleased as can be? Well, write a letter, suggests Jim Dacyczyn, former co-publisher of *The Tightwad Gazette* newsletter in Leeds, Maine. He tells of the time his fishing reel snapped. He wrote to the manufacturer, expecting an offer to replace the part. Instead, a few days later, the mail brought a brand-new reel. It was the tone of his letter that did it, he thinks. He was the loyal, lifelong customer hurt by what seemed almost a personal betrayal.

"Be polite," he advises. "Don't rake them over the coals—that will likely get you a form letter back." Tell them that everything you've bought from them over the years—and it has been lots and lots—has worked beautifully. But your good luck ran out, this one broke, and what can you do about getting it replaced or repaired? "They will probably bend over backward on behalf of a good customer."

"Don't be abusive," adds Larry Roth, editor and publisher of the *Living Cheap News* newsletter in Kansas City, Missouri. "Write as if Miss Manners had first right of approval. But state exactly what the problem is. Don't ask for freebies; ask only that they do what they're supposed to do."

On the other hand, "if they have a product you really like, write to them. Tell them," says Dacyczyn. "You'll likely get coupons for the product or for other ones they manufacture."

"Be specific," Roth adds. "If you're praising a service, tell them what happened and when, and who treated you especially well. One such letter got me a $25 certificate from Trans World Airlines. I wasn't expecting that."

itor of the consumer newsletter *The Best for Less*, based in New York City. "Some sales start in early November. You can probably get 25 percent off then. You can make this a science and note each store's sale times on your calendar so that when the time comes, you're ready." Remember to only buy clothing on sale that you would buy at full price. A suit that you never wear is no bargain, no matter how little it costs.

Be a friend to charity. Undercover cops who must look moneyed say they befriend people at charity designer sales or resale shops, who let them know when a cashmere coat or Bond Street blazer can be had cheaply. The cops claim it's just a matter of stopping by occasionally. You can do that.

Don't wear out your wardrobe. Matching pieces—like a jacket and trousers—should be cleaned together. That way one won't wear out faster than the other. Don't let shaving lotion, cologne, deodorant, or antiperspirant touch your jacket. They can affect the dyes. And if a stain appears, hustle the clothes to the cleaners quickly so the stain won't set and disfigure the garment. The more careful you are about cleaning your clothes, the less often you'll have to buy new ones.

Clean your clothes with coupons. Sometimes your favorite dry cleaner will accept competitors' coupons, offers Amy Dacyczyn, former publisher of *The Tightwad Gazette* newsletter in Leeds, Maine. It can't hurt to ask.

At the Grocery Store

At least master meatloaf. "Men should learn how to cook," points out Amy Dacyczyn. "It's dramatically more expensive to eat at a restaurant or to eat a frozen dinner."

But you work all day; you come home tired. You don't want to prepare dinner from scratch.

On weekends, you should cook a large quantity of one dish, Amy Dacyczyn suggests. Chili, maybe. Next weekend, lasagna. Then meatloaf. Package it in meal-size portions and put them in the freezer. After five or six weekends, you'll have quite a repertoire of dinners, she says. Of course, you don't have to eat meals from your stockpile every night. Just eating them three nights a week will save you hundreds of dollars a year.

Go on bended knee. Inside the store, "learn to take your time," says Jean Kwiatkowski, former editor of the *Money Talk* newsletter in Wilkes-Barre, Pennsylvania. "Invest 10 minutes to learn the prices of different products."

And remember that supermarkets put the most expensive items at eye level; the better deals are on the bottom shelves. You can get tinned crab meat and sardines in oil just by reaching out. The big cans of tuna packed in water require squatting down.

Consider couponing. There's a trap here: Nice savings in one area can tempt you to overspend in others. The fact that you use coupons for bread and dishwashing liquid does not justify splurging on a jumbo-size box of sugar bombs cereal. And be careful to use coupons only for products you would buy anyway. Kwiatkowski suspects that you're already an expert in this area. "In college, men learn they have limited amounts of money. So they have to save in areas where prices are not fixed, like groceries. I know young men who grab the coupon section in the paper before the women."

Appliance Shopping

Watch for good news in the paper. No, not the big, colorful inserts from the local superstore. Appliances and electronics can be had for amaze-your-friends prices by reading the classifieds, says Larry Roth of the *Living Cheap News*. "Someone is always leaving town or upgrading, and selling everything from stoves to stereos to computers. The merchandise is often nearly new, and it can cost as little as 10 percent of new items."

Know when it's show time. Electronics manufacturers display their new products at winter and summer consumer shows. These are usually in January and June. So it's a good idea to shop in February and July, when dealers may be discounting old stuff to make room for the new.

Go soft on supply stores. Once, computers were so intimidatingly complicated that you had to buy your software—plus computer disks and paper—from the dealer. Now a better deal can be had from the mammoth discounters like Staples and Office Depot. And they deliver free if your order is more than $50. Similarly, many retailers run low-price businesses by showcasing their wares in catalogs or on the Internet. With no physical store to maintain, they pass their overhead savings right on to lucky old you.

Wait for the mail. Ignore those good-sounding deals on computers from the discount houses, says Jim Dacyczyn of *The Tightwad Gazette.* Most discounters don't offer technical support (at least, not for free), and trust us, a computer expert on the other end of the phone can be worth his weight in gold when the kids have the day off and the Super-Karate CD-ROM won't boot up. Most mail-order companies, it turns out, will talk you through a problem on the phone, without a support contract. "If they can't, they'll make arrangements to have somebody pick up your computer the next day and ship it to them at their expense. They'll repair it and get it back to you."

Be first to be second. A first-time computer buyer could really get burned, says Shel Horowitz, author of *The Penny-Pinching Hedonist.* "Read the trade publications at the library. Go through a year's worth of *PC World* or *MacWorld.*" Read the articles. Get the evaluations. Then consider a model that was introduced from eight months

Members Only

There are two benefits to joining the organizations mentioned here. The first is that you don't have to go to meetings. The second is that you can save some money.

If you were in the military for longer than 180 days and you received an honorable discharge, you are considered a veteran. Give your local veteran's association a call and see what membership makes you eligible for, suggests Jim Dacyczyn of *The Tightwad Gazette.* "I got a 10 percent discount on my car insurance," he says. "It amounted to more than my annual membership fee. So it was worth joining."

It sounds obvious, but another resource you shouldn't overlook is the public library, he says. "You can check out movies for free, including offbeat ones the video stores don't have. And you can go online with their computers to conduct searches."

Membership in motor clubs like the American Automobile Association (AAA) entitles you to discounts on hotel rooms and car and truck rentals.

Warehouse clubs probably don't strike you as hotbeds of controversy, but Dacyczyn takes a decidedly partisan approach when the subject comes up. "A lot of them are selling merchandise designed strictly to be sold at these discount warehouses," he says. "They are not big savings; you can do just as well or better at other places."

While the advantages of airline frequent flier programs are well-known, less known is the frequent-eater's club known as Dining A La Card. For a modest annual fee, you can get a 20 percent cash rebate on your total dining credit card bill in participating restaurants. A check is mailed to you each month. Find the club on the Web, or call directory assistance for the toll-free number.

to a year ago: Sometimes you can get it for more than half of its original list price.

Ask the mail-order company if any rebuilt computers can be had at a discount, Jim Dacyczyn adds. "There are deep savings here, but be sure they give you the same warranty the new ones have."

At the Restaurant

Keep the cards. Restaurants often give out little cards that they will stamp each time you make a purchase, "like the pizza joint that gives you your tenth pie free," says Horowitz. "Anything that doesn't cost money to do, do it."

Follow this menu for saving. Ordering à la carte can be a big savings, the experts say. Or you can make a meal of two appetizers. If you're with another person, the two of you can split an entrée and an appetizer. Beware: Some tony restaurants actually have the gall to tack on an extra charge for sharing.

Order pasta. It's almost always the cheapest thing on the menu. It costs the restaurants almost nothing to prepare, Horowitz says.

Eat at the bar. At places with a salad bar, consider ordering the soup-and-salad-bar combination. It's cheap, it's filling, and it's usually rather healthy. Learn to load your plate with the good stuff: chickpeas, tofu, spicy peppers, and fresh fruit. Put the lettuce on top.

Be an early bird. Some restaurants offer savings if you order your dinner prior to 5:30 P.M. You'll end up eating the same dinner for less money, and you'll have less of a wait because it's off-peak.

On the Road

Get a deal for your wheels. The best prices on rental cars, says Roth, come on the weekend, when business travelers aren't using the cars.

"Plan ahead," adds Horowitz. "As soon as you have the dates, start calling." Rent-a-Wreck and Ugly Duckling, two agencies that rent out used cars, may have the best prices (and the cars aren't bad). But these two chains don't have franchises everywhere. So pick a company and just ask for its best price. Savings will vary by up to as much as 50 percent.

If you're in a frequent flier program, you may receive car rental coupons in your monthly mailing; they even turn up sometimes in those fat coupon packets the postman brings.

Two extra tightwad tips: Fill the gas tank before you return the car. Check if you really need the collision-damage waiver. You should have that coverage through your own auto insurance or through a gold or platinum credit card.

Know the plane truth. If you're traveling by air and don't want to waste money, be prepared to work the phones. Pepper those airlines with questions. "Sometimes they have discount prices in the morning," says Roth. "Or there are special rates on night flights. Ask." The greatest savings come when you make reservations in advance. Two to three weeks ahead is best, though sometimes two-weeks' notice is cheaper than three-weeks'. And don't forget that changing a reservation will cost you $75 just to rewrite the ticket.

Cast the net. If you have access to the Internet, enter "airline + bargain" into your computer's search engine to see what's out there. You can't, unfortunately, use the information to negotiate with the airlines, but if the numbers are good enough, you won't have to. Several discount airline agencies have the ability to search across all the airlines' databases to seek out the cheapest flights, then report that information back to you so you can make your reservations.

Don't spend a week's pay for a night's sleep. Roth raises thriftiness to the level of psychological warfare when he suggests that if you go from hotel to hotel on foot. "Go without luggage. They figure if you set down luggage, you'll take what they have to avoid picking it up again. If you're without luggage, they may offer a better rate to keep you from walking off."

Redial. When you're checking rates, Horowitz says, "call the hotel's toll-free number and the directory number. You may get a better rate from one than from the other."

Call the chamber. Contact the chamber of commerce of the city to which you're traveling and ask that a visitor's packet be sent to you. Stress that any discount coupons are to be included.

For Entertainment

Usher in a bargain. One thing anyone can do to see a free movie or play, says Horowitz, is to get a job as an usher. "You need no special skills: Just hold a flashlight, wear a black jacket, and remember where the bathroom is. And you see the show for free." Call your local entertainment venues to find out about their ushering needs and hiring practices.

Listen up. "I usually win 5 to 10 sets of free tickets every year by listening to a radio station that has a lot of giveaways and a relatively small audience," Horowitz says. "I don't compete at big commercial stations, where they have 100 people calling in for the tickets."

Go by the book. A company called Entertainment Publications offers books of coupons for meals, including half-off for single diners as well as the usual buy one, get one free. There are also discounts for movies and sporting events. There is a different book for each city, and the price is about $30 for a year's supply of coupons, though charitable groups offer them for a few dollars less. Call your local chamber of commerce and find out how you might find the one for your area.

When to Splurge

On your first date with Cindy Crawford, you will not pay for dinner with a two-for-one coupon. At that moment, nothing is more important than Cindy. Not even saving money. Later on, when she's sure you're stashing cash to buy an engagement ring . . . well, that's different.

There are times when the tightwad inside should be told to shut up. A splurge is called for, so let the dimes or dollars fall where they may.

Vacation is one such good time to loosen up, because you're there to get away from your normal routine, says Larry Roth of the *Living Cheap News*. Also, you've spent a bit of money to get where you are, why not splurge a little if that's going to help you enjoy your trip a little bit more?

Sometimes, a show of money is called for. Stint and you won't come off as sensible, just . . . stingy. Take your daughter's wedding. No, the ceremony is not about you. It's about the two ladies in your life. The bride. And the bride's mother. This is their show. The wedding is very important to them. Don't let them down by being frugal. Anniversaries and birthdays are also times to open the snap on the granny purse.

On a more thoughtful note, consider spending serious money on those things that you are going to have around you all your days and that you may wish to pass on to your heirs. Master tightwads Jim and Amy Dacyczyn of *The Tightwad Gazette* "splurge big sometimes on antiques" because nice things are nice to be around. You might consider first editions or artwork. You can buy what you like, and if you do a bit of homework before you buy, in the years to come somebody else might like your treasure, too. Remember that the purpose behind being frugal is so that you will have enough money to spend on the things that you really do want, regardless of the cost.

Shopping

What's in Store for You?

Many Americans regard shopping as a form of recreation, surveys show. What the studies don't discuss is the kind of shopping that we find fun. Hint: browsing a bookstore or guitar shop or tool warehouse or golf display can be recreation for a guy. Stopping for bread and milk and discovering they're on opposite sides of a two-acre supermarket is not. Nor is wandering the aisles of a crowded discount department store wondering where that laundry stain stick is.

Truth is, there is little reason to do the latter. To help you, we've brought together a collection of experts in time management—subhead: shopping—to give advice on minimizing time and maximizing effectiveness in your forays into consumerland. Shop smart, and you'll not only get exactly what you want but you'll also save time and maybe twice as much money—after all, time is money.

Gathering Intelligence

Your first order of business when it comes to smart shopping: stay put. Don't leave your house. Get a pencil. Some paper. Decide what you want. Write that down. That's step one. Step two is to decide what level of study is needed to make the purchase smart. If your list consists only of milk and bread, you need not study. But the other stuff—the tools, the appliances, the clothes, the vehicles, the vacation packages—needs some research. Spend a little time in the comfort of your home, researching what you'll soon be shopping for, and you'll be five steps ahead of the next guy. Here's where to look.

Read all about it. You can get information about the things you want to buy by checking out publications like *Consumer Reports* to see how they rated several products in the category you're curious about. And from a simple pricing perspective, few things are easier than browsing the Sunday paper and comparing the prices at each of the megastores in your area.

Pick up the phone. A good way to save both time and money is to let your fingers do the walking. Use the yellow pages. "Why spend four hours walking around the mall looking for something when you can pick up the phone book and call everybody? When you find what you're after, have them put it aside so you can go straight to that store," says Sunny Harris, president of Sunny Harris and Associates, the Carlsbad, California, publisher of the *Traders' Catalog and Resource Guide.*

This is a crucial point. If you want to buy something—be it a pair of jeans, a portable compact disc player, or a new car—you should not leave your house until you know pretty much which one or two models you might buy, exactly which stores carry them and at what price, and whether they have them in stock. By the time you hit the store, all that's left is to get a hands-on look at the models you've focused in on and to cut a deal once you make the final choice.

Trolling in the Aisles

Now that you're a well-armed (read: well-informed) shopper, it's time to actually go to a shop. But there are still things you can do to further maximize your time in the stores. What we offer here are time-saving tips to help keep you focused on your goals—and keep you from buying stuff you didn't want in the first place.

Avoid special trips. "Management experts make prioritizing a big deal," says Ken Cooper, himself a management consultant based in St. Louis. They categorize some things as "gotta do," others as "oughta do," and the rest as "If there's nothing else to do in the entire universe, do this." The last category could include cleaning out the garage and pouring concrete on the driveway.

The whole concept of shopping, Cooper says, is to ensure that nothing you need is a "gotta do." It should all be on the "oughta do" list. "You don't need anything this minute." (Okay, if your wife's eight months pregnant and is having a craving for cheese doodles *now*, we'll grant an exception). But generally, if you run out of copy paper or toothpaste or light bulbs or logs for the fireplace, and you have to stop everything and go get them, that's a waste of time. Instead, keep an eye on things and notice what is running low.

Build critical mass. Your next move in getting control of this unwieldy process is to minimize travel time by "batching up" your work, as Cooper puts it. "In an auto plant, they don't make each part for each car as it comes down the line, they make 500 of this and 500 of that." It's the same with errands. Since everything is on the "oughta do" list, you have the leisure to make some considerations. Are the stores you have to visit close together? If the computer store is a few miles north of you and the home im-

You're Outta Line, Mister

That isn't a line in front of you at the grocery checkout, it's the flippin' Democratic National Convention. There's only one cashier on duty, and if you crane your neck to catch a glimpse of her standing several miles up ahead, you see the process has ground to a halt. The customer at the head of the line has turned up an anomaly: whatever it is he's trying to buy, it's the only one of its kind ever found, and nothing is happening now because employees are racing around trying to find out how much whatever-it-is might cost. He's stalled, she's stalled, you're all stalled, and NASA will be on Jupiter before you get out of this place.

You're only toting a few items: a jug of orange juice, a sack of bagels, and a packet of flashlight batteries. What gods of injustice have put you behind all these people pushing overloaded carts? And what might you do about it?

- **You might say, "I have just a few items. Mind if I go ahead of you? Thanks much." That's fair, and it might work.**
- **A long line at the store isn't your problem; it's management's. So march over to the customer service desk and ask them to open another lane. Find out which one they intend to open and position yourself there until a cashier arrives. Go to the head of the line.**
- **It's for times like this that you carry a pen and your organizer. Make a to-do list. Do some brainstorming about a problem at work. Use the time productively.**
- **Use the zen approach. Take five slow, deep breaths. Relax. Grab one of the magazines on display and ponder bathing suits, martian creatures, Victorian furnishings. Or be completely radical—talk with a stranger. Pleasantly.**

provement store is a few miles south, trekking to both on the same afternoon doesn't make any sense.

Let the list build, wait until you have at least three or four things to get, and get them the next time you're in this particular part of town. Always ask, Is this convenient? Can I do it quickly? If not, let it sit on the list until the trip is worthwhile.

Live off-peak. The other time saver is learning to do things when most people don't. In nearly all things—and all stores—there is a peak-and-valley pattern. Master it, and it will be the easiest way to make it through the world. And you can cut down your time to one-third of what it usually takes to do things.

As a general rule of shopping, avoid Friday night and Saturday after midday. For grocery stores, steer clear of the right-after-work hours—everyone is stopping in to pick up something on their way home. The opposite is true at malls, though.

"People don't say, 'I want to grab that shirt on the way home,'" says Cooper. "They're rushing to get home and eat. So most of the stores in the mall are dead empty from 5:30 P.M. to 7:00 P.M." In general, good off-peak hours are later on weeknights (when the rest of the western world is parked in front of the TV) and early Saturday morning (because most people have an aversion to getting out of bed).

Don't be distracted. Never forget that all stores are designed to lead us astray. "It's important in time management to buy only what you want and not spend your time browsing," says Harris. It's important to the wallet, too, to never buy anything that you didn't know existed until you saw it in a store window.

Here's a strategy for getting in and out of any store fast, suggested by Elaine St. James, author of *Simplify Your Life.* "The moment you walk in the door, nail down somebody. Tell him you're looking for faucet washers or whatever. He'll gesture and say, 'Go two aisles down and turn left. Bottom shelf.' Then you say, 'Will you come with me and show me?' He'll do it."

Make lists. No, not a shopping list—you already knew enough to compose one to keep you on track. But there are other lists you'll want to make, too.

One is what St. James calls a 30-day list. "If you come across something or see an ad for something that you'd like to have, don't go buy it right off. Put it on a 30-day list, and reconsider it when that much time has passed. There's a very good chance that at the end of 30 days you won't be able to remember why you thought you wanted it." Many an exercise bike, rowing machine, and bread maker has bitten the dust after 30 days.

Another list, suggested by Beverly Chapman, an independent financial planner based in Boston, takes it a layer deeper. "In order for these strategies to be effective, you must first make a list of three or four things you really enjoy doing, like walking the dog or reading a book or playing golf. Anything that is more fun than shopping. Then you will want to save time shopping so you can get to these other things. Otherwise, all of the little time-saving strategies won't work."

The Smart Consumer

Buying a new television? A lawn mower? A car? An airplane ticket? Computers are drastically changing how people shop for such big-ticket items. Here's how to use your modem to make buying faster, easier, and cheaper.

Get rated. If you subscribe to a service like America Online, often one of the free offerings is access to product ratings, such as those done by *Consumer Reports* magazine. So before you buy a toaster, five minutes of hacking could get you to independent ratings of the best and worst toasters, along with sharp-shopping techniques.

Check the source. Woe to the product manufacturer who doesn't offer product information online these days. Say you're interested in a product from ZZZ Corporation. Chances are extremely good that if you search the Web for http://www.zzz.com, you'll get connected to a ZZZ Corporation Web site that offers a huge amount of useful information. Product specifications. Warranty information. Whether there's a rebate program. Authorized retailers. Authorized repair shops. Available accessories. Whether it's for sale direct from the company (skip the middleman and save bucks). Photos of the products. Prices. So if you're shopping for, say, a new refrigerator, your first step might very well be going onto the Web and perusing the Web sites of General Electric, Maytag, Sears, and any other brand you're considering. By the way, all fit the formula above: Just type in "GE" or "Maytag" or "Sears" in place of the "zzz" in the hypothetical Web address above.

Buy services. You can use computers to research and buy not only products but services as well. A great example is airline tickets. You can access all major airlines and reservation systems directly through the Internet or through online services such as America Online. You can search for flights by price, date, time, airline, whatever. You can see a schematic of the plane and see which seats are available on a particular flight. And then you can book your tickets and have them sent to you overnight, often at no charge.

The List You'll Like to Make

A list of chores and duties should begin with the opposite—a list of three or four things you would really rather be doing. Ideally, they should not cost much money. But you must get control of the time you spend on obligations so you can have more time for . . . listening to your Duke Ellington collection? Watching Bogart films on video? Surfing the 'Net?

Estimate now how much time you must set aside for the following.

Paying bills

Balancing your checkbook

Monitoring investments

Doing accounts on the computer

Grocery shopping

Mall shopping

General errands

Jot down the time you spend on each every day for a week. Then you'll know how much time you must set aside for these matters. After that, you can begin to whittle down the time spent in three areas—grocery shopping, mall shopping, and general errands—by mastering the tips we've outlined here. Thus, you'll have more time for important matters. Like the ones on this list.

Walks on the beach

Candlelit dinners at home

Watching the game

Having sex

Get the idea?

Sales Tax

Is There Any Way Around It?

"A penny for the governor," the sales clerks would say cheerfully as they added up our purchases, calculated a percentage, and added that on, too. It was rarely just a penny. It probably didn't go to the governor either. It's called a sales tax, and is thus in a category not especially loved by the citizens. That's why we address envelopes to City Haul and the Infernal Revenue Service.

Sales taxes are tricky business. Here in the United States, the way we tax our purchases changes from state to state. Some states have no sales tax whatsoever. Others have sales tax rates even higher than the 7 percent that the federal government levies for Social Security. Some states tax food or clothes; others don't. Some states let their counties or cities levy sales taxes. Sometimes, a state levies temporary sales taxes to pay for a big state project—a new freeway or rebuilding after a catastrophe. Don't even try to sort it all out.

Tax Loopholes

Note this well: The law does not look kindly on discussions of how to circumvent sales taxes. Why? Because often, you are breaking the law when you do it.

For example, one of the easiest ways to bypass a sales tax is to buy merchandise in another state and have it shipped. "But a different tax does apply," says certified public accountant Ira Bergman of Bergman, Schraier and Company in St. Louis. "It is called a use tax be-

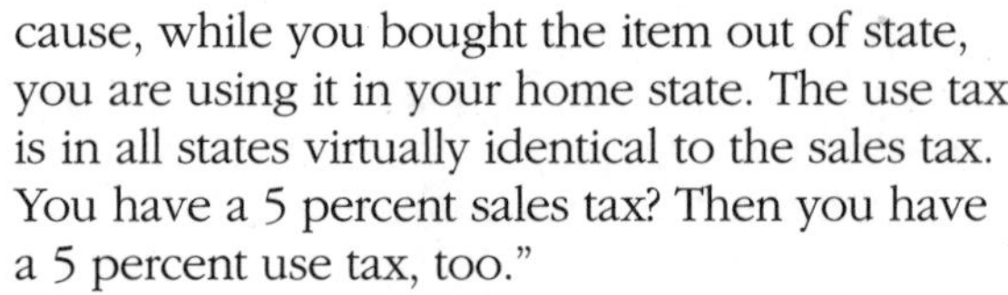

cause, while you bought the item out of state, you are using it in your home state. The use tax is in all states virtually identical to the sales tax. You have a 5 percent sales tax? Then you have a 5 percent use tax, too."

Strictly speaking, you need to voluntarily report that tax on a use tax form. You can get the form from the state department of revenue. Write down the purchases you made that year from out of state, and calculate how much use tax you owe.

We suspect, however, that if you complete this process, you will likely be the only person in recorded history ever to do so. As one source put it, "As a practical matter, there is little or no attention paid to the use tax form."

So we give you this warning: slippery ground ahead, proceed at your own risk. Consider what follows as something presented solely for your entertainment, like a newspaper astrology column. We do not advocate breaking the law. But if you are curious about how evil people circumvent sales taxes, read on.

Support your neighbors. If you're within a reasonable driving distance of a border or two, "be aware of sales tax differences in your area," suggests Larry Roth, editor and publisher of the *Living Cheap News*. For example, Missouri recently eliminated its sales tax on food. This is of the liveliest interest to people in Kansas, who can get 3 percent off by crossing the state line. And every now and then throughout the year, New York state has a period of no sales tax. It lasts about a week. It gets publicity.

Ship it in. It was a solemn moment, unfortunately lost to history, when the first traveler bought an item in a store far from home. How did he react when he was told, "If you take this with you, we have to charge you sales tax. But there's no sales tax if we ship it to you. There's a shipping fee, but it's less than the tax would be. Cheaper to ship." So it remains today: ship a purchase across state lines, no sales tax is charged.

Go by the book. Buying from catalogs is a world of commerce that is worth getting to know. "Many places have 800 numbers, so there's no charge for the call," says Roth. "And they may have a flat shipping fee, as low as $4 or $5 per order. But there's usually no sales tax."

The seller of the catalog items may or may not be registered to do business in the state where you live, says Bergman. "If the seller is not, then chances are they won't charge you a tax—they don't file the paperwork in that state. That doesn't eliminate your liability, though." He means that the transaction should go on the use tax form—next time you send it in.

Be a Web slinger. Things are equally ambiguous when you start buying products from companies with storefronts on the Internet. Some will announce, "If you live in Iowa, add 5 percent sales tax. In Illinois, add 6.25 percent." But most don't mention it, and that's in your favor. "Say you purchase some computer software on the 'Net," Bergman says. "If it's sent to you electronically and you download it, it is not subject to sales or use tax, because the laws typically say that the tax applies only to tangible personal property. But if it's sent to you on a $2.50 disk, it's tangible, and you may owe use tax."

Similarly, you may order books and magazines through the Internet. But publishers also offer the option of buying the book or magazine *on* the 'Net, in electronic form. Are the ones you can hold in your hand taxable while the others are not? Well, it depends.

"If you buy a tangible item through the 'Net, title passes to you the moment you give the company your credit card number," Bergman says. The transaction may not be subject to tax because it was done electronically outside the state and all they are doing is delivering your product. "Under current law," Bergman says, "the best way to buy is electronically, if possible."

Buy through contractors. Cultivate relationships with people who are able to buy things for business purposes, advises Alan Lechner, a financial consultant in New York City. Not only will they be able to get you some hefty discounts but you won't pay sales tax, because the contractor has a resale license that exempts him from paying the tax. A contractor can buy major appliances—a stove, a refrigerator—for you. An interior decorator can get furnishings, rugs, designer items. In the jargon, these folks are not the "end users" of these products and therefore not liable for sales tax.

Live Tax-Free or Die

If avoiding sales tax is a major concern for you, your last, best option is to move to a place like New Hampshire, whose motto—"Live Free or Die"—applies not just to life, liberty, and the pursuit of happiness but to sales tax as well.

And the Granite State isn't the only one. Here's a complete list of states that have no sales tax.

Alaska
Delaware
Montana
New Hampshire
Oregon

As long as we're talking about moving, here are the states with the highest sales tax, in case you feel the need to avoid them.

Mississippi (7 percent)
Rhode Island (7 percent)
Minnesota (6.5 percent)
Nevada (6.5 percent)
Washington (6.5 percent)

Negotiating

How to Name Your Price

The ancient Babylonians knew that life was a marketplace. Everything was for sale, all prices were negotiable. And when they approached the stall and asked, "How much?" they knew not to believe the first number they heard.

It's supposed to be different 5,000 years later. We have mass production and shelf pricing now. Things cost what they cost. No haggling.

You know that's malarkey.

It's still a bazaar; you can still find treasures amid the trash. And that price stamped on the item you're looking at? Standard pricing be damned. It's nothing more than somebody's idea of where to start the bidding.

If this chapter is going to resonate for you or save you money at all, you need to recognize one incontrovertible fact: It's all negotiable. From a refrigerator to a TV to a diamond to a compact disc player, there's a price advantage to be had for those who seek it. And right now, you're looking in the right place if you want to know how to get a good deal on just about anything you want.

The Theory of the Deal

Now, we're not advocating that you walk into the local drugstore and demand 10 percent off your next tube of toothpaste. For small, commonly available items, negotiating is implicit—you pick the store with the best price or service and buy there. There are only three scenarios in which you should *always* negotiate.

1. When the item or service you are buying is priced at more than $250
2. When you are buying something used
3. When you are in a here-today-gone-tomorrow buying opportunity, such as a garage sale, farmers' market, flea market, or craft show

"The reason for negotiation is to satisfy the interests of the two parties," says Charles Craver, professor of law at George Washington University Law School in Washington, D.C. He translates: "The salesman has the item you want; you have the money he wants." Your strength and the salesman's weakness are the same thing: competition. If you don't buy it from him, you'll buy it from somebody else.

"Preparation is the key to getting to that point," Craver says. "You must know the market, and the value of whatever it is you're going to talk about. If you don't, you're not going to have much belief in your position, and the other guy can take advantage of you." Here's how to keep that from happening.

Hit the books. "Give yourself a minimum of 30 days to look and read, and maybe listen," says Mike Phelps, owner of Audio Video Solutions, an electronics store in Washington, D.C. Especially when you're shopping for high-performance items like electronics. That way, you won't rush into a decision you'll regret later, after you've bought a set of speakers that are such a dog that the woofers actually bark. Take advantage of both print and electronic information to find out about the product you want to buy. "Read *Consumer Reports.* Look up the product on the Internet and learn the base price," he suggests.

Focus on features. Before you go looking at different models of the item you want, sit down and draw up a list of features it has to have. Then make a list of features that would be nice to have, but that you can

Sneaky Sales Schemes

The people you are buying from are not in business to pass the time. They know the negotiating ploys you are going to hit them with, and even if the ploys are effective, they have some of their own. They like to say that the money they didn't make off you they get—in multiples—from the next guy because things have a way of balancing out. What they don't like to tell you is how they do it. They told us, though. Here are some of the tactics salesmen pull. Be wary—in case you're the next guy.

Fine-tuning. **The TV monitor with the highest profit margin is the only one on the showroom floor with a perfect picture, sharp and vibrant. The others have had the fine-tuning or color knobs adjusted ever so slightly, to give a hint of haze over the picture. Your eyes—and wallet—are drawn to the pretty one.**

The show in the showroom. **Just as in a theater, store lighting can be contrived to give almost any effect. That refrigerator looks like a prop on a set because it is. This is another trick to lure you to the item with the highest profit margin.**

The name game. **The big stores have lines of appliances with their own labels on them. The house brand TV is $200 cheaper than the RCAs and Panasonics. A bargain? Not really. The name brands' prices have been inflated $200 so the house brands will look like a deal and move fast. You can guard against this one by doing a bit of the research that experts advise.**

Pigtails and rabbit ears. **Makers of heavy appliances, like stoves, don't know whether the electricity service in the area where the product will be sold will be 208 or 230 volts, so they leave it to the retailer to put on the electric plug, the "pigtail." After you've finished negotiating, the store can tack a $10 to $15 "pigtailing" charge onto the bill. Similarly, about five years ago, TV manufacturers stopped putting antennas on their sets. As with the pigtail, this gives the dealer a chance to pick up another $10. Don't pay it.**

The free fee. **Some stores offer free delivery to your house. Notice they don't say *into* your house. If you want that refrigerator carried into your kitchen, that's $20. Otherwise, they leave the thing on the porch.**

live without. This will help you keep your priorities straight when you enter the salesman's lair.

"Decide which features are benefits and which are fluff," says Frank Jones, president of Jones Appliance in St. Louis. "TV manufacturers love picture-in-picture, but customers think it's a pain. It adds 10 percent to the price. One brand of compact disc player boasts it holds 61 discs. Who needs that? Surround sound has up to seven speakers, but if your television doesn't broadcast that way, what's the point? It has to look and perform the way you want. The hell with the specs."

Be a model student. "After you've spent the time to decide what model you want," says Corky Pollan, *New York Magazine*'s shopping columnist, "call the manufacturer's toll-free number." They may possibly have a version of what you're after in a discontinued—and discounted—model. This works best for heavy items like stoves and refrigerators; for other appliances, the newer models may be superior.

With a model in mind, "call at least three stores and mention the prices you've seen for it," Pollan says. "Can they do better? Almost always, they can. Even high-end stores will usually negotiate."

Let competitors compete. Discount houses like Best Buy and Circuit City advertise their willingness to match—or beat—competitors' prices. Look through the sales brochures in the Sunday paper, says Larry Roth, editor and publisher of the *Living Cheap News.* "If they have the item you're after, take the brochure to the stores. Watch the prices go down."

Use coupons. Ask your store if they will honor competitors' coupons, Roth says. This tactic, by the way, can work with any store that has competitors, from electronics shops to dry cleaners.

Get tomorrow's discount today. In a department store, Roth says, "Ask the salesperson if there will be a sale on the item in the near future. They may offer a discount just to move it."

Stop in at the end of the month. Or if there's a sale going on, go to the store on the last day of the sale. In both cases, the merchant "may have equipment he wants to get rid of," Jones says, "or he may wish to stimulate business by taking a smaller profit margin." Translation: He'll give you a break to move merchandise off his shelf.

Check your personality. It's tempting—and a blunder—to become a gimlet-eyed, hard-voiced, you-can't-pull-the-wool-over-my-eyes type. This is what the experts call the "adversarial style," says Craver, and you'll end up "trashing whatever the person is selling in hopes of talking them down. You're saying, 'I don't really want this—so give it to me for half price.' It never works."

While it's not a good idea to look as though a coconut fell on you, a little innocent-seeming fondness for the product is in your interest. "I really love this," you tell the salesman. "I just can't afford $500. Would you consider taking something less? Or do you have something similar that might be less expensive?" You've thrown it back to the salesman, Craver says. "You've invited him to please you and given him a way to save face while he does it."

Show you're a player. "Let the salesperson know you're not kicking tires," Phelps says. "You brought money. You're there to buy or to go to the competition. A seasoned company will always negotiate." Make sure your first offer is not too big a cut; that way you'll have room to maneuver.

If you're not hearing what you want, Jones says, make him a final offer. If he says no, excuse yourself and walk out. Perhaps he has given you his best price, and that's it. Or perhaps he's thinking what every footstep is costing him. So don't disappear without leaving the salesperson information about where he can find you.

Take a friend. Hate to haggle? Do you find all this horse-trading off-putting? Do you wish everything had a shelf price, like canned corn? Take someone with you who likes to negotiate, advises Craver. Be discreet about this, though. It can turn the salesman against you if he realizes too soon that he isn't negotiating with the buyer but with the buyer's next-door neighbor.

If you're married, take your wife and work as a team. Let one person play the role of the eager buyer and the other person the role of the we-don't-want-to-spend-that-much-money-Honey spouse. This can drive a salesperson crazy, but it's highly effective in getting prices down.

Stay quiet. If you really take no pleasure in negotiating, Jones says, try this: Ask the salesman just one question, "What's your best price?" Then be quiet. For as long as it takes. Silence becomes a powerful weapon. The pressure is on the salesman, and if he's going to lower the price at all, he'll do it now.

Part Three

Tactics for Smart Investing

Safety Net

How Much Should You Have Tucked Away?

According to recent figures, the average American saves an abysmal 2 to 5 percent of his income. That means that as the economy chugs along, many of us are pouring our money into cars and clothes and daily living, rather than putting away some hard-earned cash for that proverbial rainy day.

Now that you see it in print, it doesn't seem like such a smart thing to be doing, does it? Naturally, financial planners agree with you.

"Sometimes you need to save beyond what you think you'll need," says Peggy Ruhlin, chairperson of the International Association for Financial Planning and a financial planner with Budros and Ruhlin in Columbus, Ohio. Life's little snafus and unexpected events can be costly. And life's big realities, like buying a home, can be time- and money-consuming. Good planning for both requires saving and investing. Saving is for short-term needs. Investing is for long-term goals. A disciplined mix of the two can alleviate the pain and frustration of trying to afford something now that you could have paid for yesterday. The discipline just takes some forethought and some assumptions, which we'll go over here.

When to Start Tucking

First, you need to enumerate—in your mind if nowhere else—the reasons for weaving your financial buffer against disaster. Some reasons are pretty obvious and pretty scary. But they all bear going over, one by one, before we discuss how to save or invest for them.

Unemployment. The biggest need for that money you can get at—as opposed to long-term investments—is during unemployment. That's when being liquid can save you from taking money out of other investments, such as retirement or college funds, just to pay basic living expenses. The general rule of thumb is that you should have at least three months of salary tucked away in a conservative savings account.

Of course, everyone is different. You might be able to find a new job in an hour. Then again, it may take someone else a year to gain new employment. That's why you need to have a game plan and understand your finances, your job security, and your long-term goals. Inclusive in those sobering plans should be a lot of "what ifs?" And "what if" situations usually occur when you least expect them.

Crises. There are a few typical scenarios in which people need immediate money for emergencies, Ruhlin says. "Number one, you die and your family needs money for living expenses. Most people think their life insurance will cover this, but often there is not enough or there is a delay in getting the money. Number two, you become ill or disabled. Sure, there is disability insurance to cover your living expenses, but this may not kick in for six months or more. And if you think Social Security will help, forget it. Social Security only applies if you are permanently disabled and can never work again." Other money-draining crises might be a serious illness in your family or the sudden need to put your ailing parents into managed care.

Big-ticket purchases. It doesn't matter if you are saving for a $20,000 car or a $500,000 house. The killer is scrounging up a large enough down payment to avoid major interest and financing charges.

This is especially true of houses. Most people put 10 to 15 percent of the purchase price down on a house. Considering relative income scales, that's a big chunk of cash to save.

Again, financial planners emphasize the word save. In the case of a house, if you know you are going to be in the market for a house in fewer than five years, you should be stashing money in a more secure investment vehicle than stocks or bonds. This means you should be putting money in a bank savings account, certificate of deposit, or money market account, says Mary K. Sullivan, a financial planner with Protected Investors of America in San Francisco. Because the saving process is usually planned well in advance, however, there is more room to navigate amongst investment instruments, albeit very conservative investments such as short-term treasury bills.

Most of the same principles that apply to saving for a house would also apply to, say, cars. Set your sights on how much you'll be able to comfortably spend, then begin to figure out how much the down payment will run. Once you have an amount in your head, you can begin the process of working toward that goal.

That rainy day. Don't forget that in life there are always things popping up that you'll want or want to do or don't expect you'll have to pay for. Everyone likes to take a vacation or go out to a nice dinner. These items should be effectively planned for as well. "I call it having fun," says Gary Greenbaum, a fee-only investment counselor and president of Greenbaum and Associates in Oradell, New Jersey. Make sure you have a little mad money tucked away—perhaps in its own little account.

Where to Stash It: Part 1

Here are some of the best places to put your money away for rainy-day savings, as defined by the Institute of Certified Financial Planners.

Money market or savings accounts. **These are the basic places to start an emergency fund. They're safe and easy to access. A money market account typically will earn more interest than a simple bank or credit union account. Shop around, because money markets vary significantly in their rates of return.**

Certificates of deposit (CDs). **These bank investments lock your cash up for a few months to a few years, your choice. The longer the period, the higher the rate. Penalties are big for early CD withdrawals.**

Short-term treasuries. **Lend the government money by investing in treasury bills, which are similar to bonds but of a much shorter term. These lock your cash up for three to six months. The returns are fairly low but don't get taxed by your state, and the investment is 100 percent safe. If you need access to the cash before the expiration date, you might be able to sell your investment on the open market. These can be bought straight from the government, but they cost roughly $10,000. Contact the closest Federal Reserve bank if you want to open an account.**

Short-term bond funds. **Some planners say go ahead and invest part of your emergency fund in a short-term bond mutual fund (or even short-term bonds themselves). Funds that hold treasury securities or highly rated corporate bonds that mature in one to three years would be suitable. They usually will earn more than a money market account. But watch the interest rates carefully—your bond fund (or bond) could drop in value if interest rates climb. A big plus: You can cash out of these investments at any time without penalty.**

Saving . . . or Investing?

The rules for savings are quite individual. The amount you should have in savings depends on what you are saving for and how much time you have to save. Financial pros like Ruhlin say that you should be saving for retirement, education, emergencies (such as losing a job), a home, and any big-ticket items you might want, including cars, appliances, and home furnishings. A smart move is to have a separate account for each of these.

As you can see, there are many variables to consider, but here are general guidelines for building your own safety net.

Know the difference. The first thing you'll have to come to grips with is the difference between saving and investing. Saving is money that is set aside for events that may occur within a short period of time (saving to buy a car next year, for example). Investing is money that you place in financial instruments for no fewer than three years. "The difference between saving and investing is timing and liquidity," says Sullivan.

One factor often left out of the scenario, though, is risk. "Some people are just not comfortable with their money in the stock market no matter what the time period," says Sullivan. "Then, they should have it all in savings."

Plan in layers. To help people figure out where to save their money and how much to tuck away, financial planners have people break down their lives into wants, needs, and goals. Then, these groups are further sliced into specifics, and an attainable plan is put in place.

Greenbaum says he plans in layers. "First, we have the life necessities—food, shelter, and clothing. Then, we pay off high interest rate debts. Then we plan for emergencies," says Greenbaum. This type of money should be in accounts to which you have immediate access.

After the basic savings plan is in place, he begins to plan for long-term goals. And the first two items he plans for are death and dis-

Where to Stash It: Part 2

Aside from savings and emergency funds, we all need that stash of mad money, the mini-nest egg we crack open when we really deserve a treat. Where's the best place to hide this little present to yourself? Here are some expert suggestions.

Sock it away. You can keep your mad money at home, in a lockbox or safe, if you want. But you don't have to get all formal about it. "The safest place is one where it won't be disturbed," says Moriarty Financial Services president Christine Moriarty. "Where you won't be going to it every five minutes. Inside an old shoe, deep in the closet. In a sock at the bottom of your dresser. Between the pages of a book (perhaps this book). Where you have to think about it in order to go get it."

Just don't put it in the freezer—that's the first place burglars look. And you needn't bother with those hollowed-out shaving cream cans you see for sale in the spy shop catalogs, along with telephone taps and books on how to get revenge. You're not the only who gets those catalogs, you know.

Start by keeping a small roll of twenties—a hundred bucks, let's say—then add to it now and again. And if you tap it, replace it as soon as you can. If you don't have the discipline to do that, don't bother with a home stash.

Check it out. Open a second checking account. The

secondary account is a more cheerful option than safes and bank boxes because this is where you begin letting a bit of decadence into your life. This is the money for single-malts, way-cool Ray-Bans, and the courting of profound women. But the problem with self-indulgence is that it takes discipline to bring it off properly.

"The primary checking account is one that pays a little interest," says Sunny Harris, president of Sunny Harris and Associates, the Carlsbad, California, publisher of the *Traders' Catalog and Resource Guide.* It may exist in relation to a savings account, a money market account, or a stocks-and-bonds account, all of which are attached as a means of keeping the checking account from going into overdraft. This account is a financial workhorse: it exists to cover the car payment and the light bill and the rent and the rest, the one from which you buy stocks and bonds. You want to be able to write these checks when the time comes.

When the time for bills has come and gone, put $50 in the secondary checking account. Deposit more if you have it. Watch it build. It's nice if the account pays interest, but it doesn't matter that much. There's a psychological key here: Since bills are taken care of by the primary account, "you don't run the risk of blowing your bill money on a CD player," Harris says. "You have a special account for that. A real slush fund. One with which you can play."

ability. The first step is to buy appropriate disability insurance. He says he will then do his "death planning," which includes wills, life insurance, and trusts. "Lawyer fees will cost you between $1,000 to $2,000," he says.

After all of the legal planning and insurance policies are in place, Greenbaum says he looks to fund retirement and education. A basic rule is to set aside 10 percent of your income to cover these two items, he says. Or you can do away with the idiot rules and have a financial plan assembled by a professional. "It'll cost you $2,500 every three to four years, and you won't have to guess. You'll know exactly how much money you'll need to save each year and what rate of return your investment portfolio needs to earn over the long run," Greenbaum adds.

Go to the market. "I recommend that people have their savings in a money market account as opposed to a bank savings account," says Sullivan. A money market account will pay at least 2 percent more interest than a savings account. Sullivan says some money market accounts allow the same accessibility and check writing features that a traditional bank account offers—but at a higher interest rate. "I tell my clients that they should have three to six months of living expenses in their money market account and that they should only touch it for emergencies," Sullivan says. "I don't recommend that they hold this money in a mutual fund or a stock or anything else that invests in the stock market."

While money in the stock market is not totally inaccessible, it takes more time to get the funds. "You can usually get the money in a couple of days, but it could take three to five days," says Sullivan.

More important, if you have money in the stock market, you should view it as an investment. Liquidating such funds for short-term needs could be costly. "You might have to do it on a day when the market drops and you would have to sell at a loss just to get at it," says Sullivan. "Besides, there are transaction costs every time you buy and sell."

Balance

Spreading Your Cash Around

Let's assume you have a stable job and a financial plan. You want to save money for retirement, you want to save for your kids' college educations, you want to park a chunk of cash for emergencies, and you want a small slush fund for bold investments and wild vacations. What to do?

The obvious answer—start shopping for investments—is wrong. See, a hodgepodge of random investments makes little sense. In a good investment portfolio, the sum of the investments is greater than the parts.

One of the most-used terms in the investment world is *asset allocation.* It refers to the pattern in which a person has spread his investments: One hundred percent in stocks? Fifty percent in stocks and 50 percent in bonds? Or a more complicated mix of stocks, bonds, certificates of deposit, and other investments?

Your asset allocation says an awful lot about you. It reflects how willing you are to take risks. It says whether you are investing for the long term or parking for the short term. It says you are smart enough to spread your investments across a diverse blend of options, or bullheaded enough to believe that you know how to tell the future.

A Matter of Risk

To simplify your asset allocating, you might wish to look at all of your investment goals through the prism of "risk." Many people see investment risk as the possibility of losing part or all of their investment. It's a legitimate concern. But a better way to define investment risk is

volatility: how much, and how frequently, the value of an investment fluctuates. You see, markets can be erratic in the short term, but they generally are stable in the long term. This is particularly true of stocks. Sure, stocks might turn sour for a few days or a month or a year or two. But over 15 years or more, you can be pretty assured that the market will be far ahead of your friendly bank savings account.

This is why the question of risk is so closely linked to your investment plan. If you are in your thirties or forties and you are investing for retirement, then you can afford lots of risk—time will heal any short-term wounds inflicted on your investments due to market volatility. But if you are approaching retirement age or if you will need your money in three years to buy a house, then low-risk investments are key since a down cycle could last that long.

"People have a tough time understanding risk," says Frank Campanale, president and chief executive officer of Smith Barney's Consulting Group, headquartered in Wilmington, Delaware, and Birmingham, Michigan, which conducted the study "How Behavioral Idiosyncrasies Impact Investor Decisions and the Stock Market." "Too often they take too much risk at the wrong time and too little at the right time."

What follows is a very basic look at the risk factor of the most common investments.

Stocks

Stocks, typically, are considered the most risky investment class. Why? Essentially, because they are linked to a company's financial performance, which as you know, can vary wildly month to month and year to year. Historically, stocks are the most volatile of all investments that are capable of high percentage fluctuations from day to day.

Of course, not all stocks are equal in risk. Financial experts have lots of ways of categorizing a stock. Here are a few.

By size. The bigger the company, the more stable the stock, generally. Analysts break down stocks into three categories: "small-cap" stocks, meaning the company is worth $500 million or less; "mid-cap" stocks, meaning the company is worth $500 million to $5 billion; and "large-cap" stocks, meaning a value of at least $5 billion.

By growth. Here there are two general categories. A "growth" company is doing just that: steadily growing in revenue and profits. You invest in them with the hope and expectation that the company will keep growing. A "value" stock is considered to be selling at a bargain. You invest in them when you think the stock price is below what the company is really worth.

By location. By this, we mean the United States versus overseas. International stocks are inherently more risky than domestic stocks since they are subject to additional forms of risk. For example, fluctuations in the value of the dollar affect the stock's value almost as much as the performance of the company, warns James Pupillo, chairman of the Asset Allocation Committee for the Institute of Investment Management Consultants in Scottsdale, Arizona. "They are more volatile but may produce higher returns," he says. International stocks are also subject to political risk. (Hint: An overthrow of a government is not good for stocks.) And they may not be as well researched as companies that are subject to the reporting requirements of the United States.

By income. Stable companies like utilities offer dividends to shareholders. Since you are guaranteed some return on investment, dividend-paying stocks are considered less risky than stocks with no dividends.

By industry sector. To twist John Donne's words, "no stock is an island." If computer software stocks are having a good week, Acme Software's stock may surge for no good reason other than that it is riding on the coattails of the industry. There are dozens of industry sectors, ranging from biotechnology to railroads, from banking to food. As goes the sector, often go the individual stocks within that sector.

Why You Should Be Patient

In any given year, stock prices bounce around like superballs. But if you can step back—far, far back—then a pattern emerges. And it is a very pretty pattern, indeed. Unquestionably, the stock market has been the place to make money over time. The American Association of Individual Investors says that for the past 50 years, small-company-stock investors have received an average annual return of 12 percent, large-company-stock investors 10 percent, bond investors 5.5 percent, and those who kept money in cash (short-term treasury bills and money market accounts) received 3.5 percent.

Compare that with a one-year period of an investment in large-company stocks. Depending on the year, you could have had a gain of 50 percent or sustained a loss of 30 percent, according to the Forum for Investor Advice. The group points out that investment data show "averages." So, one down year may be offset the next year with a gain. In other words, time is on your side.

Bonds

When you buy a bond, you are lending money to a government or a company with the promise that they will repay you at a set time, at a set percentage rate. You can hold on to the bond or you can trade it on the open market, with its value changing based on daily changes in interest rates.

There are several ways to measure a bond's risk.

By the issuer. If the U.S. government is issuing the bond, it is safe. Supremely safe. If it is a state or municipality bond, the risk is minimal. If the bond is from a big company with a good financial rating, it is more risky but generally a fine investment. If a Third World government is issuing it, hold on tight. And if it is from a company in a Third World country, take your Dramamine right away.

By its rating. Several top-notch organizations with names like Standard and Poor's and Moody's issue independent quality ratings for all publicly traded bonds. These range from supersafe AAA+ ratings to wild-and-woolly junk grade.

By the due date. The longer the term of the bond, the more volatile its price in the open market. In other words, a bond that is payable in 15 years will generally see greater price fluctuations than a bond due in 1 year.

Cash

The third category of investment is "cash," though when an investment advisor says that, he really means safe, liquid investments like money market funds or certificates of deposit. These are by far the safest investments. In fact, they should not fluctuate at all in value.

Unbalanced Choices

As you look to balance your portfolio and seek out the investments you can take advantage of, remember that there are more than a few people out there willing to take advantage of you. Before you start spreading your cash around, take note of these opportunities—and avoid them. According to the experts, they're the biggest investment scams around.

Pump-and-dump stocks: **Online financial message boards and chat rooms have traditionally been great places to learn about promising investments. But things are changing, says Colorado Securities Commissioner Philip A. Feigin in Denver. Nowadays, touts who share insider information with "five million of their closest friends" often convince gullible investors to buy big into a certain security, thereby driving up its price. The tout then dumps his share at a profit, and you're left holding an overpriced stock.**

The soft-sell cold call: **Normally, you wouldn't invest your money with a stranger, of course. But this scam gets around that rather neatly, says Nancy Smith, director of the Securities and Exchange Commission's office of investor education and assistance in Washington, D.C. A caller with apparent credentials asks whether you'd like to make a lot of money. Sure, you say. The voice then replies that he doesn't have anything right now, but he'll keep an eye out for you.**

Balancing Your Assets

All of this brings us back to that notion of asset allocation. Here is some advice for finding the right balance of investments for you.

Pick a model. There are three basic asset allocation models. A conservative model will garner less investment return (typically less than 8 percent, when averaged out over several years), while an aggressive model will bring in a higher return (targeting 15 percent). A moderate asset allocation model will bring in returns somewhere in between. For a conservative portfolio mix, investments would be mostly bonds and cash. In a moderate portfolio, investments would be divided almost evenly between bonds and stocks. And for a truly aggressive portfolio, investments could be 90 percent or more in stocks. (For more on choosing the right mix of investments, see Timing on page 72.)

This simple act of not asking for money immediately dispels your suspicion.

A week or so later, the voice calls back saying he may have found something but he needs to check into it further, adding that if it pans out, you need to move fast. But he still doesn't ask for money, thus pulling you along a little further. On the third call, the scam unfolds. The big opportunity has arrived, but you have to act now, your new pal informs you. You're so convinced the guy is on your side, you don't ask a lot of questions. As a result, you lose a lot of money.

***A wireless wonder:* You're listening to your favorite radio show when you hear an investment pitch for wireless cable. Sounds great. Who wouldn't want to ditch those wires and clumsy boxes for wireless freedom? In fact, you remember hearing something about this technology somewhere else, perhaps CNN. Yeah, CNN. Hence, you fall into the trap. You're associating the pitch with facts you've heard from legitimate sources, and congratulating yourself for being so perceptive. We're so close, the scammer says, we just need a little more investment money to finalize the design and make you rich. But the only firm this huckster represents is himself, and once he has enough money, he'll split—no wires attached.**

Use mutual funds. Small guys like you and me are easily trampled in the world of stocks and bonds. That's why mutual funds exist. In a fund, thousands of investors pool their money and let a seasoned money manager spread it across many investments, all linked to a well-articulated strategy. Want to invest in large, dividend-paying stocks? There are mutual funds that do just that. Want to invest in bonds of foreign governments? No problem. You name the strategy, a fund exists.

Consider segregation. Often it is healthy to look at your retirement money separate from the rest of your money. Why? Well, it *is* a separate category, if you've put it in tax-free individual retirement accounts or 401(k) plans. These are shielded from taxes and are meant to go untouched for many years. Your asset allocation mix for your retirement stash will be aggressive, spread across many stock investments. As for the rest of your money, it likely has more short-term goals, and thus requires a low-risk investment strategy. Thus, the asset allocation for that cash will be more toward bonds and cash.

Diversify. It's a tired cliché, but it bears repeating: don't put all your eggs in one basket. So what is a smart number of investments? Let's say you have a retirement account between $50,000 and $200,000, and you have many years before retirement. Somewhere from five to eight distinct mutual funds would make sense, with all but one being stocks, and the last one being a bond fund.

Choose a lifestyle. Some mutual funds have devised "scenarios" that broadly target groups of people. These funds, called Lifestyle Funds, target your age and invest in stocks or bonds. For example, a fund for 25- to 35-year-olds would invest 90 percent of its assets in the stock market and 10 percent in the bond market. The fund for 35- to 45-year-olds would have a 70 percent stock to 30 percent bond mix. And so on. But investment pros say that while those funds may be good starting points for some, they do not take into account individual needs or changing needs. "It's a pretty general and generic asset allocation," says Pupillo.

Timing

How to Know When to Do What

Imagine that you go to work every day, but payday comes only four times a year. Essentially, that's what happens to your investment portfolio: just four measly days out of a whole year account for some 95 percent of your annual return, according to Ibbotson Associates, a Chicago company that tracks investment data. When will those four days fall? Well, if you knew that, you wouldn't need this book. Fact is, no one knows with any certainty which days are going to make the difference on your investment.

This is why investment professionals are always touting the virtues of long-term investing. But it's tough to figure out when you should jump into the market. The day after you decide to invest, the market could fall, and you could lose money. Then again, if you wait that extra day, the market could skyrocket, and you could lose out on catching those gains.

Developing a Sense of Timing

"People ask me when the best time is to buy, and I always tell them the same thing: The best time is sooner. The sooner, the better," says Harold R. Evensky, author of *Wealth Management* and a financial planner at Evensky, Brown, Katz, and Levitt in Miami. He says that investors shouldn't care what the stock market looks like. "Just put the money in," he recommends. Of course, Evensky isn't talking about a haphazard investment. After a thorough look at what type of investment you

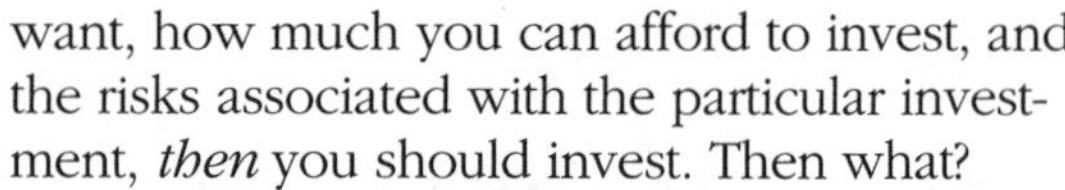

want, how much you can afford to invest, and the risks associated with the particular investment, *then* you should invest. Then what?

Invest regularly. There is no better way to ride the ebbs and flows of the market than to spread out your investments over time. So set up an automatic investment program, and throw a few hundred dollars each month into that mutual fund. Sure, at times you'll buy at top dollar, but other times you'll buy when the price bottoms out. And all those peaks and valleys will be leveled in the long run.

Buy 'em, then hold 'em. It's never easy figuring out when your stock or mutual fund might rise in price. And it's even more difficult watching your portfolio decline in value. But even the best money managers and stock pickers have their off days.

But remember that no other investments have been able to successfully outperform the stock market in the long run. So buy sound investments that you've checked out thoroughly and hold on to them. Warren Buffett, the greatest investor of all time through his company Berkshire Hathaway, is a buy-and-hold money manager. He doesn't time the markets; he buys investments that will pay off over time.

Know when to sell. A bad investment isn't necessarily one where you are losing money. Most of the time price fluctuations on shares of stock, mutual funds, or fixed income instruments are just that: fluctuations. In fact, many top money managers like it when their investments go down; then they can buy some more at lower prices. But if a business stops growing or if a mutual fund stops investing in the way that you had imagined, then it's time to sell.

Still, price is an indicator. And financial pros will often chart their investments. The thumbnail picture is that if a security falls below its 200-day average, it is time to sell. Though this does not hold true in every case, a drop beneath the 200-day average price is generally a good indicator that some variable is out of whack with your investment, and it's time to take a look at what it is and understand it. "The 200-day average is a pretty good telltale," says Tom Lydon, president of Global Trends Investment in Newport Beach, California. "I use it and so do a lot of other financial planners."

Be wary of the fall. It just so happens that the stock market crash of 1987 was in the autumn. But the fall season for investing may mean more than what its name suggests. Mutual funds typically make their annual shareholder distributions during this time of year. That means if you invest in a mutual fund on December 1 and the mutual fund makes its distribution on December 2, you will be liable for the tax consequences built up within the fund over the course of the year—even though you were invested only for a day. So, you will have to pay a capital gains tax and an income tax on the distribution you receive.

Basically, you'll be paying a tax on money that other people made and you didn't. "Some fund companies will be making 20 percent and 25 percent distributions, and their shareholders aren't aware of the consequences of that," says Lydon. He says an easy way to avoid getting stuck with undue taxes is to call the mutual fund company you are considering for investment and ask them when their annual distribution date is.

Watch December-May romances. December through May is the most popular investment season. "A lot of investors have New Year's resolutions or begin to make plans after the first of the year," says Lydon. "This is when the stock market has typically performed best." Also, corporate earnings tend to be stronger in the first and second quarters, which means stock prices have a greater tendency to rise.

"In the summer, people don't pay much attention," says Lydon. "In the first half of the year, people are more serious about their investment plans, then that begins to fade."

Of course, no one should invest by season alone. Investing for a year is even short. Most investment professionals recommend putting your money in the stock market for 5 to 10 years to experience any kind of strong performance and consistency.

Why the Herd Can Lead You Astray

There's a story of a money manager whose trick for investing was to attend company shareholder meetings and count the number of money managers in the room. If there were more than a handful, he would promptly leave the room, call his office, and sell whatever stock he owned in the company. His theory was that, had he kept the stock or bought more of it, he would be buying what everyone else would be buying.

What's wrong with buying what everyone else is buying? Nothing—if you truly believe in the long-term growth potential of the investment and are willing to hold on to it for a long time. A problem emerges when a stock becomes a fad, the current rage, every analyst's hot pick. Often stocks will jump because of this kind of short-term news or market excitement. But that's not value. Those stocks could easily experience a market correction and fall. Buying high and selling low is not the path to investment success. Buying an investment because of its potential to increase in value on its own business fundamentals, not because other investors are pushing up the price by creating demand, will increase the long-term chances of your gaining better returns on your money.

Choices

Smart Picks for Every Risk Level

We're unaware of anyone who has counted them all up. But if we were to guess at how many publicly traded investments are available to you, there's no question it would peak at 100,000. It's true. There are tens of thousands of companies in the United States that sell stock to the public. Add to that the 6,800 mutual funds traded here, all the government and corporate bonds, all the commodities contracts, stock options, gold investments, and real estate investment trusts (mutual funds that buy property—most often industrial space, but also retail and apartment—and then leases it out, with the goal of income from rentals plus capital appreciation), and your mind will get as bloated as a hog belly. And we haven't even touched overseas investments yet.

Breathe easy. Finding good investments is easier today than ever before, even as the number of investments skyrockets. Why our optimism? Because there are so many terrific tools available to you.

Moreover, you should not even consider most of those 100,000 investment options. If you are relatively new to the investment world, focus your attention on one area: mutual funds. Mutual funds exist for nearly every investment category. And the amount of top-quality information available on these funds will give peace of mind to the most fretful of investors.

Identifying Funds

So you want to find a mutual fund that invests in, say, high-grade corporate bonds? Well, here's how to proceed.

Hit the magazines. All of the major personal finance magazines regularly put out special issues that summarize the performance of virtually every mutual fund. These tables offer ratings, performance statistics, comparisons with other similar funds, and phone numbers with which to order a prospectus.

Consult Morningstar. Morningstar, a highly respected Chicago-based mutual fund tracking firm, rates funds on a one- to five-star scale, with five stars being the best. You can get Morningstar ratings a few ways—from their publications, by going onto the Internet, or even by asking the funds you are interested in. Your financial advisor will usually have access to this information. Also, many libraries subscribe to Morningstar and will have their reports available.

Grab a newspaper. Preferably, the *Wall Street Journal* or the *New York Times.* The big papers—plus certain regional newspapers, like the *Orange County Register* in California and the *Dallas Morning News*—have daily mutual fund listings that are jam-packed with useful information. Long-term results, comparisons with other similar funds, annual fees, and more are there daily. Studying the tables and reading the rest of the section for a few weeks will give you outstanding leads on the best funds to buy.

Consult the funds themselves. Most mutual fund companies offer a range of individual funds. These fund "families" have wonderful literature that describes their full range of products. If you are new, start with the big fund families like Fidelity Investments, Scudder, Vanguard, and T. Rowe Price, to name just a few. Ask for a brochure that details their full range of offerings. They'll be thrilled to help.

Look to the manager. Where mutual fund investments are concerned, look at the record of the manager of that fund. How much risk does he take in managing the portfolio? "Buy the manager, not the fund," recommends Roy Diliberto, vice president of the International Association for Financial Planning and president of RTD Financial Advisors in Philadelphia.

Don't go back to the future. One mistake many investors make is to make investment decisions based on recent performance rather than future prospects. Sure, a fund may have had a good year last year, but what does that have to do with next year? Focus more on a fund's long-term performance—does it consistently beat its competitors?—and most of all, its future strategy.

Quick Tips on Asset Allocation

"A good rule of thumb is to take your age and subtract that from 100; the resulting number is the percentage of your investments you should have in stocks," says Jeffrey Bronchick, a partner and portfolio manager at Reed Conner Birdwell Investment Management in Los Angeles. He says this is a rough estimate for conservative and moderate investors. "It's not 100 percent accurate but it gives you a good idea of where you should be."

He also warns investors not to be afraid of risk. "Most individuals think of risk not as volatility, but as the prospect of losing money. It's an important point because it's one thing to be risk averse and it's another to be risk intolerant. You have to risk some money short term to make money in the long term." Bronchick believes in diversification, of course, but he takes a minimalist approach to it. "You really only need four mutual funds to diversify properly: two U.S. stock funds, one foreign stock fund, and one short-term bond fund." Otherwise, he notes, you are overlapping investments.

Investing by Personality

Are you willing to take risks in pursuit of maximum gain? Or are you a more timid soul who would rather sleep easy with low-risk investments? Here are some strategies for the three main investment personalities.

For the Aggressive Investor

An aggressive investor wants growth and better returns. Here are some ways to reach those goals.

Take stock. Stocks historically average about 9.5 percent over inflation, according to Ibbotson Associates, a Chicago company that tracks investment data.

This is one reason that Greg Sullivan, a financial planner and president of Sullivan, Bruyette, Speros, and Blayney in McLean, Virginia, suggests that between 90 and 100 percent of an aggressive investor's portfolio be in stocks or stock mutual funds.

About 50 percent of that portfolio should be in large and mid-sized stocks, 30 percent in "small cap" companies that are worth $500 million or less, and 20 percent in international stocks, advises Malcolm A. Makin, a certified financial planner and president of Professional Planning Group in Westerly, Rhode Island.

Don't overdo diversifying. While it's certainly important to diversify investments—no matter what type of investor you are or what type of investments you are buying—an aggressive investor might be prone to overdoing it, says Jeffrey Bronchick of Reed Conner Birdwell Investment Management. A sign that you might be holding too many mutual funds is when you have different funds with the exact same financial goal.

Hedge your bets. A very aggressive investor may also want to invest in other asset classes like commodities (such as precious metals or grains), energy, or hedge programs. Hedge programs allow investors to use options or other financial instruments in place of money to buy more investment product. Here, the risk is extreme because additional money may have to be paid if you lose the "bet" on the investment trade. By hedging, you're locking in the current price. If the investment goes up in price, not only does the investment have value but your option to buy the investment at that price has value, too. But if the price goes down, you still have to buy the investment at the higher price you locked in. So, not only can you lose your principal but you may end up paying more for a bad investment. Know what you're getting into: many financial professionals liken this to gambling.

Risk versus Reality

File this under "sensible advice." The Forum for Investor Advice says you should understand what you are getting into when you invest. Here are some of the risks and realities of investing.

Risk: **The value of your investment can go down.**

Reality: **Time mitigates risk. Over the past two decades, there's been just one five-year period when the U.S. stock market lost ground.**

Risk: **Your investment isn't guaranteed like a certificate of deposit.**

Reality: **The steady return from a fixed-income investment will lose ground, over time, to inflation.**

Risk: **The prices of individual securities can vary dramatically.**

Reality: **The diversification inherent in a mutual fund substantially reduces the impact of any individual declines.**

Risk: **The market value of securities changes frequently.**

Reality: **Be thankful. If market value didn't change, there would be no reward for investing.**

For the Moderate Investor

A moderate investor is someone who is willing to accept some risk as the price of doing business, but only for a certain period of time. This type of investor doesn't want to be without access to his money for too long. Here's what the experts suggest for the moderate man.

Do a balancing act. For this type of investor, a balanced approach to money management works best: a close split between stocks and bonds or similar investment products.

"A moderate investor wants to cushion his downside," says Diliberto. "He wants to balance growth with income and understands that there will be highs and lows."

"But he doesn't want the extremes of volatility that an all-stock portfolio may have," adds Makin. "Essentially, he wants a safety net. For example, he is willing to accept slightly less in total return in the hope that the low swings may be more like 7 percent to 10 percent rather than 20 percent or more."

Most people fall into the moderate investor category. Hence, the mix of investments varies greatly because of each person's specific taste for or interest in certain kinds of investments. Financial pros say the moderate investor

Risk: **Bond issuers can default.**

Reality: **Missed payments of interest or principal are rare, and diversification minimizes their effect.**

Risk: **Interest rates could go up (or down).**

Reality: **They will. Then they'll go the other way. Again and again.**

Risk: **Investments outside the United States are subject to fluctuating currency values.**

Reality: **Over time, currency fluctuations tend to balance out. Diversification helps, too.**

Risk: **Unstable political and social conditions can hurt investments overseas.**

Reality: **Every day brings bad news for some U.S. company as well, but you'd never know it from the long-term trend of the U.S. stock market.**

Risk: **Global investments are subject to different securities regulations, accounting standards, and tax rules, and sometimes information can be hard to find.**

Reality: **Mutual funds are managed by full-time professionals whose jobs depend on their thorough knowledge of markets and companies.**

should have 60 to 75 percent of his portfolio in direct ownership investments like stocks or real estate, while 25 to 40 percent of holdings should be in bonds with a relatively short payback period (maturity) of 5 to 10 years.

Favor domestic products. For stocks, Sullivan would lean more toward roughly 75 percent of the portfolio in larger domestic companies, with the rest in smaller companies. He also says that roughly 25 percent of the stocks he would choose would be international companies. "Some diversification is necessary to help out," he says.

Spread out. An aggressive investor may opt to concentrate his holdings for the prospect of a bigger return. But a moderate investor needs to be spread out more among different asset classes and investment types, he says. Indeed, of Diliberto's 60/40 recommendation between direct ownership stocks or real estate and short-payback bonds, he advises 35 percent be in U.S. companies, 15 percent in international companies, 10 percent in real estate, 35 percent in domestic bonds, and 5 percent in international bonds.

Follow the S&P. A core group of stocks to focus on for the moderate investor are those in the Standard and Poor's 500 index. These are larger companies that are often used as indicators of how the broad market of stocks is performing. Some of these companies will be "value" companies and some will be "growth" companies. Diliberto sees a moderate investor having two-thirds of his holdings in value stocks, or those that are out of favor with the market and therefore trading lower. "Over the years, value beats growth," says Diliberto. He says these stocks fall out of favor, but over time they fall back into favor and their prices move higher. Of course, for the moderate investor this may mean waiting through some down times, too. But for those times, the fixed income side of the portfolio should ensure that not all of one's principal is at risk in the stock market.

For the Conservative Investor

The conservative investor "wants the peace of mind that his money is not lost," says Sullivan. To that end, Sullivan suggests these strategies.

Risk Rating

Suppose that you have $100,000 lying around. Now, you could buy a Ferrari (with a really nice sound system). Or you could invest it. Assuming you choose option B, what's the smart way to spread that money around?

We asked money manager Roy Diliberto of the International Association for Financial Planning. Here's how he would handle it for the three different styles of investor.

You already know this, but we're obligated to tell you anyway: Make sure you thoroughly investigate each of these options on your own before you invest your hard-earned cash. Some investments are riskier and require a higher financial aptitude than others.

Aggressive Investor	
$8,000 Fixed Income (Bonds)	**$92,000 Equity (Stocks)**
$4,000 international $4,000 U.S. bonds	$14,000 Standard and Poor's 500 index $16,000 large company (value) $8,000 large company (growth) $11,000 small company (value) $6,000 small company (growth) $15,000 real estate investment trusts $22,000 international companies

Moderate Investor	
$40,000 Fixed Income (Bonds)	**$60,000 Equity (Stocks)**
$5,000 international $35,000 U.S. bonds	$10,000 Standard and Poor's 500 index $10,000 large company (value) $5,000 large company (growth) $6,000 small company (value) $4,000 small company (growth) $10,000 real estate investment trusts $15,000 international companies

Conservative Investor	
$60,000 Fixed Income (Bonds)	**$40,000 Equity (Stocks)**
$5,000 international $40,000 U.S. bonds $15,000 money market/1-year treasury	$8,000 Standard and Poor's 500 index $8,000 large company (value) $4,000 large company (growth) $4,000 small company (value) $2,000 small company (growth) $5,000 real estate investment trusts $9,000 international companies

Climb the ladder. The conservative investor should invest more in bonds (more about what kind in a moment). These bonds should be "laddered" in investments of 5-year, 10-year, and 15-year maturities so an investor can get some capital back, or at least have access to capital, at different periods of time.

Don't play it too safe. The conservative investor needs investments he can count on. He needs to have access to capital with less time constraints or fear that his money will fluctuate in value. It might be logical to think that the conservative investor should place all his assets in bonds—but that's not the case. Too safe of an investment position would, in fact, put the conservative investor at a disadvantage because he would be losing money relative to inflation.

"The riskiest thing in terms of finances is running out of money before you die," says Diliberto. "You don't want that to happen. But it can if you invest too conservatively." He says a conservative investor should have no less than 30 percent—and preferably about 40 percent—of his investments in the stock market, albeit mostly in larger domestic companies. The remaining 60 to 70 percent would be in bonds. Any less than 30 percent in equity investments is akin to saving, not investing. For the equity portion of the portfolio, Sullivan recommends large-company stocks, of which 95 percent should be based in the United States.

Bond with your money. Diliberto's suggested mix works out to 26 percent in domestic stocks, 9 percent in international stocks, 5 percent (if any) in real estate, 40 percent in U.S. bonds, 5 percent in international bonds, and about 15 percent in cash or cash equivalents such as a money market account or one-year treasury notes. The bond selection should also be short- to medium-term notes (5 to 10 years in maturity), Diliberto says.

While the conservative investor is skewed toward fixed income investments, not all of those investments have to be government bonds. High-grade corporate bonds may also be appropriate. Financial pros say to stick with investment-grade bonds. These have ratings of BBB, A, AA, and AAA. These ratings means that the bond has been reviewed and is considered secure. U.S. treasuries, which are backed by the full faith and credit of the United States, carry an AAA rating. Another example would be, say, bonds from Exxon Corporation, a very large and secure corporation that has little chance of ever going bankrupt.

Another option may be zero coupon bonds, says Sullivan. These are securities you buy at a discount to face value and cash for face value when they mature. For example, if you bought $50,000 worth of zero coupon bonds, in 12 years they would mature at $100,000. You would double your money in that time.

The risk of zero-coupons is inflation; the value of the $100,000 at maturity may be far less than what it is today. Still, these securities are completely safe and can be an alternative to other types of fixed income investments.

All in all, conservative investors have fewer investment choices and alternatives than aggressive and moderate investors do. Conservative investors should be looking for stability and reduced volatility from their investments. That narrows the list of appropriate choices.

Stick to your guns. Buying and selling stock, or any other security for that matter, should be based on fundamental financial assessments of a company's earnings, management, and business strategies. It should not be a chimpanzee effect—doing what other people do just because they are doing it.

If you are comfortable with your investments and understand why they are moving up or down, then you should stick with what you have. Constantly shifting mutual funds, or buying and selling stocks and bonds, does little more than put commission dollars in someone else's pocket. Stick with your investment plan and ride out the bumps in performance. Just be aware of when you may fall off a cliff. And the only way to do that is with a solid investment plan that has been mapped out thoroughly.

Reading Prospectuses

How to Know an Investment Is Right

Not many people read the manual before they buy a car. They take a test drive, get a feel for how the car handles, and see if the car has the right options and performs well. But in the investment business, most people read the manual before they get behind the wheel. And that manual is called a prospectus. Every mutual fund and partnership that is sold to the general public has a prospectus. Prepared by lawyers and certified public accountants, a prospectus spells out everything from how risky your investment is to how much salary senior officers take. Usually quite lengthy (about 30 pages or so), the prospectus will lay out in booklet format exactly what you are buying.

What It Says

"It's almost easier to look for what a prospectus *doesn't* say than for what it says," says Robert M. Shepard, a partner with Ballon Stoll Bader and Nadler in New York City who has reviewed and prepared hundreds of prospectuses. "But in order to know what not to look for, you have to know what to look for." Here's a page-by-page look.

Front cover. Here, the name of the investment will be spelled out as well as where it's located. If it's a company, the company address will be listed. If it's a mutual fund, the address of the money management firm will be listed. The front cover also states how risky the investment is relative to similar types of investments. It says how much is being offered for sale and at what price. And it will tell you what the minimum investment is. Finally, the front cover will tell you how you can obtain shares of the investment through either particular financial institutions or through the company itself. To get the full story of your investment, you can't judge this book by its cover. You'll need to read on.

Inside front cover. Your guide through the maze of legalese ahead will be on this page—it's where the table of contents is located. It will also point to a glossary of terms that are used throughout the prospectus.

Fee and expense table. Mandated by law, the fee and expense table will show you exactly what you are buying, for how much, and what the maximum sales commission should be as well as any other associated charges. The table will usually be accompanied by a hypothetical investment and will map out the fees and charges that will be incurred over a 1- to 10-year period.

Investment objective section. Right after the fee and expense table, you'll find an investment objective section or a use-of-proceeds section. It is one of the most important parts of a prospectus. This section lays out exactly what your money will be going toward. If it's a mutual fund, this section will lay out how your money will be invested, in which types of companies, and for how long. Here, you can also get a better idea of whether what you are looking to buy is risky or conservative. Risky investments include a new company offering (initial public offering), a company that hasn't been in business for a long time (fewer than 10 years), or a mutual fund that invests in those types of small growth companies. Lesser degrees of risk are associated with medium-size and large companies that have been in business for decades.

Read the investment objective section carefully. Get into the fine print. "It's more important to read what the investment objective says than to read the title of the prospectus. Sometimes you can't tell anything by the title at all," says Andrew Blackman, a certified public accountant/personal financial specialist and certified financial planner with Shapiro and Lobel, an accounting firm in New York City.

Footnotes. Footnotes to the financial statements will often be more telling than the financial statements themselves, says Shepard. "They boil down a lot of things and describe what the business is about very succinctly."

The back end. Potential investors should look for "things that are special" about an investment, advises Shepard. And these items are usually found in the back of the prospectus. Included here are special risk factors. Easily missed because it's near the back, this section lays out how the product or investment idea will work. If it's a new company or investment fund, watch out. Sometimes these special risks will say that the company has no idea of what it will do with your investment. These are called blind pools.

Mutual Agreement

According to the Investment Company Institute, there are nine questions you should ask yourself when reviewing a mutual fund prospectus.

1. **What is the fund's goal? Be sure the fund's objective matches your own.**
2. **What is the fund's investment strategy? The prospectus describes the range of securities the fund may purchase, how it selects them, and the types of securities it emphasizes.**
3. **What are the fund's most significant risks and how has it performed? Although past performance cannot predict future results, looking at performance will give you a good idea how the fund has behaved in different market conditions.**
4. **What are the fund's fees and expenses? You'll find them in a table at the front of the prospectus.**
5. **Who manages the fund? The advisor/management company is the firm responsible for deciding how, where, and when to invest the fund's assets.**
6. **How can you buy fund shares? Some funds offer their shares through brokers, bank representatives, and financial planners. Other funds offer shares directly to investors or through employer retirement plans.**
7. **How can you sell fund shares? By law, the fund must stand ready to buy back your shares on any business day.**
8. **How are the fund's distributions made and taxed? Funds must make distributions at least once each year. It may be important to determine when distributions are made and how they're taxed.**
9. **What services are available to you? If any particular feature or service—such as check writing or automated information—is essential to you, check to be sure that it's in the prospectus.**

Buyer Beware

Prospectuses of regulated securities have to be examined by the National Association of Securities Dealers and pass muster with the Securities and Exchange Commission. But that doesn't completely protect you. If a company says in its prospectus that it is going to do absolutely nothing but spend your money on vacations for its management staff, then it can. And there is not much recourse for the investor. "I'm amazed by how many people who make investments don't even read these things," says Shepard.

The point is that when you invest, you should read about what you are investing in. Buy the manual. Or in this case, the prospectus. You may be able to avoid buying a lemon.

Buying Investments

Slash Fees and Buy Like a Player

Rule number one for investing is the same rule number one that applies to every other item for sale in the marketplace: Price is negotiable. Yes, even with investments. *Especially* with investments. You just have to know what you want and how to ask for it.

"Shop," advises James Cloonan, Ph.D., chairman of the Chicago-based American Association of Individual Investors, which educates consumers about opportunities in stocks, bonds, mutual funds, and other investment products. Not only are brokerage services negotiable but many do-it-yourself investment options carry reduced charges, too. And the more money you save, the more you can invest.

Cutting Out the Middleman

Mutual funds, stocks, and bonds can be bought on a direct basis with no middleman or go-between institution. Better prices can certainly be had. But be prepared. You are completely on your own.

There is a plethora of ways for you to reduce investment costs. Here are a few of the best.

No-load mutual funds. Right now there are more than 6,800 mutual funds alone from which to choose, but many of these can attach a sales charge, most often called a load. By law, this load can reach as high as 8.5 percent of whatever amount you invest, although most funds charge far less. Some of the best deals are the no-load mutual funds, where the fund manager may waive sales charges for consumers who buy directly through his company.

The "i" rate. Sometimes, a no-load option simply isn't available on a particular mutual fund. In that case, ask for an institutional rate. These "i" shares are the lowest prices offered by a mutual fund company, usually to large institutions who buy in large amounts. But, "you can get these rates if you are trading online or directly with the institution," says Ross Levin, a certified financial planner, president of Accredited Investors in Minneapolis, and author of *The Wealth Management Index.*

Levin also notes that the same type of deals exist with company stocks, bonds, and even U.S. treasury securities.

Buying straight from the company. Many companies are now offering "no cost" stock themselves. That means no brokerage or trading commission. In fact, the price of some of these shares is typically 15 percent below the market price. You have to browse the Internet or call the company you are interested in to see if they offer such a program. Don't forget, however, that you may want to sell these shares someday. Be sure that you can easily do that by verifying that the stock is actively traded on a major exchange.

Buying company (corporate) bonds is slightly more complicated. "If you buy them the day they are issued, you will almost always get the same rates as the most savvy institutional money manager," says Levin. However, these bonds are only offered through brokerages, and you have to find out which financial institution is offering the bonds, and on what day, to get the best rates. A quick call to a company's investor relations department should point you in the right direction.

Buying straight from the government. U.S. government bonds can be purchased from the treasury in an easy and less costly way as well. "If you are buying treasuries, you are almost always better off buying at auction than through an institution—and you don't pay any commissions," says Levin. He says you can call the U.S. treasury office in Washington, D.C., to find out auction dates and how to go about buying treasury securities directly.

Investing online. The absolute ultimate do-it-yourself investing—exactly like the professionals—is offered through the Internet. There are online brokerage services and actual exchanges offered via the Internet where shares of certain companies trade at a lower price than on the New York Stock Exchange or the NASDAQ (National Association of Securities Dealers Automated Quotation) quote system.

For example, if XYZ company is trading between 3¼ ($3.25) and 3½ ($3.50), a broker at a Wall Street firm may only be able to buy it at the 3½ price. On the Internet, however, you may be able to go through an online trading system to buy the company's stock at 3¼. On a 100-share order, you would save $25. Over time, this can add up, especially if you buy and sell often.

Going for Broke

Even if you're a do-it-yourself kind of guy, it's important to note that a broker can sometimes be a great investment in himself. For instance, a broker may be able to assist you in getting in on a larger block of stock that his firm purchased (known as a round lot), as opposed to placing your individual order, which will most likely be smaller and more expensive to execute. These smaller odd lots, as they are known, cost you more because there is less leverage in getting a lower price with a seller. So, in some cases, it's worth having an advisor or broker who can facilitate your trades.

However, the basis for choosing the right broker or advisor to assist with your investments is comfort. Like a good ski instructor, a good broker will get to know your risk tolerance and your objectives. Here are some guidelines to keep in mind as you explore your brokerage options.

Do some discount shopping. Perhaps the most obvious place to start shopping is at discount brokerage firms. These firms advertise their lower costs and offer most of the same products that you can find at full-service institutions—less the advice—with no sales charge attached. Discount brokerages such as Charles Schwab and Company or Fidelity Investments target the individual who basically knows what he wants and when he wants it, and who doesn't require or expect a great deal of personal service.

Watch out for hidden costs. Discount brokerages often claim to have lower administrative costs and fees than full-service firms or firms that offer advice, like Merrill Lynch, Smith Barney, or Paine Webber. But even at discounters there are handling charges. Check your account statements thoroughly, and ask your institution if there is a way to reduce these charges.

Negotiate his fee. Almost every financial services firm allows their sales professionals a certain amount of discounting latitude. So don't be shy about negotiating commissions with your broker or asking him to lower his fees. You don't expect the broker to work for free, you just want to be treated fairly. It's standard business practice.

Put all your eggs in a basket. One thing to ask your broker for besides a reduced fee is a program that best suits your style of investing. Being honest about how much you'll be involved with your investments could save you big money. For example, if you buy and sell stocks often, you may want to consider a "basket" or "wrap" account. These accounts allow investors to buy and sell stock (or mutual funds) up to a certain number of times per year for a set fee.

Keeping Up

What You Need to Know about Your Investments

Sports fans turn to the sports sections of their newspapers to get the results of last night's game or season statistics. Investors can turn to the business sections of their newspapers to get the results on their teams of investments. Every day, stock tables list the performance of every company that is traded on an exchange. And mutual fund pricing is now also included in these pages. Select bond prices (such as the 30-year treasury bond and 3-month treasury bill) will also appear along with the prices of most commodities (gold, for example).

There are numerous online services and software packages that will allow you to better track your investments—including those investments that might not readily appear in the newspaper. Certainly, there are enough tools available that will allow you to track your investments closely. But many financial pros and investors alike warn that overscrutinizing your investments can cause too much anxiety, especially if your financial plan has a long-term time frame. To be sure, you don't want to be a fair weather fan of your investments, haphazardly making changes based upon short-term events and making rash decisions to buy or sell based on one day's market condition.

Fluctuation Fretting

The trick is discovering when an investment is just fluctuating and when it is underperforming.

"Most investments will swing," says Donald Robinson, chief investment officer at Lockwood Financial in Malvern, Pennsylvania. "If they are underperforming, something has gone wrong. But how would you know that? It's not an easy thing to figure out." The way to begin to at least understand whether an investment is behaving unusually is to "look at how it has done over different business cycles," says Robinson. "Look at its volatility in up and down markets." Some well-performing investments fluctuate the most. These may be good investments, but they are also very volatile. So, their strong underlying financial positions may have little effect on the price swings in the market and vice versa.

The premise to stick with is that your investment is behaving in a consistent manner. If Babe Ruth struck out a lot but hit mostly home runs every time he did bat the ball in play, would you say he was a bad baseball player? If he began hitting singles instead of home runs, however, you might begin to change your mind. He would have become a different type of ballplayer. When an investment changes type, it's time to take a look behind the price movement. Here are some suggestions for keeping tabs.

Read the reports. The fundamentals of an investment are brought out in the prospectus and through shareholder reports, published either quarterly or annually (and automatically sent to you if you are an investor). Reviewing these reports is far more important than checking on the trading price of your investment.

Within the confines of a prospectus or a shareholder report will be some key data that may hint at a change of which to be wary. Look at the fine print, says Lewis J. Altfest, a financial planner and president of his own consulting firm, L. J. Altfest and Company in New York City. "Read the management discussion section. It's there that the company will talk about what it's doing."

While many investment gurus use complex formulas and

Keeping Up with the Business Section

For decades, the format for newspaper stock listings stayed pretty much the same, day in, day out, year in, year out. You'd learn closing prices, how much prices rose or fell that day, the day's trading volume, and a few other bits of this and that. But in more recent years, there has been a quiet revolution in many business sections' listings, particularly at big-city newspapers, that is very much to your benefit.

The primary source of investment data for newspapers—the Associated Press—has greatly expanded its data offerings to newspapers. Now, a newspaper can build stock, bond, mutual fund, and other tables as big or as small as they like, with a far greater choice of information.

You'll find some of the changes in the stock tables. An example: Some newspapers are using bold-faced or underlined type to designate a stock that has hit a 52-week high or has had unusually heavy trading or is merely a stock of local interest. Others are offering longer-term performance measures.

The revolution has been far greater in the mutual fund tables. The old listings typically had four columns of information. The first one listed the name. The second showed the net asset value (NAV)—how much you would earn if you had actually sold the stock at the close of business the previous day. The third listed the asking price—what you would pay if you bought shares. (This is the NAV plus sales charges. A fund that does not carry a sales charge is known as no-load, and its NAV and asking price will be the same.) The last column showed any changes in the NAV from the preceding day's business.

But today, you'll often find other useful data in the fund listings as well, much of which rotate through the trading week so as to give you the most data possible over five days. Some of the new information you might find includes:

- A designation of the type of fund it is (such as aggressive growth, international, health care)
- The fund's long-term performance (this can be anywhere from the three-month to the five-year change in NAV)
- Performance ranking (which compares the fund to others with the same goal; usually these ratings go from 1 to 5, with a 5 meaning it outperformed at least four out of five funds in its sector)
- Annual cost of ownership (the little bit of cash fund managers take out of the sale of the funds in order to pay expenses; this amount is usually stated as a percentage)

There is just one drawback in all this: the types of financial listings that papers choose to feature vary from city to city.

models to evaluate a stock, many of the most brilliant investors use the zen approach to investing: Ask simple questions. Can I easily explain the company's strategy in one sentence? Are its products good? Are they priced fairly? Strip away the justifications and qualifications in the quarterly reports, and you'll find many of the answers. Any change in management or business direction, or if there are adverse conditions that are affecting the industry in which a company operates, should be a flare that the business may be changing type and therefore may not perform as expected.

Meet the press. Reading the financial press keeps him informed about the investing world, says Tom Lydon, president of Global Trends Investment in Newport Beach, California. If you're invested in local companies, keep track through your local paper.

Do a little typecasting. The type of investment you choose will give you an indication of how it should perform. If it has been a good year for investments in health care companies, it's not unreasonable for you to expect your Acme Health Services stock to have had a good year, too. If the Japanese stock market has gone flat, your Japanese stock mutual fund likely has gone flat, as well. But if your investment is going south when comparable investments are going north, it's time to ask for more information and make the hard decisions. But be careful: never compare apples with oranges, such as stocks versus bonds. In fact, the two sometimes move in opposite directions. Be reasonable in your comparisons.

Apply appropriate scrutiny. "I don't think you have to know what bond prices are every day," says Altfest. "But I do think that with stocks you have to be a more active manager." He advises investors to review their bond holdings once a year, their stock holdings every quarter, and to check on how their mutual funds are being managed at the end of the year. "You don't have to do anything more than check prices and make sure they are performing as expected. If they aren't, then that's telling you something." In addition to reading shareholder reports, Altfest recommends searching online for any relevant news or information that may effect your investments. "You can do it at the same time you conduct your annual review," says Altfest.

Moderate your monitoring. A long-term investment strategy should preclude the practice of daily monitoring your investments for any reason other than the comfort that they are still there. You wouldn't call the barber every day to see if you needed a haircut, would you? But you probably look in the mirror every day and check on your hair; hopefully it's still there. That doesn't mean you have to change it in any dramatic fashion. Similarly, daily price action may not mean anything. When you think it does, that's when you get into trouble.

The phenomenon of price movements often causes investors to act irrationally. Investment pros warn not to get caught up in this behavioral pattern. A study by the University of Wisconsin and Cornell University, cited by the brokerage firm Smith Barney in a report to its clients, says that stocks that rose or fell sharply in a day smoothed out, or "corrected" themselves, in later months. "As these price adjustments occurred, they represented a correction of the initial trading activity, which did not reflect substantial changes in the fundamental outlook for the companies," the report says. So while prices changed, the companies basically didn't. Buying or selling into this panic mentality would affect the future results of your investments—usually for the worse. It's only when the fundamentals of an investment change that a review of your portfolio and change may be warranted.

Keep long-term goals in mind. "Investments are volatile to begin with. If they are underperforming, something has gone wrong with the process," says Robinson. The process he is speaking about is the long-term investment plan you should have mapped out for your financial future. If your expectations on the road to your goals are being met, then keeping up with your investments is all you will have to do.

Part Four

The Big-Ticket Issues

Income Taxes

Pay Your Fair Share and Not a Cent More

It's been said that death and taxes are the two certainties in life, but the income tax, at least for Americans, is a relatively new concept. The tax became law in 1913 with the passage of the 16th Amendment, during the Woodrow Wilson administration. (Incredibly, Wilson was reelected three years later.) Even since, the government has collected revenues through income taxes in order to support an astonishing variety of services, some arguably more helpful than others.

That's something to think about as you prepare each year for the great American trial of life—the filing of your income tax return, and, all too often, the mailing of your tax check to the Internal Revenue Service. But you don't have to take it lying down.

Tax Relief: It's All an Act

Another landmark year for income taxes was 1997. Congress passed the Taxpayer Relief Act of 1997, which introduced the largest package of amendments in over a decade. Among the highlights: A new individual retirement account came on the market; tax credits for education got better; and estate taxes softened, according to John F. Oteri, a certified public accountant and tax partner with Di Pesa and Company in Boston.

Experts generally applaud changes like the 1997 act, but worry because laws could be repealed at any time. "Government occasionally decides that it gave away too much to the public through past tax reforms," says Martin Nissenbaum, the national director of personal income tax and retirement planning for Ernst and Young in New York City. The government can simply change the rules at will, even retroactively, and the Supreme Court will invariably back the decision, he says. "The power to tax is absolute."

That's no reason not to plan ahead, says Vernon Jacobs, a certified public accountant in Prairie Village, Kansas. Jacobs practices what he calls premeditated tax avoidance. "Simply put," he explains, "you can't reduce your taxes at tax time. When people ask me if I can save them money, I tell them that 'save' is a relative term because I can't alter what happened during the tax year."

Only you can do that, and understanding some income tax strategies could help put a few more bucks in your pocket.

Set aside for retirement. To goad more Americans into saving for their senior years, the government lets workers invest a portion of their pretax earnings in funds like a 401(k) or an individual retirement account. The benefit is twofold: In many cases, the money you invest is exempt from current income taxes, and you don't pay tax on interest, dividends, or capital gains until you start cashing out in your senior years. There are all types of retirement accounts and a lot of rules about who can invest in them, how much can be invested, and how much of what is invested can be deducted. For an in-depth discussion of retirement investing, see part 5, Retirement Planning.

Get schooling on Ed IRAs. Education IRAs are somewhat of a misnomer. They cannot be used for retirement; instead, they're vehicles for funneling money toward your child's education, while deferring income taxes.

Here's how they work: Deposit as much as $500 a year per child into an Ed IRA. The money you invest is not exempt from taxation, but the subsequent investment earnings are. This could mean serious tax savings as the Ed IRA grows older. Withdrawals are tax-free as long as the money is put toward college education. This plan is not available for joint filers earning more than $150,000 per year or individuals earning more than $95,000. (Grandparents can also set up Ed IRAs.)

"If the child doesn't go to college, he has to wait until age 30 to withdraw the funds, and he has to pay a tax at that time," says Oteri.

Take stock in charity. If you are the charitable sort, consider making your donations in the form of stocks rather than cash, Nissenbaum suggests. "There is practically no better tax shelter than using property as a charitable donation, and not many people do it," he asserts.

Let's say you want to donate $1,000 to your favorite charity. Giving cash would entitle you to a deduction of the same amount on your income taxes. But you could save yourself money by donating that $1,000 in stocks. Here's how. If you had bought stock for $800 and watched it earn $200, you would be liable to pay tax on the gain. But if you sign the stock over as a donation to charity, you qualify for the $1,000 tax deduction, plus you get off the hook for the $200 gain. To qualify for the tax break, Nissenbaum notes, you must have owned the stock for at least 18 months prior to giving it away.

Use your home. Buying a home is a smart investment, and houses are possibly the most comprehensive tax shelter ever devised. Not only is mortgage interest one of the biggest tax deductions you will have year after year, but the government has backed away from taxing the profit

Returns That Raise Eyebrows

Many things can trigger an IRS audit, gross mistakes and discrepancies being just a start. In fact, the IRS keeps an eye out for several things that may be perfectly legal and correct but that often indicate trouble.

For example, merely filing a Schedule C form (used to calculate taxes for unincorporated businesses) can make you more likely to come under IRS scrutiny, says Louise Tieman, a financial planner with Gilligan, Ryan, Jorgenson, and Company in Tacoma, Washington. Your odds of being audited go up to about 4 percent, she says.

The most common cause for an audit? Unusually large deductions when compared with the total size of your income, according to Tieman. If your deductions amount to 44 percent of your income, "that's an automatic flag," Tieman says. Mathematical errors account for roughly 10 percent of audits.

Upon receiving an audit letter, you normally have 10 days to respond. After that, the interest penalties that you will pay if the IRS proves its case start accruing. "The hardest part of the letters is trying to make sense of them," Tieman says. Once you decipher the letter, make sure your response explains any extenuating circumstances that affected your tax return, such as the fact that you traveled more and therefore claimed more mileage deductions, Tieman notes.

There are different levels of audits, and your response should differ depending upon the type of audit and the nature of the query. "You may want to strongly consider seeking professional assistance rather than trying to go it alone," says Malcolm A. Makin, a certified financial planner and president of Professional Planning Group in Westerly, Rhode Island.

when you sell your home. "The government has repealed the law that said that in order to avoid paying capital gains you had to buy a new home equal to or greater than the value of the one you're selling," says financial planner Louise Tieman. "This change could be a gift to a lot of people."

In summary, a married couple who files jointly are free to sell their home, make a profit of up to $500,000, and buy a cheaper home with the proceeds—all tax-free. Single people can qualify if they earn a profit of up to $250,000. There are a few stipulations, though. The biggest is that the house you sell must have been your principle residence for at least two of the five years prior to the sale. (Some taxpayers, presumably, would try to claim a rarely used vacation home as their main residence to take advantage of the tax break.)

"You can buy a new house every two years and, if it has appreciated by $500,000, exclude that gain from the taxes you owe," says Nissenbaum. "This allows people to move into smaller, cheaper homes or rent apartments without penalty, which many empty-nesters will like."

Set up a home office. Telecommuting is revolutionizing the working world. Some 15 million people now work full-time out of their homes. If you're part of the SOHO (small office/home office) brigade, you should consider writing off your use of a home office, says Tieman.

"Restrictions on home offices have been liberalized," Tieman says. "Now, more people are eligible to take a home office deduction than before. This is accomplished by depreciating the value of your home on your income tax return."

For instance, if the office took up 10 percent of the home, you could depreciate 10 percent of the value of the home each year as a business expense, Tieman says. To qualify, you have to use the office on a regular basis exclusively for administrative or management activities, and it must be the only place where these functions are performed. However, if you're planning on selling your house and you're still using your home office during the year of sale, then you can't take the deduction.

Take credit for kids. The government now offers a $500 tax credit for each dependent under the age of 17, according to Nissenbaum. The provision is known as the Child Tax Credit. "If your adjusted gross income is less than $110,000, you would be entitled to the full amount for each child," he says.

Do estate planning. Estate Tax is a confiscation tax. Under it, assets that you have worked hard all of your life to accumulate must be taken away from your family and given to Uncle Sam when you die. "If you think that one of the rewards of success is leaving your wealth to your family, think again," says Robert W. Marrion, an estate planning lawyer and partner in the law firm of Waller, Smith, and Palmer in New London, Connecticut. "The estate tax is so devastating because many Americans simply aren't prepared for it. It's the federal government's nasty little secret."

There are two important elements to smart estate planning. The first is the "unlimited marital deduction," which allows one spouse to pass to his surviving spouse unlimited assets during his lifetime or at death. You may be a multimillionaire and still pass everything to your wife without fear of her having to pay any estate tax at the time of your death.

When the surviving spouse dies and the kids or other heirs inherit the assets, the estate tax kicks in. This brings us to key element number two: the unified credit. This is a direct credit against a taxable estate. For 1998, the unified credit is $625,000, and it will increase until the year 2006, when it reaches $1 million. Everyone is entitled to the unified credit. The trick is to find a way to pass on the unified credit from both of the deceased parents, so as to double the assets that are shielded from the estate tax. Actually, it's no trick: it simply requires creating a "credit shelter trust" for both husband and wife at the time you write your will. It sounds complicated and expensive, but is neither. A competent attorney can guide you through the maze.

Reject refunds. By now, you've worked long enough to become familiar with—and resigned to—your old pal FICA, the line on your paycheck that indicates how much money the government withholds for taxes. Essentially, they get their money up front and maybe, if you're lucky, you get some of it back in the form of a refund check.

"Of course, people look at their refunds as bonuses that they can play with later on," Oteri says. "But it would be better if they paid the minimum owed to the government and put that extra take-home pay in a savings account or the stock market. Anything is better than giving it to Uncle Sam." Let's say that you overpaid $30 on each of 26 paychecks during the year. That's $780 that could be earning you interest. Oteri advises paying as little as possible during the year so you can invest all you can. To follow this plan, you will have to forgo your tax refund.

Look at your prior year's tax return to see what the total tax you owed was. You must withhold an amount equal to what you paid that year, says Oteri. Once you figure that total amount, divide it over the number of paychecks you get during the year. The number you get will be the amount you'll want withheld from each paycheck. IRS Publication 919, "Is My Withholding Correct?" can also help you figure the minimum amount. You can order it by contacting your regional IRS distribution center.

Pack up. Here's an innovative, if not quite practical, way to reduce your income taxes: Move to a state that has no state income tax, says Roger Rotolante, a certified public accountant and managing partner with Olin, Gottlieb, Rotolante, Villalobos, and Maya in Coral Gables, Florida. But be aware that some states without income taxes have different taxes that more than make up the difference.

Accounting for Lower Taxes

"No deduction shall be allowed by this section to an individual for the taxable year if a deduction under section 151 with respect to such individual is allowed to another taxpayer for the taxable year beginning in the calendar year in which such individual's taxable year begins."

—Taxpayer Relief Act of 1997, Code Sec. 221(e)

So goes the arcane world of tax-law writing. Verbs, nouns, and prepositions mingle at random, often appearing to lead nowhere. Even savvy CPAs have difficulty deciphering the tax code, no matter what year it's published. "I think we all feel that tax law is almost too complicated to comprehend, and I've been doing taxes for 30 years," says certified public accountant Vernon Jacobs.

Relying on the tax collectors themselves for help is a dubious proposition as well. In 1993, reports circulated that the IRS gave incorrect answers to 8 million taxpayers who called the agency's hotline for tax assistance.

As a practical matter, you could do worse than asking a professional to handle your tax return, even if you just take the standard deductions. "I've helped a lot of people with retirement tax planning, because the decisions are quite complicated," says Jacobs. "If you have a business, you absolutely need some help. The rules are simply too confusing."

"Anyone who files the long form should have an accountant do their return," adds certified public accountant Roger Rotolante. Considering the pain and suffering an audit might cause, accountants, he states, "are a bargain" at about $150 an hour. An even more economical option would be to consult a tax-preparation service like H&R Block or Jackson Hewitt, whose preparers are trained in tax law changes every year.

Mortgages

Pay 'Em Off Fast and Cheap

If you've ever tried to buy a house, you've probably heard the following bit of conventional wisdom before: A home is the single largest expense that you'll ever incur. But just how big an investment is it? You'll likely end up paying more for the interest on your mortgage than you will for the house itself, points out Eric Tyson, co-author of *Home Buying for Dummies.*

This is why you should probably pay more attention to your mortgage than to any other single financial obligation you manage. A small shift in its interest rate, a slight change in when and how you pay, or a well-timed refinancing can add up to untold thousands of dollars back in your pocket.

Secondary Considerations

In their advertising, banks often take a down-home approach to lending money. They promote concepts like "personal service" and "friendly relationships." The image of your banker as a kindly relative or neighbor, however, belies the economic realities your bank probably faces: It can't afford to spend too much time with you. In fact, once you get a mortgage, you may never speak to your loan officer again.

That's because banks routinely sell your mortgage to other institutions, such as the Federal National Mortgage Association (known as Fannie Mae) and the Federal Home Loan Mortgage Corporation (Freddie Mac). This combination of public and large private institutions is collectively known as the secondary market. Among other things, the system helps ensure greater cash flow for the primary lenders, allowing them to make other loans.

Arguably, there's nothing devious about the practice, and your bank will notify you when your mortgage is sold. But what you should realize is that your bank evaluates you on the basis of your mortgage's viability in the secondary market, notes Randy Johnson, president of the Independence Mortgage Company in Newport Beach, California, and author of *How to Save Thousands of Dollars on Your Mortgage.* It's like interviewing for a job with someone in human resources and never meeting your future boss.

While you may have little or no control over some bank practices, you're not powerless. Here are some tips to help you cut a better mortgage deal.

Cleanse your credit. Lending institutions want to make sure you're a good credit risk. You want to negotiate a favorable mortgage. Help yourself by reducing debt as much as possible before taking on a mortgage. Pay off high-interest credit card debt and get copies of your credit history. If there is a mistake, this is the time to correct it.

Negotiate points. We're sure you know that the amount of your down payment has a direct correlation to the size of your mortgage principal. But remember also that a way to lower the interest that you'll pay on your mortgage is to pay your lender "points," in which each point is equal to 1 percent of the mortgage's value. For instance, you could propose paying 7.25 percent instead of the going rate of 7.5 and, in exchange, pay the bank one point up front, according to Marcus Stamp, an officer with Citibank in Park Ridge, Illinois. "You don't have to pay them, but they are useful in bargaining for a lower interest rate on your mortgage." Points are typically due at closing (the day the house changes hands).

But be realistic about how long you expect to stay in the house, Stamp advises. Don't make the classic mistake of paying three points for a lower interest rate, only to move two years later. "That leaves you no time to recover the costs of paying the points," he says.

Take out the garbage. During a mortgage transaction, banks may tack on charges for underwriting, loan processing, document handling, and other nebulous services. These costs, according to Johnson, are known in the lending industry as "garbage fees," and can add up to roughly $1,000 per transaction. Ask your banker what each and every charge means. If it sounds like garbage to you, put up a fight. Your bank is going to make plenty off you in interest; there's no reason why you should pay some of these add-on fees.

If you're in doubt, ask for an explanation under the government's Truth in Lending Statement, he advises. "It breaks down every single fee that the bank charges and what it's for," says Stamp. "The consumer has it in black and white."

Exploit an expert. "I would love to sell my house to a first-time buyer," says Jonathan Pond, a certified public accountant; president of Financial Planning Information, based in Boston; and the author of 11 books on personal finance. Novices tend to go blindly into the transaction out of fear of losing their bid on the house. "When shopping for houses, take along an experienced homeowner," he advises. "Have him ask the hard questions, like the cost of fixing the roof." Use his expertise to help you negotiate a lower price for the house. Remember, the lower the price, the less you'll have to borrow, and the lower the mortgage will be.

Should You Pay Off Early?

Financial planners have a lively debate going about the virtues of paying off mortgages early. On the one hand, you can save many thousands of dollars in interest and build equity faster. The flip side: The cash you reserve for early payment could potentially be put to greater use elsewhere.

Some people wonder why they should pay off an 8 percent loan ahead of schedule when they can invest more profitably in the stock market or a mutual fund—say, with a 12 or 15 percent annual return. "It's not a bad question," says Jonathan Pond of Financial Planning Information.

But the money you would use to retire the home loan may be earning less than 8 percent anyway. By their nature, securities can lose value as well as appreciate. "Mortgage money is a sure 8 percent return. It's safe money," Pond points out.

There could be a subtle ulterior motive on the part of financial planners who discourage early mortgage payoffs, he notes. "They may want people to invest as much money as possible because the planners themselves will then earn higher fees. It's a conflict of interest."

But paying early can be disadvantageous if you have access to good investment options and a low-cost mortgage, warns Eric Tyson, co-author of *Home Buying for Dummies*. "Say you're a guy in your thirties with extra monthly cash flow who can choose between paying down your 6.5 percent mortgage or socking the money away into your employer's tax-deductible retirement savings plan," he says. "In that case, it might be better to opt for the retirement plan." Another case against accelerated payments: "You don't want to pay early if doing so depletes your emergency reserve and causes you to run up high-cost credit debt when unexpected expenses arise," says Tyson.

Consider a specialist. If your foot hurts, your family doctor may be capable of diagnosing and treating the problem. But you might feel even better if you visited a podiatrist, who specializes in foot maladies. So, if you're in the market for mortgage, why wouldn't you consider consulting a mortgage company?

"Banks typically don't have a large profit margin with mortgages," Johnson says. "Therefore, the seasoned people, like the branch manager, usually won't get directly involved with mortgage matters. The decision process gets mixed in with other bank business and routinely gets delegated to less-experienced people." Mortgage companies, on the other hand, sell nothing but mortgages. "Their expertise could lead you to the most appropriate loan program," Johnson adds.

ARMs Talks

Mortgages come in two principal varieties: fixed (the most popular form) and adjustable, or variable, rate. A fixed-rate mortgage locks in an interest rate for the entire term—most commonly, 30 years. "If you like getting your daily newspaper delivered at the same time every day, you're going to like fixed-rate mortgages," Tyson points out. But that stability can work against you if the interest rate falls and you're unable to refinance the loan, he says.

This is one reason why some consumers favor adjustable-rate mortgages (ARMs): Their rates fall with the market. Some ARMs guarantee a fixed rate for a period of time, such as one year, before the rate starts fluctuating. During the stability period, you could realize savings, because the interest may start out a point or two lower than that on a 30-year fixed mortgage. But experts note that ARMs can be trouble if your income waxes and wanes—due, for example, to temporary unemployment. And, of course, if interest rates rise, you could end up paying more than the going rate on a fixed mortgage for indefinite stretches.

Unless you're actually planning to stay in your house for the rest of your life, "the most expensive way to finance your home is the 30-year fixed," adds Stamp. Why? "If the bank guarantees a rate for 30 years, it's going to charge an extra premium to secure that rate. It doesn't do any good to lock up a really low rate for a long time if you won't be staying in your house for long."

Here are some other money-saving tips to keep in mind once you have a mortgage.

Pay on time. This is a simple—but sometimes underappreciated—rule, Stamp says. "If your monthly mortgage payment arrives even a day late, the bank could penalize you 5 percent of the payment amount—maybe $50. Also, it gets reflected on your credit history."

Make extra payments. One of the best ways to reduce the overall cost of your mortgage, while building equity faster, is to make extra payments. Some people pay half the monthly amount every two weeks, which amounts to one extra payment per year; or they add extra money to their monthly checks. Whatever method you choose, the additional payments begin cutting into the loan's principal more quickly, shaving years off the life of your mortgage.

"Paying off early really becomes significant when you retire," says Pond. "A mortgage-free house creates extra spending money. It's a late-in-life trump card.

"It doesn't take a lot of extra money to retire a mortgage," he says. "If you have a $100,000 loan with 25 years to run, add an extra $100 a month to the payments and it will be paid off in 15 years." (Beware that some lenders will charge a penalty for early or extra payments. Furthermore, in sending supplementary installments, you may have to stipulate that the amount be applied against the principal, not to the next month's interest payment.)

Get a shorter mortgage. An alternative to making extra payments, 15-year mortgages can also lead to faster ownership of your house. Such arrangements work if you have a lot of spare cash, because, with a shorter-term loan, you will pay more each month. At a fixed interest rate of 8 percent, monthly payments on a 15-year mortgage will be about 30 percent higher than those for a 30-year loan, according to Tyson.

"A lot of banks are now giving a pretty hefty break for 15-year mortgages," Pond notes. In some instances, the discount may be three-eighths of a point off the prevailing interest rate. "That's nothing to sniff at," he says. As a general rule, though, he advises that you take the 30-year deal and send additional money whenever you can, retaining flexibility in your payment plan. Many financial planners recommend taking a 30-year mortgage, but paying it on a 15-year schedule.

Save as You Reduce Your Mortgage Term

By getting something other than a 30-year fixed-rate mortgage (or by paying off your loan ahead of schedule), you could realize huge reductions in your total interest payments. The following table shows your monthly payments and potential savings.

The table is based upon a $100,000 fixed-rate mortgage. Interest rates for the 30-year and 15-year loans are based on the 3-year national average between 1994 and 1996. The rate on the 20-year mortgage was calculated by splitting the difference between the 30-year and 15-year rates (8.23 - 7.77 = 0.46 ÷ 2 = 0.23) and subtracting that amount from the 30-year rate (8.23 - 0.23 = 8.00). The same amount was subtracted from the 15-year rate to extrapolate the 10-year rate.

Interest Loan Term	Rate (%)	Payment ($)	Interest ($)	Savings ($)
30 years	8.23	749.86	169,949	
20 years	8.00	836.44	100,745	69,204
15 years	7.77	942.42	69,635	100,314
10 years	7.54	1,189.11	42,693	127,256

Watch your PMI premiums. Homeowners with less than 20 percent equity in their houses have to pay private mortgage insurance (PMI), according to Stamp. PMI is not paid to the bank; the policies are issued by third-party insurance companies to protect the lender against mortgage defaults. You can figure on spending roughly $1,000 a year for PMI, Stamp says. His advice: "If you're a second-time home buyer, wait until you can put 20 percent down on the house and avoid PMI." (Most first-time buyers will not have such a large amount at their disposals.) Also, keep a close eye on your equity level. When your equity level reaches 20 percent of the house's purchase price, you can cancel the PMI.

"Believe me," Stamp says, "the mortgage company isn't going to call up one day and say, 'Hey, you've hit 20 percent. You can stop paying us now.'"

Refine your refinancing goals. At some point in the life of your mortgage, it may make sense to change the terms. Done properly, refinancing is an option that could save you thousands of dollars. Tyson recommends refinancing when you can lock in a lower monthly payment to recoup the refinancing costs; a reasonable period of time, he says, is within five years.

Stamp advises holding off until you can save 2 percent annually. Moreover, don't relocate soon after you've refinanced, because the savings won't have time to accrue. (This is the same logic behind choosing a short-term ARM over a 30-year fixed mortgage.)

Keep in mind that when you refinance, the lending institution charges closing costs all over again. That is, fees for a new appraisal on the house, a title search, and loan-processing fees may all come back to haunt you. Make sure to figure them into the payback equation.

Home Ownership

Treating Your House Like an Asset

Real estate and investment pros all counsel that your home is, first and foremost, a place to live, and an investment consideration second. Unless, of course, you speculate in residential real estate for a living. Some people who do this, like Joe Best of Freeport, Illinois, buy several homes a year. Best looks for properties he believes will appreciate in time. He's parlayed his knowledge of the local market into a second career as a realty agent for Coldwell Banker.

Best has lived in the same house for 20 years. His method is to sell his other properties for profit or turn them into rental units. "There are certain things you can do to protect your home as an investment," he says. "Still, certain factors will always be beyond your control."

The Equitable Owner

The list of things that could drive down your home's value is a long one, ranging from natural disasters to economic conditions. Those vicissitudes may make you long for the days when you were renting that cramped studio apartment above the flower shop. Certainly, you had less to lose.

Nevertheless, home ownership is a prized accomplishment for many people. And analysts at the National Association of Home Builders predict homes will continue to rise in value by 5 to 8 percent through 2002.

"If you're in a $150,000 home that appreciates 5 percent a year, that's an annual $7,500 gain," points out Marcus Stamp, an officer with Citibank in Park Ridge, Illinois. "And you don't get taxed on this until you sell the house, so it's like a deferred savings plan." And of course, owning a house is tax break in and of itself, as we explained in the income tax chapter.

Here are other ways to take advantage of your home's versatility.

Tap into equity. Equity is determined by calculating the market value of your home minus the mortgage debt you still owe. Interest accrued on home equity loans (that is, a bank loan or line of credit secured by using the house as collateral) is typically less than what you'd pay on credit card debt and is usually tax-deductible up to $100,000. The amount you qualify for will be based on your current equity position.

"These loans can help you accomplish important financial and personal goals," says Eric Tyson, co-author of *Home Buying for Dummies* and author of *House Selling for Dummies.* "I'd recommend them for investment purposes, such as your education or your child's, retirement, and starting a small business." Avoid them when buying that flashy sports car you've always wanted or taking a vacation, he says.

Put it in reverse. Some people, particularly retirees, find they need cash for day-to-day living expenses. With reverse mortgages, they can turn their homes into revenue streams. "A reverse mortgage allows you to utilize equity without selling the property," Tyson explains. In effect, you're borrowing against your home's value, but unlike a home equity loan, where you get a lump sum that you have to pay back within a certain time, a reverse mortgage is doled out in the form of monthly payments to you. You're not obligated to repay until the home is sold. Tyson points out that if you die before retiring the loan, your estate will be responsible for the repayment.

Investing in Your Home

Aside from capitalizing on the tax advantages of home ownership, the smart owner can take steps to help this key investment remain productive. Some advice will apply before you even own your home, when you're still crunching numbers to determine if you can afford a mortgage in the first place.

"What makes real estate appreciate the most is a strong job market coupled with a shortage of housing," says Tyson. "Within a given area, low crime rates, good schools, and community amenities such as parks and recreation areas attract buyers."

Among some real estate pros, convention holds that it's wise to buy less house than you can afford. "Get the least expensive house on the block," Best advises. "If you own the most expensive one, the other houses won't be as good as yours and they'll tend to drag you down."

Then again, some guys like the thought of owning the biggest house around. Your home, after all, can be a showpiece, a statement that you've arrived. (Okay, an ego trip.) We won't quibble with your motives, but one of your tasks before buying is to take your time scouting communities. You've heard the old real estate mantra—location, location, location.

Tyson recommends calling local chambers of commerce and getting a primer on the area's economic and employment picture. Keep in mind that once you've selected a neighborhood,

When Should You Move?

People move for a variety of reasons, some of them beyond their control. A few reasons include divorces, layoffs, job transfers, and deaths in their families. "Move when your house is no longer what you need, when you've outgrown it or it's too big, or when it's no longer convenient to where you work," says syndicated financial writer Humberto Cruz. "I think you should make your decision based not on financial factors but on lifestyle factors."

He admits, though, that not everyone will agree with him. The temptation to sell could be almost undeniable if your house has appreciated by $10,000 in one year.

Few people, however, are speculating in their homes, says Robert Irwin, author of *Buy Right, Sell High*, a guide to choosing residential real estate. "I don't think most of us seek to get our money out and make a big profit," he asserts. "Let's say you're living in a given town and find out your home has appreciated and you can make some money. But if you get that money out, what are you going to do with it?" Buying a new house in the same neighborhood will cost about the same as your old place, he says, plus you will have to pay transaction and moving costs. "So you haven't accomplished anything."

The experts agree that staying put makes sense if you are satisfied with the area's amenities or you see potential in your neighborhood. "I have always bought homes in new, well-located neighborhoods," says Cruz. "For awhile, when the subdivision was still being built, we put up with some inconveniences, like housing going up all around us or living four miles from the nearest grocery store. But after a few months, the neighborhood gets full and the price goes up."

you can't do much to change it, other than keeping up your house.

And when it comes to maintaining or renovating your house, don't just focus on doing things that will make the house a better value when it comes time to sell it. "You should do a renovation on your home because you're going to enjoy it," says Humberto Cruz, a syndicated financial writer with South Florida's *Sun-Sentinel* newspaper and Tribune Media Services. If you're a conscientious homeowner, you'll be putting a lot of work into your castle. Here's how you can claim some of the royalties.

Stay on top of your roof. There's nothing quite like a leaky roof to spread damage through the rest of the house. "Water seepage from a leaky roof tends to affect the ceilings, walls, and floors," says Best. "You don't want to become aware of it after it's already become a major problem—say, when your bedroom ceiling caves in."

Roof repairs tend to be expensive, too—anywhere from $3,000 to $15,000 or more, according to Robert Irwin, author of *Buy Right, Sell High*, so it pays to keep them in good condition.

Don't defer. While your roof is arguably the single most important feature, you can't afford to let other areas fall into disrepair. "What starts out as a $100 problem can turn into a $1,000 problem overnight," says Best.

"Many people live in the house and never pay attention to anything unless it absolutely breaks," Irwin adds. Solution: Inspect your house regularly. Get up in the attic when it's raining and check it. Ditto the basement. Set yourself a semiannual inspection route that has you looking over the infrastructure of your home—pipes, beams, drains, shingles, everything.

Subtract additions. In most situations, say the experts, building additions to your home is a questionable strategy. "There's nothing more expensive than adding space to a home," warns Irwin. "You have to be sure that you're getting the job done really cheaply, and even then you have to carefully examine whether it's worth it." Otherwise, you may not make any money on that annex.

Take on smaller projects. As it turns out, few home improvement projects end up putting more money in your pocket than they took out. But with certain types of upgrades, you can break even. For example, according to a recent survey in *Remodeling Magazine*, a contractors' trade journal, homeowners got a nearly full return on their investments in kitchens and bathrooms. (See "The Cost of Improvement.")

Notably, the survey considered $8,000 to be the cost of a "minor" kitchen makeover. Best says that you can trim costs while still making your rooms look like new. "For instance," he says, "in kitchens, you don't have to tear out all the cabinets. Instead, just replace the doors. A new countertop and floor, plus a fresh coat of paint, will often be enough to satisfy potential buyers."

If you do make improvements, don't go beyond what the neighborhood can support, says Best. "After you've finished all the work, your house should still be an average-priced house in your neighborhood," he says.

Analyze the market. How do you know how much your home is worth? One way of finding out is through the mail—when you receive your property tax assessment. Other means are available to accomplish the same goal. "Ask for a market analysis from one or more real estate agents," says Best.

In this process, agents will search a database of comparable residences and pinpoint what those houses sold for in the last six months. The service can be done for free, before you commit to hiring an agent, he notes. Calling the local board of Realtors and asking if the market is rising or falling will also give you a good idea of real estate conditions, Best advises. You'll generally want to sell in a rising market.

Another method: If you apply for refinancing on your mortgage, the bank will typically order a new appraisal. But, be prepared to pay for this.

Visit with your neighbors. Irwin points out that possibly the most efficient way to acquire real estate information is to attend a neighborhood cocktail party or similar community gathering. "Believe me," Irwin says, "when a neighbor's home goes on the market or sells, word gets around. Quickly."

Come back to Earth. If you're not seeing the clues around you, you could make serious mistakes before your home even goes on the market. One prominent blunder that homeowners frequently make is inflating their home's value. Indeed, an overly optimistic estimate can come back to plague you, experts caution.

"The owners know all the hard work they've put into their house," says Janice Tucker, a senior appraiser with First Appraisal Services in Phoenix. "But some things may not be quite as appealing to the typical buyer." Swimming pools, for instance, can be great fun, but some people regard them as safety hazards, she says. They tend to limit your potential buyers.

"I refused at least a dozen listings this year because people wanted more than their properties were worth," says Best. He advises setting a price that is perhaps a few thousand dollars over your most reasonable estimate. By aiming too high, you risk keeping the house on the market for months, with no one bidding.

"At that point, buyers will look at the house as damaged goods," reports Dian Hymer, author of *Starting Out: The Complete Home Buyer's Guide.* "You'll start to get lowball offers and you'll usually end up getting less money than your house is really worth." And that's no way to treat a good investment.

The Cost of Improvement

Your furnace is acting cool toward you lately. Your kitchen sink has sunk. Should you spend a chunk of money to make repairs? Most buyers are looking for homes in "move-in condition," according to Dian Hymer, author of *Starting Out: The Complete Home Buyer's Guide.* "They don't want to spend a ton on repairs right away."

Hey, it's your house; you can treat it any way you want. But if you plan to sell it one day, don't expect a bounty of bids for a house that would look right only with Jed Clampett sitting on the front porch—before he moved to Beverly Hills. Here's what various home repair projects will return on the investment.

Project	Job Cost	Resale Value	Cost Recouped (%)
Minor kitchen remodel (replace doors, oven, counters, repaint, etc.)	$8,395	$8,579	102
Bathroom addition	$11,721	$10,820	92
Major kitchen remodel (total replacement and redesign, including custom lighting and island)	$22,509	$20,340	90
Master suite addition (includes walk-in closet, whirlpool tub, separate shower)	$37,388	$35,527	87
Attic bedroom addition	$23,002	$19,839	86
Two-story addition (family room and bedroom with full bath)	$56,189	$48,943	87
Family room addition	$32,558	$27,904	86
Bathroom remodel	$8,563	$6,582	77
Window replacement	$5,976	$4,042	68
Siding replacement	$5,099	$3,593	71
Deck addition	$5,927	$4,356	73

Property Insurance

What to Protect, What Not To

In the realm of big-ticket items—the stuff you're going to spend a lot of money on throughout your life—property or homeowners insurance is probably the least-conspicuous one. Unlike life insurance, it can't be used as a savings account; unlike a mortgage, it can't help you get a low-interest loan. And unlike income taxes, a homeowners policy usually won't cause anxiety and night sweats once a year.

Homeowners insurance is ubiquitous in this country. For the most part, if you own a home, your mortgage holder will require you to buy a policy. According to the Insurance Information Institute, about 95 percent of all houses are insured to some degree. (Some people let their policies slip after they pay off their mortgages.) Since having insurance will seem routine, you may be tempted to buy a policy, file it away, and rarely look at it again.

Meanwhile, you'll spend many thousands of dollars on premiums and, unless your insurer pays annual dividends, never see a return on your investment. In short, homeowners insurance—we'll use the term interchangeably with "property insurance" in this chapter—may look very much like a cash drain to you.

Best not to think about it too much, right? Wrong. Not thinking about your policy, that is, not investigating what you're covered for and what you're not, could turn an unfortunate event (such as a burglary) into a major catastrophe.

What's Covered, What's Not

Virtually all U.S. property insurance policies have certain elements in common, according to Bob O'Brien, a chartered property and casualty underwriter and vice president of Blake, Hall, and Sprague Insurance in South Portland, Maine. He says that 85 to 90 percent of insurers use forms developed by an industry ratings bureau known as the Insurance Service Office as the basis for coverage.

"The forms are important because the contract language has to be fairly standardized for testing in courts," says O'Brien. "Standardization also helps insurance adjusters to know what's covered and what's not."

That doesn't mean, however, that you'll have the same policy as your next-door neighbor. If you own the property you live in, you will likely have the following types of coverage at your disposal.

HO-1: This is the basic form of insurance, which covers the structure of the house and its contents in the event of damage caused by fire, smoke, lightning, windstorms, hail, explosions, riots or civil disorder, vehicles, aircraft, theft, vandalism, and glass breakage. It also covers property that is lost after the owner has removed it from the house—for instance, personal effects lost while you travel.

HO-2: This is the broad form of property insurance. It includes protection from the perils listed in HO-1, plus damage caused by falling objects; hot-water pipes or heater explosions; frozen pipes; air-conditioning malfunctions; electrical surges; roof collapse because of ice, snow, or sleet; or collapse of any part of the building.

HO-3: Known as the special form, HO-3 offers supplemental coverage beyond what is included in HO-2, according to Loretta Worters, director of public relations for the Insurance Information Institute, based in New York City. "This type of policy expands on the personal property that's covered, such as clothing, furniture, and appliances. It's notable because relatively few things are excluded from coverage, and those that are will be spelled out in the policy."

For instance, the special form will insure you for losses due to almost anything except cataclysmic events. That means that if your house gets taken out by an enemy missile in wartime or if the local nuclear plant melts down, you won't collect a dime for damages.

What Are the Odds?

Homeowners insurance is designed to protect you from a range of occurrences. But what is the likelihood that you will ever file a claim? Here are figures supplied by the National Association of Independent Insurers in Des Plaines, Illinois. Statistics reflect nationwide experience from 1990 to 1994, the latest data available.

Event	Number of Claims per 100 Houses
Wind and hail	3.2
Theft	2.1
Fire and lightning	2.0
All other physical-damage losses	1.6
Liability and medical payments	0.3
Credit card theft	0.0

With few exceptions, the same goes for earthquake destruction. Although quake insurance is available, the deductible alone may be huge—possibly 10 percent of the cost of the wreckage. (In other words, you would pay the first $30,000 for repairs to a $300,000 home.) If you live in an earthquake-prone area, you should ask your agent about coverage for such occurrences, O'Brien advises.

Here are some other factors to consider when choosing a homeowners policy that's right for you.

Get an appraisal. To determine your home's value, you will need an appraisal. Don't fret too much about this unless you have already paid off your mortgage, since an appraisal is part of the mortgage-granting process. Your insurance agent or other company representative can arrange the service, and you'll have to pay a fee of about $200.

"Be sure your agent makes an adjustment every year or two," Worters advises. "If your last appraisal was 10 years ago, you will only be covered for the lower amount that the house was worth at the time of the appraisal."

Buy separately for floods. Floods are relatively common, but no insurance company offers direct protection against them. Instead, you have to buy from the federal government's National Flood Insurance Program because private insurers cannot adequately measure the risk involved, according to Jerry Bell, assistant vice president of commercial and property insurance with the National Association of Independent Insurers in Des Plaines, Illinois.

You can buy a flood policy either directly from the government or through a private insurer, but the government will always be the underwriter. Expect to pay between $200 and $400 per year for flood protection, experts say.

"There's a lot of misunderstanding about flood insurance," says Worters. "Many people assume their policies cover them for flood damage, but that's not the case. Fewer than 20 percent of people who live in flood-prone areas have flood insurance."

Get replacement value. When insuring your home, your best option, say many experts, is to have the home covered for its replacement value rather than its actual cash value. The former refers to the cost of rebuilding your current home after it has been destroyed, while cash value is replacement cost minus the physical depreciation of the house over time.

"Replacement value is one of the best deals you can get," says James Cox, an independent insurance consultant in Palm Springs, California.

You will pay 10 to 15 percent more for a replacement-value policy as opposed to a cash value one, according to Worters. For a house appraised at between $125,000 and $200,000, the typical homeowner can expect to pay approximately $600 in annual premiums for replacement value.

Opt for 80. For many years, the insurance industry recommended that a customer buy coverage for at least 80 percent of his home's value. The reasoning behind this was that most disasters left about 20 percent of the home intact, says Worters. Interestingly, the standard has changed in recent years, due mainly to the increased ferocity of hurricanes. "Most insurance companies now tell you to insure your home for 100 percent of the costs of rebuilding it," she says.

Take the "hurricane-as-culprit" line of reasoning with a pinch of saltwater, and be wary of any factor that raises your premiums. At the same time, be aware that your insurer will still require 80 percent coverage before writing a replacement-value policy.

Take inventory. Insurance experts agree that customers deal poorly with both natural disasters and man-made ones such as theft. "The problem is that you're going to forget things that you owned, and you won't be able to make an accurate list after the fact," says Bob Hunter, director of insurance for the Consumer Federation of America, based in Washington, D.C., and formerly an insurance commissioner for the state of Texas. "Without looking around, just try to remember all your possessions. It's nearly impossible."

Ways to Pay Less

With a typical property insurance policy, you may pay roughly $700 a year in premiums. Here is some expert advice on lowering your premiums.

Combine policies. Buying home and automobile coverage from the same company usually yields discounts of around 5 to 15 percent, according to Loretta Worters of the Insurance Information Institute.

Shop around. Some people think insurance prices are relatively equal, but they aren't, says Bob Hunter, director of insurance for the Consumer Federation of America.

Don't rely solely on an independent insurance agent to do the shopping for you. "Independents" may represent just six or seven companies, not the entire universe of insurers. And since agents work on a commission basis, they may recommend a higher-priced company. Remember, agents represent the companies, not you, Hunter says.

Haggling with your company agent to pay a lower premium won't work unless you are armed with information, and even then it's not a sure thing, he adds. "An agent won't lower your rates just because you ask him to," says Hunter. "But what you can do is, after shopping around for the best deal, present the agent with a few comparison quotes from different companies. Ask, 'Can you beat these prices?' He'll either walk away or work a little harder to bring the premium down. That's a good way to use an agent."

Bring your house up to spec. Insurance companies like security, so they'll give discounts for certain home improvements you initiate. You should tell your agent if you in-

stall a burglar alarm, smoke detectors, or deadbolt locks, says Bob O'Brien of Blake, Hall, and Sprague Insurance. Additionally, if every member of your household is a nonsmoker, you'll likely qualify for extra reductions.

"Insurers typically have more than one pricing tier," O'Brien explains. "They'll offer standard and preferred pricing. New homes or even older homes with new wiring, plumbing, and heating, or a new roof, will probably qualify for preferred programs. The cost difference can be substantial."

Self-insure. The standard deductible for property insurance is about $250, according to Worters. "If you increase it to $500, you can save up to 12 percent on your premium; going to $1,000 would save 24 percent; raising it to $2,500 would save up to 30 percent; and carrying a $5,000 deductible would save you up to 37 percent. Of course, you have to determine what your pocketbook can withstand if you need to make a claim," Worters points out.

Hunter set up his own "casualty account" in a bank. "What I saved by taking high deductibles every year, I've deposited. Over 30 years, I've paid myself $3,500 with a $1,000 deductible. So I can file three claims and still come out ahead."

Hunter says the typical homeowner files a claim about once every 10 years. "That means that over time, if you're an average risk, you're going to do better with a higher deductible. If you're exactly average, you'll still save 40 percent of the dollars you don't pay for premiums. My advice: Take the highest deductible you can afford."

As a remedy, Hunter says that you should create some type of record of your personal effects. "You can take a video camera around your place, recording and describing everything, or just take photos," he says. Hunter himself keeps pictures of his possessions in a safe-deposit box.

"Videotaping does offer proof of what you owned, but more important, it reminds you of items that you would have otherwise overlooked," O'Brien adds. "And obviously, keep that tape in a safe place, like a fireproof vault."

Endorse, of course. All homeowners policies set coverage limits on certain items. For your most prized and valuable possessions, you will want a separate insurance provision known as an endorsement, which will guarantee full replacement value. According to O'Brien, an endorsement is anything that changes the basic policy. You should consider placing any especially valuable object on a separate schedule.

Here are some items that commonly have coverage limits, along with the maximum amount you will typically collect to replace them. They should be considered for endorsement.

Cash	$200
Boats (not including canoes) and boat trailers	$1,000
Computer equipment	$1,000
Furs, jewelry, watches, and precious and semiprecious stones	$1,000
Stocks, deeds, and passports	$1,000
Guns	$2,000
Silverware and goldware	$2,500

O'Brien notes that when you endorse an item, you normally won't have to pay a deductible on it, but you will have to pay an extra premium. How much these premiums are usually depends on the value of the item being endorsed. Your insurance provider will be able to give you an exact quote before you buy the endorsement.

Beyond Robbery and Roof Collapse

Until the 1950s, homeowners could only buy insurance designed to safeguard against specific losses. One policy covered theft, another protected against vandalism, and yet another shielded against fire damage. So packaging together different coverages is a relatively recent—and quite sensible—idea. Imagine how much time our parents must have spent shopping for insurance. It's a wonder they managed to squeeze in having families.

Today, a good property insurance policy can help protect your home and possessions from a variety of tribulations. But there is even more that it can do. Your plan will also indemnify you for personal liability in case someone has an accident on your property.

"Homeowners insurance is built on limits," says Cox. "One set of limits applies to damage to your home, another to your possessions, and a third to your personal liability."

"A lot of people think of homeowners coverage, understandably, from a property standpoint," O'Brien adds. "They think, 'What if my house burns down?' But liability coverage is equally or more important. You know how much your house is worth, you know how much your stereo is worth. But you don't know how much you can get sued for."

Personal liability will protect you against a suit brought by someone who is accidentally hurt or whose property is damaged in your house, according to James Walsh, managing editor of Merritt Publishing and author of *What Do You Mean It's Not Covered?* The policy covers damages caused by you, a family member, or your pet. Most policies provide $100,000 in liability insurance, but you can raise the amount to $300,000 for only $10 to $20 in additional annual premiums, Walsh reports. The insurance company will even pay to defend you in court. Most financial planners recommend buying an umbrella policy that will increase liability limits by $1 million to $2 million.

Here are a few more tips about personal liability for your consideration.

Keep your credit cards to yourself. Maybe we were brainwashed by those old American Express commercials where Karl Malden turned up at the scene of a credit card crime, because many folks are surprised to learn that their cards are covered by property insurance, says O'Brien. Within limits, of course. Normally, you're covered for $500 in fraudulent use. Be careful, though: You can't file a claim if someone other than yourself lost the card or had it stolen. Incidentally, your policy will also provide coverage for other items that you may be traveling with, such as clothing and luggage. "Your possessions are covered anywhere in the world," says O'Brien.

Buy more if you run a business. These days, a lot of people run small businesses out of their homes. If you are one of them, make sure you buy a policy designed specifically for the enterprise, experts say, because your regular policy won't apply to commercial endeavors. "A typical homeowners policy limits losses on computers to $1,000," says Hunter. "Your equipment may be worth a lot more, so you'd lose big."

Liability coverage may be even more important in a business setting, Cox says. "If a worker gets hurt on your premises, then by law you're liable for medical damages that occur," he notes, adding that each state has its own laws governing such cases.

Get a renters policy. Experts say that people who rent houses or apartments typically assume they need no property insurance. They're mistaken. It's true that they needn't worry about damages to the building they live in; that will be covered by the landlord's policy. But they should get a policy known as an HO-4. "A renters policy generally protects the tenant's possessions against the perils covered in a broad homeowners policy," says Worters. "Furthermore, like a homeowners policy, it will indemnify you against personal liability."

Health Insurance

The Best Coverage for the Least Cash

If you've ever taken a close look at a hospital bill, you've begun to understand the magnitude of health care costs in this country. The average cost for a full day's stay in a hospital in 1995, the most recent year for which statistics are available, was $967.69. At the current rate of growth, in just two years, health care spending will consume almost 20 percent of what is spent on all goods and services, according to James Walsh, author of *What Do You Mean It's Not Covered?* The lion's share of services will be dispensed through doctors belonging to health maintenance organizations (HMOs).

There's a good chance that HMOs will one day play a part in your future health care, if they haven't affected you already. And though many different HMOs have similar features, by understanding their basic operation you could get better health care and even lower your medical costs.

Historically, HMOs have done a good job controlling insurance costs for employers. "HMOs have been sensationally successful in blunting medical inflation," says Paul M. Ellwood, M.D., president of the Jackson Hole Group and InterStudy organizations based in Jackson Hole, Wyoming, which advise government on formulating health care policies. (Dr. Ellwood is generally credited with coining the term *HMO* in 1970 and devising much of the modern system's structure.)

Performance Factors

Judging by their brochures, you'd think that all HMOs exceed national standards, take superb care of their members, and charge remarkably reasonable rates. Unfortunately, real-life experience with the health care bureaucracy tends to paint a different picture. Visions of George Orwell's *1984* run through your head as your coverage questions get routed from clerks to functionaries, each of whom knows less and less about your case.

If you think you can't fight the maddening bureaucracy of the health care system, you're mistaken. For one thing, HMOs and their managed care cousins, preferred provider organizations (PPOs) and point of service (POS) plans (which will be discussed later in the chapter) are getting better and more responsive, according to Karen Ignagni, president and chief executive officer of the American Association of Health Plans, based in Washington, D.C. In addition, it's in your employer's best interest to make sure the plans do the job for you since it doesn't do the company any good to have you spending your time being ill or haggling with insurance companies.

With respect to HMOs and other forms of managed care, "employers are driven by a combination of three things: cost, service, and quality," says Jim Watson, vice president of provider services for CIGNA Healthcare of Illinois in Chicago. "Cost used to be the primary driver. Now, companies are dealing more with service and quality issues since inflation has slowed."

Plan Characteristics

Typically, HMOs provide "basic coverage," including routine checkups and office visits. The plans also cover participants for what's known as "major medical," wherein benefits are characterized by high limits of insurance (frequently $500,000 to $1 million), offer copayments (a percentage of covered expenses paid by the member, usually $5 to $10 per office visit), and set a "stop loss" deductible (a maximum amount paid by the member, above which the insurer pays 100 percent of additional covered expenses).

The "gatekeeper" concept is also central to HMOs. Gatekeepers are primary care physicians (PCPs) who coordinate all care for the patient. These doctors handle routine office visits and recommend services by specialists, such as heart surgeons. In virtually all cases, the HMO will not cover you for treatment by a specialist unless you have a prior referral from the PCP.

"HMOs are the most restrictive kind of health care plan available," says Connie Barron, associate director of legislative affairs for the Texas Medical Association, based in Austin. "They limit the availability of physicians and hospitals so that, in order to receive any benefits at all, you have to use the physicians and hospitals that are contracted to the HMO."

Doctors are typically reimbursed through a system known as capitation. Under this plan, the HMO pays the physician in advance each month to deliver service to a given number of patients. For example, if a doctor (or group of doctors) wants to make $20,000 a month at $100 per visit, they will agree to see 200 patients per month.

Capitations have caused controversy because HMO critics tend to view the system as promoting "assembly line" medicine, with doctors spending less time with each patient.

For the most part, your health care programs have been selected for you by your employer, usually through the human resources department. Most larger corporations offer two plans—often, an HMO/POS option paired with a traditional indemnity (or "fee-for-service") plan. Sometimes, employees can select a PPO instead of an HMO.

Of these plans, indemnity coverage has invariably been seen as the best deal for the employee, who can visit any doctor he chooses, but a bad bargain for the employer, who must pay open-ended amounts for medical care. Accordingly, cost controls account for the rising popularity of HMOs and the shrinking demand for indemnity plans among employers, though experts say the plans must compete on quality as well. Employees are beginning to demand better service from their HMOs.

"People need to consider their own personal needs in a health care plan," Watson advises. "You need to determine, 'Am I going to need consistent health care services? If so, what is the role of the gatekeeper?'

"Then, look at the provider network," he continues. "Check to see if your current doctor is in it." The average doctor, according to Dr. Ellwood, belongs to five different HMOs.

Here are some other expert tips to help you get the best health care from your HMO.

Know your options. Perhaps the single most important thing you can do is ask your company to investigate other health plans. "You'd be surprised how often you can find a better plan than the one your company offers," Walsh notes. Employers, he says, "are as befuddled by this stuff as you are. They may offer your suggestion as an alternative to the existing plans."

Of course, your benefits professionals may listen harder if you're armed with good information. Fortunately, we're entering a period of enlightenment in which hard data on health plans is becoming more accessible, according to Dr. Ellwood and Ignagni.

Speak up. Employees should tell their employers about any problems encountered with plan doctors or administrators, suggests Barron. "If the employees aren't getting the services they're entitled to, then the employer can pressure the health plan to improve service," she says.

Hold on to a good thing. You may want to fight to keep a reliable health plan in effect. "Encourage fellow employees to join what you consider to be a good plan, because then it won't be dropped due to low enrollment or lack of interest," Barron says. HMO contracts with employers typically run for about a year, she adds, a change from the days when companies routinely signed multiyear pacts.

Read the fine print. The law dictates how insurance companies can structure their policies. One important practice mandated by law is that HMOs must point out and describe any medical services that they will not cover. "Go to the exclusions page of the contract," Walsh counsels. "That tells you what they won't cover."

Most HMOs have a master contract that defines experimental coverage, Walsh adds. This definition is critical because some procedures that are considered experimental may be denied coverage by the HMO. For instance, until relatively recently, HMOs considered bone marrow transplants for leukemia patients to be experimental, Walsh says. "Reading up on what is covered and what is not is a good way to compare policies."

Compare policies. If you or your family happen to have more than one type of insurance (for example, you have a policy paid for by your company but are also considering some sort of supplemental policy) be sure to compare the two and avoid the cost of duplicate coverage: essentially paying twice for the same insurance, says Malcolm A. Makin, a certified financial planner and president of Professional Planning Group in Westerly, Rhode Island.

Consider your circumstances. Everyone has different priorities in a health care program, says Watson. For example, young singles tend not to go to the doctor unless they're ill. They're not picky about the plans offered to them, whereas families with children tend to be more selective. In fact, say observers, HMOs are really geared toward families.

Lose Your Job, Keep Your Coverage

Layoffs have been endemic in the 1990s, as big businesses seek to slash operating costs. If you get caught in the downsizing current or if you leave your job for other reasons, you will probably need to retain your health care coverage until you find a new position.

Breathe easy: Under the Consolidated Omnibus Budget Reconciliation Act of 1985 (known as COBRA), your former company must keep you enrolled in their health plan for 18 months or until you find new work.

"Your employer is obligated to provide the paperwork for filing," says James Walsh, author of *What Do You Mean It's Not Covered?* "Some employers may be a little sneaky about it. They'll try to include a waiver of COBRA obligation and ask you to sign it." This waiver, he says, will state that you've been informed about COBRA, but it also relieves your company of the task of sending you enrollment paperwork, which increases the odds that you won't get the papers and send them in yourself. Don't bite.

"A good rule of thumb: Don't sign anything COBRA-related on the spot. Take it home, read it carefully, and send it in later," says Walsh.

He notes that you can also try to negotiate a separation under which the employer will continue to pay your benefits for a while, getting you a better deal than if you relied on COBRA provisions. "If you're being let go," he advises, "don't assume you have to take the package they offer."

"If you have young children, HMOs may be your most efficient form of coverage," says Walsh. "Kids will keep you going back and forth to the doctor's office with any number of problems. The fact that you pay just a small amount per visit is an important factor."

Older people also have a different set of health care needs, though they, too, have ample incentive to keep costs down. For instance, HMOs generally pay for most prescription medications. "I have to take a drug that costs $4 a pill," says Dr. Ellwood, "and I really resent paying $120 a month for it. So I think drug benefits are one of the best parts of the managed care deal."

Assume you're sick. "Any plan is good enough if you're healthy," says Barron. But ask yourself what you would need from a health plan if you found out tomorrow that you had a life-threatening illness. "Be sure you'd get the specialized services you would want and need," Barron warns.

Researching HMOs: Some Pointers

"Consumers will soon have access to comparative information on HMOs that's never been available before." That's the message from Dr. Paul Ellwood, the physician who coined the term *HMO*.

The information explosion has yet to occur, Dr. Ellwood continues, but when it does, health plans must be prepared for tough questions. Among those who will be asking questions are companies that offer health care insurance to employees, and individuals who expect results from their insurers.

"You should ask how good a plan is at getting people well and keeping them well," Dr. Ellwood says. Some resources are available now, of course. Data from the National Committee for Quality Assurance (NCQA) are shedding new light on the effectiveness of all managed care organizations, including HMOs.

For example, NCQA investigates whether insurers continually seek to improve their product and encourage preventive tests and immunizations. The group also verifies that insurers are screening physician histories as well as they claim to. (Notably, no comparable system monitors doctors in fee-for-service plans.)

The committee also provides accreditation of managed care organizations. That's been a sore subject for some insurers, who argue there's no way to compare the nation's roughly 1,000 health plans in a consistent fashion.

Time to Get Out?

Though HMOs try to offer high-quality care to all demographic groups, some people just don't like them. The freedom to select their own doctors or hospitals becomes the key factor in choosing a plan.

At some point, you may find it worthwhile to opt out of one plan and sign up with another. Generally, you can do this once a year for no cost, during the plan's renewal period. "You can switch at other times, but the new provider will charge a fee of possibly a few hundred dollars to enroll you," says Walsh.

Here are brief overviews of two other plans that may be available to you.

Preferred Provider Organizations (PPOs). PPOs allow a degree of freedom that HMOs reject. "The upside is that you have a greater choice of doctors and hospitals, and you can go to a specialist without a referral from the gatekeeper," says Watson. "The disadvantage is

But that rationale is fading fast because NCQA data has already become a quality yardstick of sorts.

"If you don't get accreditation, a lot of the big employers won't deal with you anymore," says Jim Watson of CIGNA Healthcare of Illinois. "Employees could therefore suggest that the human resources people look at the NCQA data as an objective source of information." The data can be found on the World Wide Web.

The Portland, Oregon–based Foundation for Accountability has a mission similar to that of the NCQA. It helps consumers find the information they need to make better decisions about health care. Other sources of HMO data include the Health Association of America and departments of insurance within each state. Also, *Newsweek* and *U.S. News and World Report* magazines publish annual rankings of HMOs.

That said, you can always ask HMOs to supply details on the success rate of their plans and doctors. While it's unlikely that administrators will share these records with you (they'll claim physician histories are confidential), it may be comforting to know that HMOs require their doctors to submit to such background checks before they can join the network. HMO administrators like Watson consult the National Practitioner Database, which reports data on every doctor who has had an adverse outcome or a malpractice suit.

that PPOs require higher deductibles and co-payments than HMOs, so it's much more costly for a family to get care."

That said, PPOs try to minimize costs by soliciting discounts from physicians and hospitals, usually in exchange for more business.

"PPOs tell doctors, 'We'll put financial incentives in place to send our members to your office, if in return, you'll agree to provide services at a discounted rate,'" Barron explains.

"Doctors also agree not to 'balance bill' the consumer," Barron adds. That means that if the doctor's normal charge is higher than the standard rate in the area, the doctor can't pass that difference on to the patient.

POS plans. A growing number of HMOs now offer a Point of Service option. These plans allow members to seek care from non-HMO physicians, but the premiums for such plans may cost more. Furthermore, the plan typically pays far less than its usual 100 percent coverage for medical services, according to Dr. Ellwood.

"POS plans offer the best of both worlds," says Watson, whose company administers POS plans. As with an HMO, you utilize a primary care physician and a provider network. The difference: "If you choose to go out of network or unreferred, you are still partially covered—usually between 60 and 70 percent. In an HMO, you would have no insurance for going outside the plan."

A private plan. While it's not the most popular choice, some people buy personal health insurance policies. For the most part, personal policies have the reputation of not being very cost-effective, but ever since the Clinton administration tried to reform health care in 1993, several insurance companies responded to the proposed changes by offering reasonably priced private insurance plans. If you're self-employed or not finding a satisfactory insurance plan with your employer, it wouldn't hurt to consider this avenue. You may be able to make a better deal on your own.

Life Insurance

Do You Really Need It?

In his movie *Take the Money and Run*, Woody Allen plays a small-time crook who does hard time in prison. While in the slammer, he breaks a rule and receives his punishment: a one-on-one meeting with an insurance salesman.

Why does the scene work so well? Maybe it's because, thanks to the insurance industry, we can speak coherently about something called a death benefit.

The purchase of a life insurance policy is "one of the most ill-informed decisions that any consumer makes. And the beneficiaries pay dearly for it," according to William McLeod, professor of business at Cambrian College of Applied Arts and Technology in Sudbury, Ontario, and author of *The Canadian Buyer's Guide to Life Insurance.*

Misunderstandings about life insurance arise because of a "paucity of independent, objective analysis of what's going on" in the insurance field, says Joseph M. Belth, Ph.D., professor emeritus of insurance in the Kelley School of Business at Indiana University in Bloomington, and editor of the *Insurance Forum* newsletter.

Choose a method. The first consideration is how much income your family will need. One simple formula, recommended by the Wall Street Insurance Group of Gaithersburg, Maryland, is to multiply your salary by 10. Thus, if you make $50,000, you would buy a $500,000 policy. Invested at 10 percent annually, that amount would produce your former annual income, leaving the principal untouched.

"The goal is to make sure your family is provided for in the same manner they were accustomed to while you were alive," according to the company.

Consider your family's situation. "You must decide how much of the insurance benefit will be invested so survivors can live off the principal and interest as long as they need to," says McLeod. You'll have to consider personal factors like the number and ages of your children, whether you were planning to send them to college, and the likelihood of your spouse working or remarrying after your death.

Pay your bills after the fact. Besides providing your beneficiaries with money to live on after you die, life insurance should address final expenses and debts, according to Dr. Belth.

So-called final expenses include funeral costs and costs associated with settling your estate, such as federal, state, and property taxes. With respect to debts, your family may have to pay off short-term obligations, charge accounts, and installment loans. Your spouse may have to decide whether to settle the mortgage in one lump sum or keep it as a long-term obligation.

Life Choices

In deciding whether or not you need life insurance, you may want to start by setting aside some very basic emotions. Life insurance, after all, asks you to imagine a world in which you're no longer around, then commit money to it.

Here are some basic guidelines to keep in mind when coming to a decision about buying life insurance.

What Type Will Do?

Meet with any agent and you'll likely hear about at least two forms of life insurance: *term* and *whole life*. Understanding the salient differences between them will set the stage for deciding which one to select. Here are the fundamentals.

Term life. This type of

insurance is simple, says William Pullano, a State Farm Insurance Company agent in Chicago. "Each year (or more often) you pay a premium, which increases as you grow older, and coverage is provided for one year. When you die, any person, group, or organization of your choice gets a sum of money from your insurance company."

With term life, you can choose a level premium plan, in which the premium stays constant for several years. Also at your disposal are annual renewable term policies. Here, the premiums are cheap early on but get more costly over time.

"When you're young, term insurance generally offers the largest insurance protection for your premium dollar," says Pullano. The annual renewable policies, however, become prohibitive if you live past 70 years old, because the premiums on those policies go up each year.

Whole life. Unlike term life insurance, the whole life option allows you to build equity in your policy. As with term insurance, your beneficiary gets a death benefit when you die. But a whole life policy is also a vehicle for accumulating cash while you are still alive. Thus, such plans are also known as cash value policies. Some have likened whole life policies to home mortgages because you can borrow against the equity.

McLeod, for one, believes whole life insurance is a rip-off. "The traditional whole life policy combines savings and insurance in the same contract," he says, "and the company steals the savings when the policy holder dies." In other words, the beneficiary gets only the policy's face value and the company keeps any savings built up in the plan.

Many financial planners now recommend using variable whole life, especially for younger clients for whom "permanent" protection is needed, advises Malcolm A. Makin, a certified financial planner and president of Profession Planning Group in Westerly, Rhode Island. The cash value is comprised of a variety of mutual fund–type investments as opposed to the usual low interest rates that whole life pays.

Alternative Sources of Life Insurance

"By and large, life insurance is purchased through agents," says Dr. Joseph M. Belth, author of *Life Insurance: A Consumer's Handbook*. Nevertheless, other means are available to get coverage.

A good starting point is your workplace. According to the International Foundation of Employee Benefit Plans in Brookfield, Wisconsin, about 91 percent of workers have some life insurance through their employers, and it's usually free.

Should you rely on this type of life insurance coverage? Not entirely, says William McLeod, author of *The Canadian Buyer's Guide to Life Insurance*. "I usually advise people to look upon their work coverage as a bonus," he notes. He also says it's safer to consider a policy that has no bearing on your employment situation.

Associations offer group life insurance plans as well. For example, the American Automobile Association (AAA) offers term life insurance to its members. Among other problems, though, the policy terminates when the membership expires, according to Dr. Belth.

You can also buy life insurance before you fly, but that strategy seems dubious. If you're flying on business, for example, your company covers you over and above any life insurance they already offer you anyway. Furthermore, if you charged your ticket on a major credit card, you're probably covered there as well.

College Planning

Guarantee Your Kid's Education

One good thing that came out of World War II was that all those returning soldiers got the chance to attend college for free on the GI Bill. Talk about a peace dividend: In 1946 alone, more than one million veterans started college with the help of the bill, and some schools were founded just to accommodate the huge demand.

Maybe that's why higher learning now seems so important to so many people. The World War II generation and their descendants venerated the benefits of college. Success at the university level still goes hand in hand with notions of advantage and opportunity.

What has changed radically is the cost of a college education. "On average, tuition goes up at about twice the inflation rate, which runs 3 percent a year," says Mark Kantrowitz, the publisher of the Financial Aid Information Page on the World Wide Web and author of *Prentice Hall Guide to Scholarships and Fellowships for Math and Science Students.* "With annual 6 percent hikes, tuition could come close to doubling in 10 years."

Catch-Up Game

Why? Colleges have a relatively high proportion of new construction expenses, Kantrowitz explains. Those outlays tend to rise faster than inflation.

Another factor is the cost of financial aid itself. About 40 to 70 percent of the student population is on aid—55 percent is about average at a college, Kantrowitz reports. Schools, then, net only about 55 percent of the tuition dollar, so they're forced to cover their expenses quickly. Kantrowitz believes schools are trying to control costs because, eventually, "they won't be able to increase tuition at all."

The surge in tuition costs is less forgiveable to Kalman A. Chany, founder and president of Campus Consultants in New York City and author of *Paying for College without Going Broke.* Like corporations, colleges adjust their prices as they see fit, says Chany "If (government) funds are more readily available and colleges figure they can charge more, they're going to do it," he says.

With every tuition uptick, parental anxiety about how to foot the bill rises, as does resentment toward schools. But financial planners and college-aid experts say there are ways to cope with spiraling college costs.

Bring the kids on board. Parents tend to assume that they have to pick up the entire tab for their children's education, says Humberto Cruz, a syndicated financial writer with South Florida's *Sun-Sentinel* newspaper and Tribune Media Services. Not so. "The first thing to consider in financing college is, 'How much am I expected to save and how much are the kids going to contribute?'" says Cruz.

When his own daughter was a high school junior, Cruz got estimates of the annual cost of attending the universities his daughter had chosen. He then talked with her about how much she could reasonably kick in. While at school, she would be responsible for this amount and would have to figure out how to get the cash if her budget fell through. "It's a good way to teach responsibility at a young age," Cruz notes.

Take risks early. "The greatest resource available to families is time," says Kantrowitz. "If a family starts saving $25 a week from the date the child is born, at 5 percent interest above inflation, they could save about $34,000 by high school graduation. To save that amount over four years, the weekly contribution would have to be $150."

"If the child is preteen, you would invest the money like you would any other retirement money: for long-term growth," says Jonathan Pond, president of Financial Planning Information in Boston. Investments would include stocks and mutual funds, which have relatively high risk but also potential for greater return.

"A lot of parents invest the money too conservatively when the kids are young," Pond says, "and they shouldn't be doing that."

Play it safe later. People typically have heavy expenses when starting a family; money is tighter then, says Terri Jiganti Stewart, a certified financial planner with Bush, Polen, and Associates in Gig Harbor, Washington. In many cases, she says, parents simply put off an investment program. If you've procrastinated, it's still not too late to do something.

As a general rule, if your child is 13 or older, Jiganti Stewart recommends more conservative savings vehicles such as certificates of deposit, treasury notes, and Series EE savings bonds. As long as they're used for college, the interest earned on these instruments is generally exempt from taxes, she says.

Pore over prepaid programs. Many schools (particularly state universities) allow you to lock in future tuition at today's prices long before your child reaches college age. Funds earmarked for a given school under the so-called prepaid programs cannot be taxed until withdrawal. Furthermore, the money will be assessed at the minor's rate of 15 percent. Nevertheless, experts see hefty risks associated with these plans.

"Would you buy a car that hasn't been produced yet—a car you'll own six years from now?" asks Chany. "Who knows what will happen to the school in six years? Its reputation could slip." Other considerations: You could move to a different state before your child starts school, meaning your eligibility to pay as a state resident could be affected. The programs may also hamper your chances of getting student aid. "For every dollar you withdraw out of a state prepaid tuition plan to pay for college," Chany says, "your aid eligibility will be reduced dollar for dollar."

And if your kid wants to go to a different school, you may get your money back, but with little or no interest paid on it. In effect, you've loaned the state your cash—and don't think it's been invested for 0 percent interest.

Infuse inflation. Say your kid is 10 years away from starting college. When estimating costs, remember that during Junior's college career, inflation will continue to rise like foam in a newly tapped keg. Here's a rule of thumb, says Chany: "Figure tuition 12 years in the future, not 10. What I do is multiply the junior-year costs by four."

Granting Your Wishes

A college education is often the second-largest expense that most families ever face, second only to mortgage costs, according to Chany. In helping your child get through school, you'll probably require some amount of aid, even if junior college beckons for a couple of years.

"People realize their children have to go to college," he says. "It's not a choice. For almost all jobs, you have to have that college degree. Financial aid is designed to bridge that gap, and parents who understand the process come out way ahead."

"Parents want all aid to be in the form of grants, not loans," adds Kantrowitz. "This is not possible. Schools and government believe it is the family's duty to pay for tuition."

Government, in fact, does fund the lion's share of student loans. Sixty-five percent of all financial aid comes from the federal government, 8 percent from state governments, and 20 percent from the schools themselves. The remaining seven percent is split evenly between private employers and scholarship organizations, says Kantrowitz.

Here are some tips to improve your chances of qualifying for grants and aid money.

Be an early bird. "Students and parents should beat the bushes for grants and work-study awards," says Jiganti Stewart. These are generally underutilized options, she says. "You're new at the process, and you're dreading it. By the time you get your act together, a lot of these things aren't available."

A couple of noteworthy programs to investigate: the Hope Scholarship and the Lifetime Learning Credit. The Hope gives up to $1,500 a year in tax savings for the first two years of college; the Credit offers up to $1,000 in tax savings for the last two years of school. (Both programs come with family income limits. At press time, those limits stood at $60,000 for the Hope and $80,000 for the Credit.)

Negotiate nicely. In their dealings with financial-aid officers, parents occasionally try to play the role of NBA free agents. They make demands that one "team" (School A) match an aid package from a competing franchise (School B). Usually, though, they come off looking less-than-savvy—or savory. In reality, says Chany, you can sometimes cut a better deal for yourself, but you have to be sly.

"In a conversation with the financial-aid officer, don't even say you're negotiating. Aid professionals are offended by that word, or anything that smacks of bargaining for a more generous package," says Chany. So how do you approach this nonnegotiating negotiating session? "Tell them you're concerned that you can't make the payments based on the current offer. Give them a reason why, too. Say that last year's salary was distorted because of greater overtime pay, for instance." Chany says to keep in mind that some schools will not give their best offer in the initial package anyway.

Also, don't let your kid negotiate with financial-aid personnel, even if you think he's the next Donald Trump. Few teenagers are up to the task. "Would you let your child negotiate the sale of your house? Similar amounts are at stake, after all," Chany points out.

Leave open leveraging. In some situ-

What's in a Name? More Financial Aid

In the effort to get as much money as they can from colleges and the government, parents wonder what advantages they gain by sheltering assets under their child's name.

"The decision to invest in your name or the child's is important," says syndicated financial writer Humberto Cruz. "The child's money will be in the lowest tax bracket."

You can take advantage of this fact by setting up a Uniform Gift to Minors Act (UGMA) account, according to certified financial planner Terri Jiganti Stewart. Here, all interest earned up to $1,300 is taxed at the child's rate. For amounts above $1,300, the funds will be taxed at the parents' rate if the child is under 14.

Most states also offer the Uniform Transfers to Minors Act (UTMA). "These accounts are slightly better than UGMAs," says Jiganti Stewart, "because you can put more types of assets into them, including real estate."

On the whole, however, experts say that keeping money in your own name is probably a better approach to getting as much financial aid as possible. "If you want to have any hope at all of qualifying for financial aid, don't put any money in the child's name," advises Kalman A. Chany

of Campus Consultants. Assets under the child's name are assessed far more heavily by colleges than parental assets.

Here's how it works: Say you established a college fund that now has $40,000 under your name as an asset. That figure is assessed in the student-aid formula at 5.65 percent, or $2,260. That means the school expects you to put up that amount toward the first year of school. By contrast, children's assets are assessed at 35 percent. "In other words, that same 40 grand in your child's name will be assessed at $14,000," says Chany.

The parents' home, retirement funds, and first $40,000 of income are also untouchable by the formula, says Mark Kantrowitz, publisher of the Financial Aid Information Page Web site. "If you work out all the math, for all but extremely rich parents, it's to your advantage to have the money in your name, not the kid's."

Keeping the money in your name also ensures that you have control over the funds. At a certain age (primarily 18 or 21 years old), children gain custody of the funds set aside in their names, and can do anything with them. Any money set aside for their educations could be gone.

ations, colleges will give more aid money (typically $500 to $1,000) to especially talented students, independent of the applicant's financial need, Kantrowitz says. Play up your kid's 3.75 grade point average, or her ability to dazzle audiences with a skillful interpretation of Rachmaninoff's Second Piano Concerto. "Some schools will also match an offer from a 'peer school'—another college in their category," says Kantrowitz. As a general rule, assume that schools will ask for documentation of the other college's competing bid.

Myth Conceptions

Finally, don't believe everything you hear. A few prominent myths about the student-aid and scholarship process can prevent you from seeking—and therefore receiving—any money. Here are three of the most common incorrect assumptions.

Myth #1: If you make $100,000 or more a year, you won't qualify for any aid. Not necessarily true. First of all, financial-aid people try to look at your total economic picture, says Chany. A big portion of your income may be in reserve to start a small business. Second, you may have more than one child in college. "In that case, you might end up paying only half the tuition and cover the rest with loans."

Myth #2: Homeowners can't get financial aid. Ignore this rather homely advice. Under current aid formulas, Chany says, "the federal government does not consider the value of your primary residence at all as an asset."

Myth #3: You'll need to pay an entry fee for scholarships. Many organizations and companies offer legitimate merit- and need-based scholarships. In virtually every case, the application process is free, and the scholarship's reputation is well-known. "If you have to pay money to get money, it's very likely a scam," warns Kantrowitz. "You'll send in your fee and never hear from the organization again."

Also, avoid "scholarship-matching" organizations that, for a fee, purport to match you with scholarships or even guarantee that you'll win a certain amount. "These organizations are essentially fraudulent," says Kantrowitz. "All they do is a search a publicly available scholarship database and send you some addresses. Nobody can guarantee your results. They can't even fill out the application for you."

Car Buying

Get the Best Deal on Wheels

Groucho Marx once said, "The secret of life is honesty and fair dealing. If you can fake that, you've got it made." This philosophy could also be applied to the art of striking a deal on a car—but don't assume that only car dealers can take advantage of this tactic. Groucho's wisdom cuts both ways. While we assume car salesmen routinely use underhanded tactics to get us to buy cars, how many of us have thought to turn the tables on them and use our guile to get what we want? Probably not enough of us, and certainly not often enough, argues Burke Leon, Ph.D., co-author of *The Insider's Guide to Buying a New or Used Car.*

Our focus here is on ways to negotiate a better deal for yourself when buying a new car. After all, what's the worst that can happen? The dealer says no. Big whoop. Actually, the worst thing that could happen is that you don't even try to get the best deal—then your wallet ends up paying the price.

Buyer's Market

If you're reluctant to go one-on-one with a car dealer, consider that the time to brush up your jousting skills has seldom been better. The Internet has begun changing car-buying habits, while freeing up information on true dealer costs.

To accomplish their financial goals and reduce inventory, carmakers maintain a steady flow of sales programs to their dealerships. These programs are known as factory-to-dealer incentives. They differ from manufacturers' rebates in that the dealer may or may not pass on the savings to the customer (it's his choice). These incentives can be substantial—as much as $5,000 per car for some models.

Additionally, floor sales personnel can earn anywhere from $50 to $1,000 per transaction, depending on the profitability of the deals they strike. On top of that, they may also qualify for bonuses based solely on the number of sales they close, regardless of profit.

"Knowing that, how can you rightfully do business with someone who wants to make as much money as he can off you?" asks Michael La Motta, founder and president of Executive Car Buying Services, an online company based in Cedar Grove, New Jersey.

We mention this because when some guys venture into a dealership, they bring their hearts—and the belief that even car dealers should be allowed to make a living. "We think dealers are entitled to a profit," says Greg Anderson, an editor at *Edmund's Automobile Buyer's Guides.* "But that profit should be a fair one, not something that gouges customers."

Here's how you can reduce the chances of a dealer using you to pad his wallet.

Do market research. More often than you'd care to admit, you've probably visited just one car dealership before buying. Maybe you were desperate for a vehicle because your old one broke down, or, even more likely, you wanted to encounter as few salespeople as possible. Don't feel too bad. As Dr. Leon points out, dealers have a natural advantage on their home turf.

You will feel more in control if you're better informed, Dr. Leon and others assert. So, how can you feel confident that any one deal on the table is a good one? You're going to have to shop around. Your options are to physically visit several showrooms, or go online to accomplish essentially the same thing.

Pinpoint the dealer's cost. The overriding goal of

your research is to find out what the dealer has paid for the car. Online services have made this a relatively easy matter. The *Edmund's Automobile Buyer's Guides* Web site, for instance, lists the dealer's cost for virtually every new car on the market. As you might guess, salesmen aren't thrilled that this data is so readily available, and Anderson won't reveal the company's sources. But knowing the dealer invoice cost, for comparison against the manufacturer's suggested retail price (MSRP, or sticker price) will serve as the basis for future negotiations with the dealership.

"Consumers should always base what they're going to pay on what the dealer pays," Anderson says, "not on MSRP, which is usually at least $2,000 more than invoice."

Of course, other factors do come into play. "Understand that, when the demand for a car is high, dealerships will occasionally disregard invoice cost," says La Motta, "and even try to charge more than the MSRP.

"So, here's my best advice to a customer shopping for a vehicle that's in high demand and low supply: Wait. Sooner or later, you'll be able to buy at a price very close to the dealer's cost."

Assume holdback. Another cushion built into new-car pricing is dealer holdback. Simply stated, holdback is a percentage of the vehicle's MSRP that the manufacturer gives to the dealership for overhead expenses (usually paid quarterly). This allowance typically amounts to about 3 percent of the MSRP, so figure a $900 cushion on a $30,000 vehicle.

"It's a profit the dealer can count on," says Anderson, "and it's a charge no one should pay. If dealers are getting 3 percent from the manufacturer, then you should just pay invoice. Al-

Get the Most for Your Trade-In

Trading in an old car is part and parcel of many vehicle purchases. And while selling your old beater to the dealership where you're buying a new car can give you quick down payment cash, it opens up a new frontier for dealer rip-offs.

For instance, let's say you haggled your heart out to buy your new car for just a few hundred dollars above dealer cost. The sales manager may try to make up for some of his loss by giving you a lowball figure on your trade-in. "That's why it's important to know the trade-in value of your old car," says Greg Anderson, an editor at *Edmund's Automobile Buyer's Guides*.

One of the most reputable names in used car pricing is the *Kelley Blue Book Used Car Guide*. While it's available in most bookstores, it's now possible to check the trade-in value of your car at one of the many Internet sites that contain an interactive version of the blue book (do a Web search using the term "blue book" to find the most up-to-date site). Then, simply plug in some data about your vehicle, such as its make and model, age, mileage, and possibly your ZIP code, and in less than a minute you'll see a dollar figure that you can take to the dealership. Edmund's and the National Automobile Dealers Association (NADA) Web sites contain used-car prices for many models as well.

"If you can't get the dealer to give you the consensus price according to these sources," says Anderson, "it's another sign the dealer is trying to make some money off you." His advice? Get the trade-in price before you ask the dealer for his best price on a new car, and tell him to put the quote in writing. "You don't want the story to change after you come to terms on the new car," he says.

ways let the dealer know you're aware they're getting this kickback from the manufacturer."

Buying a Used Car

Buying a used car is similar in some respects to cutting a deal on a new one. You always want to research the market as much as possible, negotiate from a position of strength, and reach a fair price. Nevertheless, while investigating used cars, you're probably going to use a different set of muscles than those that you employ in a new-car transaction.

For instance, you may have to search motor vehicle department records to verify the car's true mileage, if you're dubious about the stated mileage. Moreover, unlike buying a new car, you'll only have a rough idea of what the dealer paid for the car he's trying to sell you.

"New-car dealers lost whatever edge they had over the public when their costs became general knowledge," says Burke Leon, Ph.D., author of *The Insider's Guide to Buying a New or Used Car*. "Few consumers know what a used car costs." But you can be sure of one thing, he says: Dealers stand to make much more selling you a used car than they can a new model, because of these uncertainties.

Check the prices of used cars on one of several Web sites that publish used-vehicle prices, such as the *Kelley Blue Book Used Car Guide* site. Kelley uses a mix of national and regional information to establish used-car prices, according to the editor of *Kelley Blue Book*, Charlie Vogelheim. Also, read back issues of *Consumer Reports* magazine for critiques of vehicle brands. In this way, you will become familiar with a make and model's unique problems, and you can begin to narrow down the price range.

Guerilla Buying

You should reveal your insider information as it suits you, advises Dr. Leon. "Don't tell salesmen things they have no right to know, such as how you're financing or if you have a trade-in, until you're happy with the price they give you," says Dr. Leon.

Why should you be so evasive? Because your goal (getting a good car for the right price) conflicts with the dealer's aim (selling a car today at maximum profit). A car dealer is not looking out for your best interests; why should you care about his feelings?

"The best way to handle a salesman is with a technique that, when used on young children, usually induces schizophrenia," jokes Dr. Leon. "When you first get to the dealership, be a nice guy for a while," he recommends. "Say you really like the cars and want to do business there. And then just explode over some little detail. Object strongly to something minor that the dealer said, then turn back to being a nice guy again. He won't know how real his chances are with you, so he'll treat you better."

Here are some other ways to get the upper hand in a showroom showdown.

Force a direct comparison. "When I was a sales manager," La Motta recalls, "the most important thing I would teach our salesmen was to avoid comparison quotes. As much as possible, a dealer will tell you why the car you priced with his competitor is not the same as the one on his lot."

"Go to the dealer equipped with the exact model, color, options package, and time of delivery you want," La Motta advises. "Be adamant about this, and on that basis ask them why their price is $1,000 more than you could pay elsewhere."

"There's a risk in the used-car market that doesn't exist in new cars," says Vogelheim. "We call this the triple A rule: faulty airbags, air conditioning, and ABS (antilock braking system). These items can go at any time and repairs could be expensive."

Once you're on the lot sizing up the used-car selection, says Dr. Leon, mentally break the car into three pieces, each worth about a third of the car's value. Piece number one is the car's exterior. Inspect it carefully for obvious things like broken windows, missing trim strips, bent fenders, and doors that don't open and close properly, says Dr. Leon.

The second piece is the inside of the car. Take a deep breath and smell for bad odors. Check for thin carpeting, especially under the accelerator, where the driver's heel rests. Also, roll the windows up and down, move the seats back and forth, turn on the radio, and check the air conditioning and heater.

The final piece is the engine and drive train. Here, check the oil for white globs, which would indicate water seepage into the oil. Then, while someone revs the engine, get behind the tailpipe to detect any scent of burning oil. On the test drive, take the car up a hill to see how the engine runs. If you can, get a mechanic to drive the car, too. You should insist that the car pass your mechanic's inspection before you buy, says Dr. Leon.

Once you're satisfied with the overall condition of the vehicle, let the haggling begin.

Get it in writing. Dealers are not above changing the terms of a deal at closing, Anderson says. For instance, you agree to pay 6 percent financing for your new car, only to discover that a higher rate has been inserted into the contract. "The sales manager may claim the salesman made a mistake or didn't explain the terms fully," he observes. "If the salesman names a figure, have him put it in writing before closing."

Shop at odd times. Visiting a showroom late in the evening can work in your favor, Dr. Leon says. He advises stopping into the dealership 15 minutes before closing and apologizing for the inconvenience. "Ask if you should come back another time—say, three weeks from now. Then tell them you really want to buy the car tonight." This tactic puts the onus on the dealer to make the sale, and the process will go more smoothly.

Avoid add-ons. Many dealers will try to sell you a corrosion-protection package that's separate from the manufacturer's warranty. "It's junk," warns Anderson. "Don't go for it; every car comes rustproofed." Some manufacturers advise customers not to buy auxiliary warranties, because the dealer's treatment may actually ruin the factory installation, he says. Also, the markup on extra "protection" is extreme.

The same goes for auxiliary trim packages, where they decorate the sides of your car with flashy decals and other bits of automotive fluff. Dealers often try to sell you these packages, or they add them to the car without ever consulting you and then expect you to pay for them. Don't. Costs will generally be more reasonable through design shops that have no relation to the dealer.

Look out of state. Thanks to the Internet, you can now easily shop for automobiles outside your immediate area. "I recently had a customer from Texas who bought a car in New Jersey," says La Motta. "It was cheaper for him to fly here and drive the car back to Texas than to buy where he lived."

Manufacturers occasionally offer dealer

incentives in one region only. These packages could indeed yield lower prices, says Anderson. He says regional price breaks are worth checking out on the Edmund's Web site, but he advises customers to get a firm quote from the dealer before traveling to buy a car. "You should also make sure to license the car correctly so that you don't pay licensing fees in more than one state," he says.

The Lease You Could Do

In these fast-paced, life-is-always-changing times, you can rent almost anything. Art for your walls. Power tools. Computers. A nice suit. Furniture. A date for the evening. If you hate to own things, you could almost get through life owning nothing but a change of underwear. Some of it borders on the absurd. But not when it comes to autos. In this realm, the question of buying versus leasing is one to consider seriously.

In some cases, leasing an automobile, rather than buying, could be to your advantage, say experts. "Take a vehicle that sells for $30,000," says La Motta, "If you financed it for five years at 7.5 percent, your monthly payment would be roughly $640." Leasing the same vehicle for three years would cost you about $340 a month.

"Shorter term, about half the payment—the average person finds that very attractive," he notes.

But don't walk into a dealership with a one-track mind. Low installments are nice, but depending on your circumstances, lease arrangements don't always make sense. Here are some points to ponder.

Realize it's not yours. The average age of a car on the street keeps rising and rising. Buy a car, and once it's paid off, you'll likely have many years of usage without monthly payment. It's yours. You own it. Put on whatever window decals you want. Install your dream stereo. Bumper sticker away. But forget all of that if you lease. At the end of a lease contract, you turn off the engine and walk away with absolutely nothing to show for all the money you spent.

Consider your commute. Leases typically restrict your driving to 12,000 to 15,000 miles a year, according to Anderson. If you commute long distances—say 50 miles a day to and from work—you're already at 250 miles per week, or more than 12,000 miles a year. Plus, you also drive for other reasons, right? If you exceed your allotted miles, you'll receive a hefty fine at lease's end, Anderson warns.

Negotiate like a buyer. Before telling the car dealer you want to lease a vehicle, negotiate the car's purchase price as if you are going to buy it, says Dr. Leon. Afterwards, when you announce your intention to lease, insist that the dealer use the quoted price as the basis for the monthly payments. "Most of the time," Dr. Leon adds, "the dealer's terms will end up being lower than if you had announced your intention to lease before striking a deal."

Go the distance. Some people think you can terminate a lease early with no penalty. Not so, according to *Consumer Reports* magazine. The editors' advice: "Penalties can amount to thousands of dollars, sometimes costing as much as it would to keep the car for the full length of the lease." Don't enter into a lease unless you plan to keep the car for the duration.

Refuse mystery fees. At the end of the lease, says Dr. Leon, a dealer will often ask you to pay a "disposition fee"—a charge to take the car back into the dealership. Does your video store tack on a penalty if you return your movie on time?

"There is no logic for this cost; it's just a way to bleed you a little more," says Dr. Leon. Ask about the disposition fee up front and negotiate it out of the deal before you sign.

Read the fine print. Leases are complicated deals. Read every single word in the contract before you sign it. Have a complete understanding regarding the mandated condition of the car upon turn-in, what happens if the car is in an accident, and other such scenarios.

Mounting Debt

Where to Go when You Owe

Debt is like love handles. The longer it exists, the harder it is to get rid of. And escaping debt matters hugely if you want to achieve financial security. Big rewards—a nice vacation home, Yale for your daughter—accrue only if you operate lean and mean.

How do you avoid mounting debt? Let's extend that love handles analogy. The best way to lose weight is to permanently change your daily habits; short-term diets or exercise spurts just don't work. The same is true of debt: Short-term solutions don't get to the core problem. "The single most important step in getting rid of debt is to take action to reverse what gets most people in over their heads in the first place: living beyond their means," says Eric Tyson, author of *Personal Finance for Dummies.*

Tyson believes a "comfortable" level of debt is zero. Others believe that you can live with a small amount. Where is the threshold?

"If more than 15 percent of your net income goes to pay debt, then you're looking at a danger level," says Jonathan Pond, president of Financial Planning Information in Boston. At that level, it becomes truly tough to achieve any long-term financial goals, such as saving enough for retirement. (For the record: We are not talking about mortgage debt here but, rather, shorter-term debt such as car loans and credit card balances.)

Easy Credit, Easier Debt

Banks, department stores, and car salesmen are just a few of the merchandisers who tout the virtues of "easy" credit. Indeed, these days it seems that the possession of opposable thumbs is all you need to qualify for a Visa or MasterCard. Meanwhile, credit solicitations are on the rise and, as of mid-1996, Americans held more than 500 million credit cards, up from 456 million just a year earlier.

Collectively, we continue to dig ourselves deeper into the hole, at a rate of about $4 billion a month. Perhaps it's not surprising, then, that we occasionally feel besieged—not just by creditors but also by our own impulsive buying habits.

"We take on expensive short-term debt, and waste 20 to 30 percent of our money, just because of poor spending habits and practices," says Paul Richard, president of the National Center for Financial Education, a nonprofit consumer-education group based in San Diego.

Richard partly blames credit card providers for this precarious situation because they continuously engineer ways to get you to part with your money. Consider a man who opens a bank account to qualify for a secured credit card, in which the credit line is worth only the amount deposited in the account. If our unlucky fellow pays 21 percent interest on the card, "he's borrowing back his own money for $21 per $100 per year," Richard points out. We've heard of better deals through loan sharks.

Sure, getting your debt under control takes discipline, but it's not impossible. Here are some strategies.

Avoid chasing bad money with good. Keep your loans to a minimum, especially if you're borrowing to buy depreciating assets, like cars and entertainment equipment. "Instead," Pond recommends, "only get loans to buy a house, make worthwhile home improvements, and to fund education." Your home and education are appreciating assets and worth going into debt.

Turn cards into shards. Cutting up your credit cards seems radical, but that's exactly what Tyson recommends. Plastic isn't necessary, he believes, especially for people with a history of abusing credit. "Just as alcoholics should stay completely away from booze, so too should compulsive spenders and debtors stay away from credit," he says.

If you feel like you need a credit card, he advises, transfer outstanding balances from high-rate to low-rate cards. Or better yet, trade in those cards for charge cards that make you pay the entire balance every month.

"Generally," says Pond, "you can't get a better rate of return on your money than paying off credit card debt."

Avoid debt-consolidation loans. An enticing way to reduce the number of bills coming in is to arrange one large loan to erase lots of smaller ones. This method is a trap, though. "The act of debt consolidation usually results in a somewhat lower monthly payment, but this payment must be made for a much longer period of time," says Bob Hammond, author of *Life after Debt.* As a result, you'll end up paying even more interest, and therefore more money.

Think of it this way, he says: Let's say you get a debt-consolidation loan to pay off a $10,000 debt, and you agree to retire it at $265 a month over five years. Your new debt, with interest, equals $15,900—$5,900 more than what you originally owed. If you net $15 an hour, you'll be toiling for 1,060 hours (that's 26 working weeks) to pay off the total obligation. Talk about indentured service. "You can't borrow your way out of debt," Hammond points out.

A Long Recovery

That doesn't stop some of us from trying to imitate Houdini, though. Consider Mary Hunt, editor and publisher of the *Cheapskate Monthly*, a newsletter based in Paramount, California, that promotes frugal living. In the years before Hunt converted to thriftiness, she and her husband owed more than $100,000 to creditors. Their debt, which was a direct result of having paid the minimum monthly amount on bills and signing numerous consolidation loans, accumulated over a 12-year period.

"Take all of those things," says Hunt, "add them together, stir in a compulsive personality and, boy, you have the makings of a disaster."

It took 13 years of cost-cutting and learning to live frugally, but today, Hunt has just one charge card (used solely for business expenses) and pays off the balance each month. Of her time spent in financial purgatory, she says, "You see credit as 'more money'—as the answer to all your problems. You just assume that life will take care of itself."

Don't we wish. For the most part, unloading debt (or at least greatly reducing it) will require effort on our parts. Unless, of course, we never go into the red in the first place. Financial advisors, who get paid good money for their opinions, take pains to state this rather obvious fact to their clients. They point out that you could adopt a cash-and-carry lifestyle; or you could get a second job to pay for fun stuff.

But since we're stating the obvious, we should also concede that it's damned hard to avoid debt altogether. Further, it's not implausible that you could find yourself falling behind with payments. For those of us who dare to be imperfect, here are some ways to minimize problems with creditors.

Stay on good terms. If a creditor has not received payment by the end of one billing cycle, he considers the account delinquent, according to Hammond. After two billing cycles and no payment, you may start to get "past due" letters 10 to 20 days apart.

"Creditors are eager to work with people who admit they are in trouble and need some help paying," says Richard. "You'll find it easier to gain extensions by approaching the creditor first, before the late payments hit." He suggests writing a letter that explains your situation.

Show good faith. If you can afford to send small payments, even $10 or $15, companies will appreciate the gesture. Remember, at this point the creditor still wants to keep you as a customer.

Offer a "workout." Most creditors are willing to settle for a portion of what's owed them, according to Mory Brenner, a bankruptcy attorney in private practice in Pittsfield, Massachusetts and president of American Mortgage Debt Resolution, which negotiates debt workouts for homeowners in foreclosure. He ordinarily counsels his financially troubled clients, some of whom are considering declaring bankruptcy, to attempt a "workout." In such cases, the debtor and his lawyer arrange a partial restitution to all creditors. True, the workout will show up on your credit history—and usually has to be paid in one lump sum within 30 days of reaching the agreement—but it spares you the emotional and psychological toll that bankruptcy can inflict.

"Credit card companies are cutting some nice deals with folks now," says Brenner. He adds that some credit card companies will even make the initial offer of a workout to the debtor, rather than the other way around.

Cooperate with agencies. Let's say that your creditors are not in a forgiving mood, though. After about three months, they will make other appeals to get their money, in the form of phone calls and letters from the in-house collections departments.

If these efforts prove fruitless, Hammond says, the creditors will turn the accounts over to a collection agency. The agencies usually keep 50 percent of whatever they collect for the creditor. Collection agencies are a last resort for creditors who have written you off as a nonpaying customer, says Hammond.

The agencies also report to credit bureaus. "Your cooperation with an agency will make a difference in what, if anything, they say to credit-reporting firms," adds Richard.

Check Your Credit Rating

Banks, mortgage companies, and even employers will scrutinize your credit history as they see fit. When they do, you don't want them to come away with a jaundiced view of your finances and money-management skills. Having a chance to correct an inaccurate report could mean the difference between landing a job and not getting it, or getting turned down for an important small-business loan.

Getting a look at your current report is neither hard nor expensive. It's usually not more than $8, depending on where you live. Some copies may be obtained for free if you have been denied credit in the last 60 days. And, besides, it's fun. You get your information from any of the three best-known credit-reporting agencies: Equifax Incorporated, Experian, and Trans Union Corporation. Check your yellow pages for local listings.

Know your rights. Of course, horror stories about collection agencies abound. They are routinely castigated for lying, calling people at work, threatening arrest, and for other underhanded tactics.

"Agencies can call you at work once, to try to locate you," says Tyson, "but they can't disclose your debt to your employer." Moreover, if you tell a collector not to call work anymore, he must stop.

"Any collector who calls you at work to discuss payment of your debt after you've told him not to is breaking the law," Hammond states. Collectors are bound by the Fair Debt Collection Practices Act. To stop an agency in its tracks, you can write to the agency and tell it to cease any contact with you, he adds. If harassment continues, you are entitled to sue the agency.

Bankruptcy

Starting a New Chapter for Yourself

So, you've fallen on hard times. Bill collectors are tying up your phone lines. The bank is threatening foreclosure. And, perhaps worst of all, your marriage is coming apart because of all the arguing over money. Time to consider bankruptcy?

Think carefully. The prospect of escaping your creditors is tempting, but resorting to such drastic measures could have painful repercussions.

"Bankruptcy is not a little scratch," says Mary Hunt, editor and publisher of the *Cheapskate Monthly* newsletter. "It's more like a black eye that sticks around for a long time."

Still, a lot of people choose this option. In 1996 alone, 1.13 million Americans filed for personal bankruptcy protection. The numbers keep growing, too. According to Regional Financial Associates of West Chester, Pennsylvania, 1.59 million of us are expected to file in 2007.

Card Games

People go bankrupt for a multitude of reasons. Job loss, costly medical bills, and divorce are often cited as factors. There's some evidence that bankruptcies due to gambling losses are growing. But the prime culprit, according to experts, is credit mismanagement.

"I see clients with 10, 15, or even 20 credit cards," says bankruptcy attorney Bruce Strauss, a partner at Merrick, Baker, Hufft, and Strauss in Kansas City, Missouri. "They'll take cash advances on cards to pay off other cards. Sooner or later, it catches up to them, when they realize they can't possibly cut into the interest, much less the principals."

Granted, few things stir the blood more than wielding a tiny piece of plastic in return for a big-screen TV or a cash advance at Caesars Palace. But is that any reason to go broke, sully your good name, and trash your credit rating? The rational man screams "No!" The rest of us say "Gimme a minute."

"People are often looking for someone to tell them it's okay to go bankrupt," laments Hunt. "I think it's even become a little glamorous."

Those sentiments aside, it seems like a legitimate question to ask whether there is a "proper" time to file for bankruptcy. No clear-cut answers have emerged. Personal finance experts are reluctant to identify any single point at which bankruptcy becomes inevitable. What they will say is that ignoring signs of fiscal chaos could land you in serious jeopardy with creditors.

Serious money problems often result from sheer bad fortune, and they occur across the income spectrum, says Catherine Williams, president of the Consumer Credit Counseling Service of Greater Chicago. "Mitigating circumstances, such as job loss, often cause people to rely on credit," she explains. A financial consultant can usually trim $85 to $125 worth of "fat" from clients' monthly budgets as a means of reducing their debts. "But if we do this and their incomes don't even come close to meeting their payments," says Williams, "then we'll suggest that they seek out legal advice on bankruptcy."

What's Your Type?

Most people have three forms of bankruptcy at their disposal: Chapters 7, 11, and 13 of the U.S. Bankruptcy Code. While each person's bankruptcy experience will be unique, nearly every case has certain elements in common.

The court, for instance, will appoint a trustee to administer your estate. The trustee is not your lawyer; in fact, he is an advocate for the creditors, and he roots around for your assets.

Your creditors are classified into two main groups: "secured" and "unsecured." Secured creditors (typically banks and mortgage companies) have some rights over property in question and can seize that property if they choose. Practically everybody else—credit card companies, utilities, the family doctor—is unsecured.

Furthermore, your assets will be considered legally "exempt" or "nonexempt." Exempt assets cannot be taken from you in bankruptcy, while nonexempt ones can. Exemptions themselves can be classified as federal or state exemptions, but as a debtor you can ignore the federal rules and select the state exemptions if they are more favorable to your circumstances.

Simply put, in most bankruptcies, you'll probably get to keep your clothing and furniture, provided you didn't do all your shopping on Rodeo Drive. Federal rules allow for a $2,400 car exemption, though some states exempt your car altogether. Pensions and retirement plans may also be at least partly protected. Surprisingly, a number of states, including Florida, Iowa, Kansas, Minnesota, and Oklahoma, consider your house exempt property, no matter how much it's worth.

Are You in Trouble?

Worried that you might be on the path to bankruptcy? The National Foundation for Consumer Credit asks a number of simple questions to help you reveal your degree of financial distress.

- **Are you able to make only the minimum payments on your credit cards?**
- **Are you at or near the limit on your credit cards?**
- **Are you borrowing from one credit card to pay another?**
- **Are you unsure of how much you owe?**
- **Do you skip payments on some bills in order to pay others?**
- **Do you have insufficient cash saved for an emergency?**
- **If you lost your job, would you be unable to pay for your basic living expenses?**
- **Are you receiving calls from creditors about overdue bills?**
- **Do you find yourself arguing with your spouse or others about money?**

A yes answer to two or more of these questions should sound a clear warning bell that you need help, according to the Foundation.

Getting It Straight

There are differences between the three sets of bankruptcy laws, however. Chapter 7 is the most common form of personal bankruptcy in this country, and it is sometimes known as "straight bankruptcy." Under these laws, the debtor turns over his nonexempt assets to the trustee, who sells them and distributes the proceeds among the unsecured creditors. Any individual can file for this type of relief.

"The point of a Chapter 7 is complete liquidation of your assets," according to Mory Brenner, a bankruptcy attorney in private practice in Pittsfield, Massachusetts. In return, you are discharged forever from the debts you owe at the time you file. That discharge includes your personal liability for missed mortgage payments, but you could still end up losing your house: Though Chapter 7 puts a temporary stay on foreclosure proceedings, the bank may seize your house after bankruptcy if you continue nonpayment of your mortgage.

After Chapter 7 bankruptcy becomes effective, you're still liable for those pesky exceptions that apply to all forms of bankruptcy. You cannot, for instance, usually escape payments on alimony, child support, student loans, or taxes. You must settle with your lawyer and the court, too. Expect to pay anywhere from several hundred dollars to $1,000 or more, depending on the case's complexity.

Have Any Plans?

Chapter 13 is a less-common recourse, in which you agree to repay some or all of your debts, usually over a three- to five-year period. "You're placed under the court's wing, and they oversee your finances for the duration," says Williams. Like Chapter 7, Williams says, Chapter 13 puts a temporary halt to all collection activity, and you're allowed time to draft a monthly repayment schedule.

Under the plan, your lawyer will typically propose a partial payment to your unsecured creditors. After the trustee approves the plan, Chapter 13 allows you to keep most of your assets, though you may have to sell some. "Say you owe $80,000 to a credit card company," says Strauss. "The company may settle for just 50 percent of the balance. But to make good on the $40,000, the trustee will sell your Porsche and pay off the company."

Not everyone will accept a partial payment, though. Your mortgage holder, for instance, will want the full amount. "The major reason you would file for a Chapter 13 is to stop foreclosure on your house," says Brenner. "I had one client who was 29 months behind in his mortgage. He agreed to pay the old debt over 60 months, plus he had to meet the regular monthly obligation."

Individuals can also file for Chapter 11 bankruptcy. Here again, the aim is to retain your assets while working out a full- or partial-repayment schedule. Think of this as Chapter 13 on a larger scale for both assets and debts; it's used mostly by businesses. Unless you have more than $250,000 in unsecured debt and $750,000 in secured debt, you probably won't qualify for Chapter 11, according to Bob Fishman, president of the American Bankruptcy Institute and an attorney with Shaw, Gussis, Domanskis, and Fishman in Chicago.

If You Decide to File

Now that you've read up through all the Chapters, we feel compelled to point out a few things before you proceed.

You can't do this every day. Once you've filed for discharge under Chapter 7, you have to wait six years before doing so again. A quirk in the law, though, allows you to file for Chapter 13 bankruptcy within a year of getting your 7. Sometimes this is done to continue making payments on your house once your other debt has been dismissed under Chapter 7.

It stays with you. Any bankruptcy remains on your credit history for 10 years. But that's just the beginning. "A lot of people think bankruptcy is erased after that period, but it's not," says Hunt. "Anyone doing a thorough background search on you is going to find it. It's still a matter of public record. And whenever you want credit, you'll be asked if you've ever filed for bankruptcy." If you have, then lenders could deny you credit or demand that you pay higher interest rates than someone with a clean record, she says.

It could affect your career. More companies are asking for credit reports as part of the job-screening process, according to Williams. "Bankruptcy could be viewed as indicative of your character or your management ability," she says.

With those factors in mind, consider bankruptcy not as skillful bobbing and weaving but as a desperate measure to keep from getting KO'd.

Part Five

Retirement Planning

Strategies

Planning for the Future

Anyone who follows demographics knows that one trend overwhelms all others: the aging of America. Seniors are living longer; the baby boomer generation, by far the biggest population blip in this country, is fast approaching 50; the birth rate is at best stable. It all adds up to an American citizenry with a steadily rising average age. Which begs the obvious question: Who is going to pay for all these people to live when they stop working? It's a complex issue.

While the idea of quitting the 9-to-5 forever and retiring to a sunny place may sustain many a baby boomer worker, the media hasn't been quite so positive about the financial fate of future retirees. In fact, the message in the papers and the news weeklies is primarily one of fear. It goes something like this: Tomorrow's retirees, driven by a desire for instant gratification, can't possibly save enough money to retire comfortably. Social Security is bound to go bankrupt. The cost of living is only going to get higher. What can you do except continue working through your seventies or contribute to your 401(k) plan and hope for the best? You can do plenty.

What You Can Do

"When it comes to retirement planning, it's never too soon to begin and it's never too late to start," says Suze Orman, president of Suze Orman Financial Group in Emeryville, California, and author of *Nine Steps to Financial Freedom.* "There are three ways to make money in life. You can earn it, inherit it, or have your money earn money for you. By the time you reach retirement age, you want option number three to be your primary mode."

To get there, though, you'll have to follow one of three basic strategies that Orman offers as well as some more general tips for making sure that you—and your bank account—are ready for retirement.

Save what you can. This means putting aside $50, $100, $300, whatever you can each month, starting now. The younger you start, the better. You need the appreciation of money compounding over time to make up for the relatively small amount you're setting aside. As any financial planner who crunches the numbers can tell you, this will eventually add up to substantial savings.

Save what you should. This is the proper strategy for people within 20 years of retirement. This requires that you sit down and work out how much income you'll need on a monthly basis once you retire, and then calculate how much principal you'll need to generate that revenue stream. Although your numbers will involve some guesswork (such as the interest rate and cost of inflation), you'll have a realistic figure that will allow you to work backwards to develop an accurate savings plan.

Save what you must. This strategy entails an element of panic: you have 10 years or less to fund your retirement plan. This can mean that you will need to continue working, investing aggressively in the stock market, or scaling back on your retirement lifestyle. "These are not doomsday options," says Orman. "I think everyone needs to invest for growth. After all, you might spend just as much time as a retiree as you did as an employee—you have to let your money compound throughout retirement, too."

So how much of a nest egg do you need at retirement? Here's a simple way to come up with an amount, says Malcolm A. Makin, a certified financial planner and president of Professional Planning Group in Westerly, Rhode Island: Figure out how much income you'll need each year to live on, and multiply that by 15. For example, if you think you'll need $40,000 a year to live on, your nest egg should be about $600,000. At that amount, you can invest the money conservatively and yet still live off the interest.

Save in little ways. There are all sorts of obvious and not-so-obvious ways to save for your retirement, often in ways you'll hardly notice. Save your change at the end of the day—by the end of the year, it can add up to the value of a U.S. savings bond. Use automatic deductions to make saving your first priority. Take advantage of any automatic savings plan offered by your employer, bank, or local organizations. Concentrate your savings in tax-deferred accounts such as IRAs or company-sponsored 401(k) plans. Contribute to a company-sponsored stock purchase plan—and reinvest the dividends. Once you pay off a credit card debt or car loan, keep making a payment of the same amount to your own savings account.

Don't forget human values. "In retirement, your self-worth has to be as great as your net worth," adds Orman. "If all you know how to do in your spare time is to go shopping, you're going to deplete your savings in a hurry."

"Preparing for retirement means more than accumulating money," says Ralph Warner, a lawyer based in Berkeley, California, and author of *Get a Life: You Don't Need a Million to Retire Well.* You also need to maintain your health, activities that stimulate you, and close emotional ties with your family, long-term friends, and your community, he notes.

Insurance for the Long Term

Health care eats up an increasing share of our disposable income. Last year, the United States spent more than $1 trillion on health care. "This trend will only increase as we get older," says Rebecca Chekouras, a consultant with Age Wave Communications Corporation, a publisher of senior newsletters and magazines in Emeryville, California.

One of the smartest investments you can make when you reach your fifties is to buy long-term–care health insurance. "Long-term care gives you the ability to pay for an in-home nurse or physical assistant, to rent a special hospital bed, or purchase additional medication," says Chekouras. "It can be a real lifesaver."

Long-term coverage is purchased based upon the following factors.

1. **Amount You Need: You usually pay this in $10.00 increments, based upon how much the insurance company assumes it will cost to take care of you.**
2. **Deductible: The longer the time between the onset of your illness and the point at which the policy must begin to pay benefits, the lower the premium.**
3. **Duration: Policies cover specific periods of time. They may be one year, two years, three years, five years, or unlimited.**

You may find it helpful to check with such resources as the American Association of Retired Persons (AARP) and your state's Area Agency on Aging (AAA) for more information.

Social Security

What to Expect

Social Security, signed into law by President Franklin Roosevelt in 1935, is one of the most enduring safety nets that arose from the crucible of the Great Depression and the New Deal. Today, it pays out nearly $1 billion a day in benefits, providing the main source of income to more than half of all current retirees.

Most unretired folks, however, are growing increasingly cynical about the future of Social Security, believing it won't be around when they turn 65. Baby boomers especially underestimate the significance of Social Security's contributions to their retirement incomes.

"The maximum benefit available to a 65-year-old in 1995 was about $14,500 a year," says Joseph Coyle, senior editor of *Money* magazine. "If that person's spouse also worked and was the same age, this couple could conceivably receive $29,000 a year from Social Security alone. To achieve the same results on your own, you'd have to build an investment portfolio worth $350,000, generating an 8 percent return," he points out.

Unlike the majority of corporate pensions, Social Security payments rise with inflation. Recently, Congress has been granting cost-of-living increases of approximately 3 percent each year. "It's an excellent program that will still be around in one form or another when the baby boomer generation is ready to retire," says Coyle. Even though that day may be decades in the future, it pays to understand how Social Security works today. Here are the basic facts you need to know.

Age matters. While most people think of 65 as the age to apply for Social Security, only people born before 1938 can receive their full benefits at that time. If you were born between 1943 and 1959, you must wait until age 66 to receive your full benefits. People born after 1960 must wait until they turn 67. If you're willing to forgo about 25 percent of your payment, you can apply for Social Security as early as 62. On the other hand, if you're willing to wait for your benefits, you'll get a lifetime bonus—a 4 percent increase in your ultimate yearly disbursement for every year you hold off from applying, up to age 70.

You can keep working. It is possible to work and continue receiving benefits. The rule of thumb is that Social Security will reduce benefits by $1 for every $2 you earn. But this doesn't kick in until your earnings reach a certain threshold. As of 1997, beneficiaries under 65 can earn $8,640 before Social Security benefits are affected. Between the ages of 65 to 69, $13,500 in earned income (as opposed to investments, pensions, or annuities) is exempt before Social Security levies a $1 reduction for every $3 you earn. Keep in mind that these numbers continue to change. As of this writing, legislation is pending that in the year 2002 would more than double the earnings allowed before Social Security benefits are reduced. Also, such rules apply only to people younger than 70. Once you cross that milestone, you can earn all you want with no reduction in benefits.

Benefits do get taxed. A certain amount of your Social Security benefits may be taxed, depending on your total income. The government looks at all sources of income reported in your IRS filing. If your adjusted gross income, plus half of your Social Security benefits, plus half of your tax-exempt investments (such as interest from tax-exempt municipal bonds) add up to $34,000 or $44,000 for a couple filing jointly, then up to 85 percent of your Social Security benefits are taxed.

Learn What You've Earned

Want to know what you can expect from Social Security when you're old enough to collect? Just ask. The government keeps a computer record of your earnings, which they can track through your Social Security number. Based on those figures, you can get an estimate of what your retirement benefits would be if you were to apply at age 62, 66, or older. To get yours, you can write to the Social Security Administration, c/o Wilkes-Barre Data Operations Center, P. O. Box 7004, Wilkes-Barre, PA 18767-7004. Ask for Social Security Administration form 7004, also called the Personal Earnings and Benefit Estimate Statement. You should receive a statement within three weeks. Better yet, visit the Social Security site on the Internet (http://www.ssa.gov) and request an estimate of your earnings online.

"It pays to check up on your record of Social Security credits and earnings," says Joseph L. Matthews, an attorney in Berkeley, California, and author of *Social Security, Medicare, and Pensions*. "Employers are only required to keep records of your income for four years, and Social Security gives you a three-year window to correct mistakes."

Social Insecurity

What we need to know about Social Security right now seems to be of less importance to many people than what we need to know about Social Security in the future. The burning question is: Will Social Security be solvent when the first wave of baby boomers turns 65 in the year 2010?

The reason for such concern? In a word, demographics. Today there are 76 million baby boomers, born between 1945 and 1964; every seven seconds for the next 16 years, another member of this cohort will turn 50. What that means is, between 2010 and 2029, a tidal wave of applications will descend upon the Social Security Administration. And since our generation faces an increased life expectancy, living perhaps an additional 30 years after retirement, that translates into a constant financial pressure on the Social Security Administration for the foreseeable future.

However, the sheer number of baby boomers does not tell the whole story. The generations following the boomers are considerably smaller in number. Twenty years ago, there was a ratio of 40 employees contributing to Social Security for every recipient. By the year 2010 (when more than a third of all Americans will be 50 or older), that ratio will dwindle to nearly one to one. If that day arrives without any change in government policy, by the year 2012, Social Security will run at a deficit, paying out far more than it will take in.

The upshot? You'll still receive benefits but you might have to wait longer to claim them or you may not receive quite as much as was promised to you. "Unless some type of correction is made, such as a tax increase or means testing (which reduces entitlements for the wealthy), expect your benefits to be to reduced by half, if not two-thirds, of what Washington is currently promising you," says Ken Dychtwald, author of eight books on health and aging issues and president and chief executive officer of Age Wave, a business development company based in Emeryville, California. "In addition, we'll all probably be responsible for our own health care, with Medicare more likely to undergo substantial alterations than Social Security is."

Pension Plans

Banking On Your Company

When pensions were introduced in this country, you had to fight to get them—literally. The first official pensions in the United States were disbursed to Civil War veterans. The corporate pension, meanwhile, is a twentieth-century invention, originating in 1913, when AT&T established a fund for workers aged 60 and older with at least 20 years of service. The pension plan's true heyday came during peacetime, not wartime.

"Company-funded pensions, which typically extended life insurance and health care coverage to retirees, were prevalent during the economic boom of the 1950s and 1960s," says Paul Yakoboski, senior research associate with the Employee Benefit Research Institute in Washington, D.C. Although nearly 50 percent of all U.S. employees still earn such pension coverage, that number has dropped from 87 percent in 1975, reflecting the trend within corporate America to replace pensions with voluntary 401(k) plans. If you work for a company that offers a traditional pension (one which takes your age, salary, and years of service to calculate a monthly, lifelong annuity upon retirement), consider yourself one lucky employee.

Knowing the Formula

Ninety days after joining a defined benefit plan, you are entitled to receive a summary plan description from your pension manager. This will explain how the program works. Most pension plans, minus the jargon and legal mumbo jumbo, have one of three formulas for calculating your retirement payments. Here's how they break down.

Final-average payment. Also known as a highest-average payment, this figure is based on your average annual earnings over the last three or five years of employment. Such a plan would take your years of service, multiply that number by a small percentage (say, 1.25 percent), and multiply again by a five-year average of your final salary to arrive at a yearly payment.

Career-average payment. This calculation is similar to final-averaging, except that it's based on the average salary of your entire tenure with the company. Needless to say, this could well translate into a smaller pension.

Cash-balance plan. This third formula is becoming increasing popular. It works like a more generous 401(k) in that the company socks away a percentage of your yearly salary (say, 5 to 10 percent). Although you can't make direct contributions, like you can with a 401(k), you can check on the value of your pension plan now. "People like these plans because they're visible and they're portable—you can take the pension with you if you leave the job after getting vested," says Joseph L. Matthews, author of *Social Security, Medicare, and Pensions.* "But realize that your highest wages will be earned at the end of your career. Final-average payments are the most lucrative ways to calculate a pension." For you, that is, if not for your company.

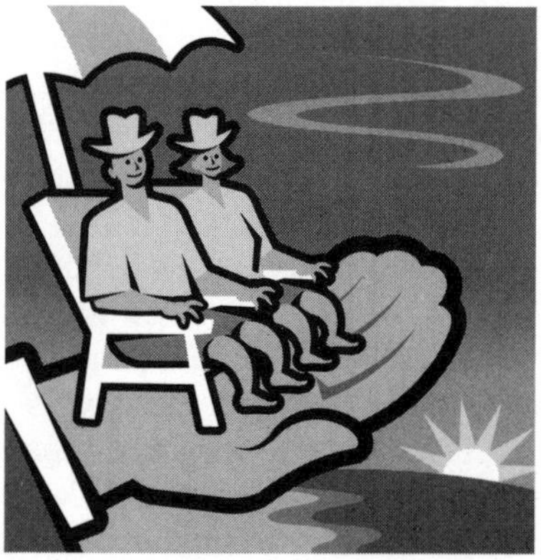

What You Should Know

While there's not a lot you can control about your pension before you get it, there are several steps you can take now to have a firm grasp on this annuity. And you should. Because the decisions you can make regarding your pension can have far-reaching—and not easily reversed—effects.

"Certain decisions about pensions are final," says Nancy J. Wartow, a policy analyst with the U.S. Department of Health and Human Services' Administration on Aging. "Leaving a job before you get vested is just one of the situations that can have tremendous financial implications. Understanding arcane pension rules and concepts early in your career is crucial and can save you tens of thousands of dollars once you retire." Here are some tips to help you take full advantage of your pension.

Know the vesting schedule. Pensions are based on your salary, years of service, and your age. "Therefore, you want to know the vesting schedule," says Yakoboski. "Do you earn the right to keep your pension after 5, 7, or 10 years of service?" In this era, a typical man will have worked at an average of 10.7 companies during his career. That's a lot of jobs, and a lot of potential pension benefits you need to keep tabs on. "While only a small amount of earnings will accrue between 5 and 10 years," says Yakoboski, "you want to know if you can take it with you, or whether it's worth it to stay one more year at the company."

Roll it over. If you do change jobs and have some pension coming to you, avoid getting it in a lump-sum payment. Or at least, avoid spending that lump sum.

"Roll that money over into an IRA or your new company plan, if possible," says Wartow. "Statistically, the majority of pension payments are being paid in lump-sum distributions. Each year, many of those who get lump sums at any age spend the money—a terrible temptation and tremendous mistake. Only 60 percent roll it over and save it for retirement."

Ask for an estimate. You should ask for an estimate of your earnings and look it

Looking for Warning Signs

Some common questions you may have about your pension plan.

What if my company is bought out? **If your plan is terminated as a result of a merger, your new benefits must be at least equal to the pension you would have received under the old plan. That's the law.**

What if my employer terminates the plan? **If your plan terminates, you immediately become 100 percent vested in all the earnings you've thus far accrued. Furthermore, if your plan is insured by the Pension Benefit Guaranty Corporation (a quasi-independent government agency), the agency will guarantee your payments up to certain limits. Contact the Pension Benefit Guaranty Corporation at 1200 K Street NW, Washington, DC 20005-4023.**

What if the company has made a mistake? **The National Center for Retirement Benefits will review pension disbursements for free. If they discover an error, they keep 30 percent of any funds they recover. Another consumer advocacy group is the Pension Rights Center, located at 918 16th Street NW, Suite 704, Washington, DC 20006-2902. The center will evaluate your pension plan, answer questions, and help you recover missing funds. "These problems are fixable," says Karen Ferguson, an analyst with the Pension Rights Center. "The key is to send someone looking. If you don't look, you can't fix it."**

over once you get it to make sure it's correct, says Yakoboski. There's no evidence that pension administrators are fraudulent, but there is always the potential for mistakes. Treat it like your checking account. Go over your statement very carefully and if need be, seek out professional help.

Keep your own records. "You must think like a private detective," says Wartow. "The importance of keeping your own records cannot be overemphasized. Keep track of your dates of service, if you've had any breaks in service, and what your employer is contributing and to whom. For example, if you are a union contractor, you might have several employers during the course of a year. Make sure they're making the appropriate contributions to your union's pension account."

Act on your age. The age at which you retire will also affect your final payout. If you take an early retirement, say age 55, your benefits will be less than if you retire at 65.

While it's somewhat unsettling to confront these numbers, it's a fact that pensions are also based on your life expectancy: The earlier you retire, the longer they expect to pay you. Thus, the smaller those monthly payments will be. Conversely, you will get larger payments if you work past age 65, not only because you'll accrue more years of service but also because your life expectancy after retirement will be less.

There is an exception to this rule of thumb, and that is when corporations offer early retirement packages. "For most people, early retirement is not a choice. It means being downsized," says Suze Orman, president of Suze Orman Financial Group in Emeryville, California. "To entice you into accepting a voluntary layoff, they'll change certain aspects of the pension formula in your favor. Of course, it will never be as much money as you would earn with an additional 10 years of employment, but it's always a better deal than if you decided to leave on your own."

Check the Social Security link. Finally, find out whether the value of your pension is dependent on Social Security benefits. Dubbed integrated plans, these pensions are reduced by either the full amount or a percentage of your Social Security benefit. However, federal law passed in 1988 requires that integrated plans leave you with at least half the value of your pension.

Cashing In

Once you have a grasp of these issues, get ready to face the big enchilada of pension payment decisions. The big day has arrived—do you want to receive a lump-sum distribution or a monthly, lifetime annuity? Frankly, financial planners are divided as to which approach is better. On the one hand, a lump-sum distribution is likely to be the biggest check you will ever receive in your life, and it's tempting to hold what could easily be a check for a million dollars in your hands.

"But that's a terrible reason to choose a lump sum," says Orman. "This money has to support you for the rest of your life, and probably for the rest of your spouse's life, too. What you should do is reinvest this money," says Orman. But not everyone does.

Why a Lump Sum?

The main reason to choose a lump sum over an annuity is because you think you can get a higher rate of return if you invest it yourself. In fact, that's what companies are trying to accomplish—they want to give you a pile of cash big enough that investing it will generate an income stream equivalent to the lifetime, monthly payments they had promised you.

To make the best decision, your real objective is to figure out which payment option is going to give you the bigger pot of gold in the long run. Of course, determining that requires some number-crunching, plus a bit of guesswork.

First, you have to confront the cold,

hard number of your life expectancy. (The Internal Revenue Service provides actuary tables for every age group.) Currently, 65-year-old men are expected to live until age 82; women at 65 are expected to live until 86. But unlike standardized actuary tables, you know whether your parents or grandparents lived into their nineties or passed away in their sixties. And you know the state of your health, whether you're exercising regularly and adhering to a healthy diet. "If you think you'll live longer than the charts say you will, an annuity has the edge," says Orman. "If there are serious health complications in your family background, I'd go for the lump-sum payout."

The last piece of the puzzle is to ask what interest rate the plan is using to calculate your lump-sum distribution. There's a tricky relationship between pensions and interest rates. When rates are high, companies know that it won't take much as much capital to generate the monthly annuity they promised you. In such market conditions, you'll receive a lower lump-sum. But when interest rates are low, you'll receive a larger final payout to generate the same income stream. As a result of 1994's General Agreement on Tariffs and Trade (GATT) treaty, companies can now use one of two interest rates to measure how large your distribution will be: either the rate on a 30-year treasury bond or a standard rate determined by the Pension Benefit Guaranty Corporation (PBGC). However, treasury bonds can be more than 2 percent higher than the interest rate offered by the PBGC, resulting in a substantially different payout.

One caveat: Unless you direct your pension plan administrator to deposit your lump-sum payment into a rollover individual retirement account (IRA), this large amount of money will be taxed by the IRS. However, people ages 59½ or older qualify for a one-time tax break called "forward averaging." The IRS allows you to calculate your payout as if it had taken place over a five-year period, separate from all other income that you may have. This way, although you still have to pay the taxes at once, they may be calculated at a lower rate.

Why An Annuity?

For one thing, annuities do pose less of a mathematical challenge than lump-sum payments do, but you're not out of the woods quite yet. Annuities come in three forms. A single life annuity only pays benefits to the retiree. When the retiree dies, the benefits stop. A second option is called a continuous or 2/3 joint and survivor annuity. This pays a slightly smaller monthly benefit than the first option, but continues to pay benefits to the spouse after the retiree passes away. The benefit paid to the survivor is less than the monthly payments made while the pensioner is living. The third option is called 100 percent joint and survivor annuity. This pays both the retiree and the surviving spouse monthly payments for life. Although the monthly check for this option is smaller than with single life annuities, the benefits are paid out over a much longer period of time. Also, many state and municipal plans as well as some company plans offer a "pop-up" option, says Malcolm A. Makin, a certified financial planner and president of Professional Planning Group in Westerly, Rhode Island. Under this option, if the beneficiary dies prior to the retired employee, the payment option reverts to a single life annuity.

"Some husbands choose the single life annuity, thinking that if their houses are paid off, their wives can get by on Social Security or savings," says Orman. "But they forget that fixed expenses don't change whether it's one person in the house or two. Also, their wives, by virtue of living longer, might face additional health care expenses. I've had to counsel widows to either sell their houses or take out reverse mortgages to get through their final years." In fact, the value for married couples of the joint and survivor annuity over any other option is so clear that companies require both spouses' signatures for any couple that chooses single life annuity or lump sum.

Making the Most of Your 401(k)

It's Your Most Powerful Tool

Fast-forward to your last day at work before retiring. What are you expecting? A goodbye lunch, the ubiquitous gold watch, and a comfortable pension paid for by your steadfast corporate employer? Well, you can probably count on the lunch. However, the watch may be plastic, and you'll be lucky if you're one of the increasingly small number of employees who will earn an all-paid, company-sponsored pension.

In 1975, nearly 87 percent of full-time employees were covered by traditional "defined benefit plans." By 1993, that number had fallen to 53 percent, and it continues to drop. In all likelihood, the cornerstone of your retirement will be the money saved and earned in your 401(k) plan. Otherwise known as defined contribution plans, 401(k)s—and their siblings, 403(b)s, for employees at nonprofit firms, and section 457 plans for government workers—are fundamentally different from traditional pensions.

"Your 401(k) plan is a tax-sheltered, salary reduction plan," says Neil Grossman, of William M. Mercer/Washington Resource Group, an employee benefits consulting firm with offices worldwide. "It's completely voluntary—the government does not mandate your participation, nor does it mandate your company to provide matching funds, although many do."

Today, more than $675 billion is invested in 401(k) plans. Participation rates at large companies (defined as having more than 1,000 employees) are as high as 78 percent. But at smaller firms, approximately 47 percent of employees sign up. The difference, most analysts agree, is basic financial literacy.

"There is no single more powerful way to save for retirement than joining a 401(k) plan," declares Suze Orman, president of Suze Orman Financial Group in Emeryville, California. "Unlike individual retirement accounts (IRAs), which limit your contributions to $2,000 a year, you can sock up to $10,000 a year in a 401(k). Many employers will match some or all of your contribution to the plan, and that's the only free lunch still on the menu. Also, you're saving with pretax dollars, and you're compounding interest without being subject to capital gains taxes." When you withdraw the money at retirement, you'll be taxed on it, but by then you'll most likely be in a lower tax bracket.

Mastering the Basics

When you begin a new job, ask your human resource manager how soon you can sign up for the company's savings plan. Most companies require that you be employed for six months to a year before joining. Your ability to participate will likely start prior to the company matching your contribution. That might kick in after anywhere from one to five years of employment.

Having signed up, you're now faced with two decisions: First, how much of your pretax salary do you want deducted from your pay? You can choose from a low of 2 percent to a high of 15 percent, with a maximum contribution of $10,000. Next, you must decide which investments to participate in. The majority of companies offer five to eight investment vehicles that typically range in performance from conservative, such as certificate of deposits, treasury bills, or guaranteed invest-

ment contracts offered by insurance companies; to moderately risky vehicles, such as bond mutual funds or high-income stock funds; to high-risk investments, like aggressive or overseas stock funds.

"Even with a lot of choices, companies do a service and a disservice," says Cynthia Oti, host of the San Francisco radio talk show *Financial Fitness: Your Weekend Workout.* "They say, 'Here's a list of 12 mutual funds—do with it what you will.' But they won't teach you a darn thing about investing, because they fear the liability. And most people, if they don't know what to do, don't do anything."

Here, then, are 10 things you should always do where your 401(k) is concerned.

Contribute the maximum. In the early 1990s, Orman consulted for Pacific Gas and Electric as it prepared to downsize, offering early retirement to 7,000 people. "After a while," says Orman, "I began to notice that, among people who had been working for the same amount of time, some had saved more than $400,000 in their 401(k)s while others had only saved $150,000." The difference? The first group of people had been contributing the maximum amount from day one.

For some, it may be hard—impossible even—to part with this much money. Orman suggests trying it for a while. "Why not see if you can live with the maximum monthly deferment for a period of six months? If you can, great." If you can't, scale back a bit until you reach a number you can live with.

Invest appropriately. Even if you're in your mid-fifties and planning to retire at 62, you should treat your 401(k) plan as a long-term investment, with at least a 10-year time frame. "People in their forties invest as if they're 92," says Oti. Younger people don't need bond funds, they need growth. "You need to accept a certain amount of risk or you'll never reach your savings goals."

That means not only investing in the stock market but earmarking a good part of your portfolio in aggressive, high-risk funds. "There's a difference between high risk and silly risk," says Oti. "You don't want to pour your retirement funds into Uncle Marvin's ostrich farm."

Still, if you think being in the stock market as opposed to the bond market is a high-wire act in itself, consider the following definition: High risk within the stock market refers to sector funds (mutual funds that invest in a single industry, such as technology or biotechnology) because they're volatile and there is tremendous potential for growth and appreciation. A low-risk stock would be a high-dividend-paying blue-chip company, such as General Motors Corporation or Kraft Foods. The

Monitoring Your Investments

If any of the following problems occur, contact the Pension and Welfare Benefits Administration, U.S. Department of Labor, 200 Constitution Avenue NW, Washington, DC 20210-0001. The Administration has 15 field offices nationwide and also gives out educational information about retirement.

- **You notice a steep drop in the value of your account that can't be explained by fund performance.**
- **The deductions on your paycheck don't match your 401(k) contributions.**
- **Your statements arrive late or at irregular times throughout the year.**
- **Your employer failed to transmit your contribution to the plan on a timely basis.**
- **You hear of former employees having trouble getting their benefits paid on time or in the correct amounts.**

stability of these firms can be measured in decades.

Develop a strategy. There are several ways for you to pick a winner. *Growth funds* have managers that look at the momentum of companies. Managers of *value funds* pick unloved, out-of-favor companies with a strong financial base. Allocate your money in different types of funds by percentages.

"From your twenties to your early sixties (or five years before you plan to retire), 100 percent of your money should be in growth funds," says Oti. In your twenties and thirties, 25 percent should be in high-risk, aggressive funds and 75 percent in moderate-risk growth funds. "At this age, you have between 40 and 50 years until retirement. If you can't handle risk now, when can you?" In your forties, you should change that only slightly—20 percent higher-risk, 80 percent moderate risk. In your fifties, 20 percent should go to high-risk funds, 40 percent to moderate-risk, and 40 percent to conservative growth funds.

Why not put all your money in the most aggressive funds? "The narrower the focus, the greater the risk," says Oti. "You would never want a large percentage of your investment in such a fund, because one loss—caused by deregulation, a bill passed by Congress, a localized natural disaster—could have a huge impact on you."

As you get closer to retirement, evaluate what kind of lifestyle you plan and how much it will take to maintain it. You may not need your retirement income until your seventies; others may want to tap into it much earlier. In either case, when you are five years before retiring, move 20 percent of what you have invested in high-risk funds to a new category—fixed-income investments such as bonds. Take 50 percent and put it in moderate-risk stock funds, and put the remaining 30 percent in conservative growth funds.

Improving Your Company's Plan

If you're dissatisfied with your company's 401(k) plan, chances are it's because your employer doesn't match your contribution or you have a paltry number of low-performing investment options. Whichever the case, there are steps you can take to improve your retirement program.

Make an appointment with your human resources manager. If you don't have one, contact your accounting department or the chief financial officer. Explain that you're researching general information about 401(k) plans. Ask how your company decided on their particular fund provider. Was it by committee, senior management, or the human resources person making recommendations directly to the president? You want to find out so that you can address your research to the key decision makers.

If your goal is to convince the company to change their matching structure, it's equivalent to asking for a pay raise for everybody. Before you write a memo, evaluate the financial strength of your company. Are they having a profitable or difficult year? How does the coming year look? Research statistics on the number of corporations that provide matching contributions. This will help you position your request as a way to make your company more competitive.

If your goal is simply to improve the number of fund offerings or replace them with better-performing funds, begin by asking your human resources person for the phone number of the outside company that manages your funds. By law, companies are required to offer three 401(k) investment options. Learn the precise investment parame-

ters of your existing funds. Ask your fund manager for their average rate of return over 1, 3, 5, and 10 years of performance. Next, ask if additional fund families are offered by the sponsoring financial institution.

"Once your company has selected a provider, it's a big pain to switch," says Randy Hardock, a senior partner with the Washington, D.C., law firm Davis and Harman. "There are fees and administrative costs to pay if they terminate a plan. Far better to call the provider and see if they have more investment options. The average financial institution usually has many more mutual fund choices than are offered in a 401(k) plan."

While this tactic might seem obvious, try to obtain as much supporting material as possible to submit with your memo requesting specific additional funds to be added to your company's mix. Ask your fund manager for a prospectus of the funds you'd like to add. Obtain a Morningstar financial rating and the average rate of return over several years of performance. See if you can get any additional supporting material, such as articles on diversification from the financial press that will buttress your point. In your memo, be sure to explain the differences between the funds that are already being offered and the ones you're proposing the company add.

"Human resources people are swamped. If you make it as easy as possible for them, they'll get back to you much more quickly," says David Wray, president of the Profit Sharing/401(k) Council of America in Chicago.

"Whatever you do, don't diversify yourself into oblivion," says Oti. "Remember, a fund itself is diversified." You should have about four funds—five at the most. Even if your 401(k) is worth between $100,000 and $200,000, you probably need no more than six or seven funds. "I once had a client with $200,000 in 72 mutual funds," Oti recalls. "Can you imagine what her mailbox looked like? There is no way you can monitor this."

Invest unused vacation time. If you can't roll over unused vacation time or if you simply don't have time to take all of it, you can ask your employer to contribute the dollar equivalent of your unused days to your 401(k) plan. Such a contribution is exempt from Federal Insurance Contributions Act (FICA) taxes. "It avoids these taxes as well as the $10,000 401(k) plan limit," says Grossman. Vacation pay contributions "must comply with other IRS limits on retirement plan contributions," he adds.

Spread out your contributions throughout the year. If you're a high-wage earner making more than $65,000, you'll reach the $10,000 maximum before the year is through. That could mean you'd miss a month or more of your employer's matching contributions. Better to spread your contributions evenly throughout the year so you will maximize the value of your plan.

High-wage earners can also make excess contributions to 401(k)s. You are allowed to kick in the difference between the $10,000 cap and 15 percent of your salary. However, you must contribute using the taxed portion of your salary.

Stay put. Don't keep switching in and out of investments throughout the year because you think a fund is performing too high or too low. This is an emotional response to normal ups and downs. Resist it. Think long-term, not moment-to-moment.

Be cautious with company stocks. Investing in company stock is a double-edged sword. Often, employers will only match your contribution via participation in an Employee Stock Ownership Plan (ESOP).

"Naturally, you want to invest in your own company if it's doing well and making exciting new products," says Oti. "But beware of investing all your eggs—salary, career, and retirement—in one basket, especially if it's a start-up company."

Leave your 401(k) alone. Some employers will loan you, without penalty, up to 50 percent of your account balance, or $50,000, whichever amount is lower. This loan must be paid back over a maximum of five years with payments made no less than quarterly. A loan for the purchase of a primary residence may be repaid over a longer period.

"People take out loans, thinking there's no cost because you pay the interest back to your plan," says Orman. "But as long as that money is missing, you are missing an opportunity for growth."

Many people aren't aware that the money is due in full the minute you leave the company, get fired, or the company is sold. If you can't repay the full portion, you'll be charged a 10 percent distribution penalty and the unpaid balance will be counted as additional income, subject to year-end taxes.

Keep some cash in your 401(k). Many people choose to roll over their 401(k) funds into IRAs in order to gain more control over how their funds are invested. If this strategy appeals to you, be aware that experts advise that you keep some portion of your money in your 401(k). The reason for this is that if you are 55 in the year you actually leave employment, IRS rules allow you to make early withdrawals from your 401(k) without incurring a 10 percent penalty. (Otherwise, you must wait until you're 59½.) But you are not given the same break if you try to withdraw that money from an IRA.

Separate your rollover money. If you're younger than 55 and have wondered what to do with your 401(k) when you leave or change jobs, you do have several options. Some plans will allow you to keep the money in the plan administered by your old employer. Typically, they don't charge any additional management fees, but you can't make any more direct contributions. You may also be limited in flexibility. Many plans will only make changes once a month or at other specific times. Your other option is to roll the funds over to a 401(k) plan at your new job, if they allow it. If not, you can roll it over to an IRA. Be sure, however, not to mix these funds with an existing IRA. As long as that original 401(k) investment isn't co-mingled with other funds, it will eventually be portable to a new 401(k) plan.

Moving On

Should you leave the company, you are entitled to take with you 100 percent of your own investment. However, if you leave after fewer than seven years of employment, you may be entitled to only a percentage of the company's contribution. The percentage to which you are entitled increases the longer you have been with the company, usually by 20 percent for every year of employment. This process is called vesting, and the Department of Labor requires all companies to vest their employees 100 percent after seven years of continuous employment. Consult with your employer to see what the vesting schedule of your own plan is.

When requesting a 401(k) distribution, always let your plan administrator make the transfer directly to your new IRA or qualified plan. If you ask for a check while researching your options, the IRS requires all companies to withhold 20 percent of your money for taxes and penalties, just in case you don't roll it over. Should you appropriately roll over the full amount (including the missing 20 percent) within 60 days, you will be reimbursed by the government. But this is one headache that's easy to avoid by letting your plan administrator make the change for you.

Individual Retirement Accounts

When and How to Use Them

Like 401(k) plans, individual retirement accounts (IRAs) are simply an additional way to save for retirement with tax-sheltered income and earnings. But the similarities end there. IRA contributions are not linked to an employer-sponsored plan or conveniently deducted from your paycheck automatically. You have to set up an IRA yourself through either a bank, a brokerage house, or a financial planner. The savings limit is different, too. You can sock away up to $10,000 per year in your 401(k). In general, the most you can save per year in an IRA is $2,000.

"There's no question you should participate first and foremost in a company-sponsored savings plan," says James Poterba, professor of economics at the Massachusetts Institute of Technology in Cambridge. "But IRAs are extremely attractive if you are self-employed or otherwise don't have access to a 401(k) plan, if you're a high-wage earner and want to save more than the maximum allowed through your company plan, or if you simply want the freedom that an IRA allows."

Unlike company-sponsored plans which are typically limited to six or so fund groups, IRAs are self-directed. You can pick any investment vehicle—be it stock, bond, or mutual funds, annuities, or government securities.

Your money is also more liquid. While you can't borrow from your IRA, you can get at it if you deem it necessary and if you're willing to pay the penalty and taxes that would result from an early withdrawal.

In 1997, the government not only changed the original rules governing IRA contributions and withdrawals but also added two new ones. Need a scorecard to keep track of your options? Here it is.

Traditional IRAs

This is the basic model. The most you can contribute is $2,000.

You can always open an IRA even if you participate in a 401(k) plan. But you may not be able to take a tax deduction for your IRA contribution unless you fall within certain income limits. You're eligible for IRA tax relief if your adjusted gross income is less than $35,000 as an individual or $50,000 if you're a couple filing jointly.

Bear in mind that these IRAs grant you a tax deduction in the same year you make your contribution. Because they're tax-deductible in the first year, these are beginning to be referred to as "front-loaded" IRAs. Your investments grow tax-deferred but you are taxed in your later years when you start withdrawing the money—which you are allowed to do as early as age 59½ and you are absolutely required to do by the time you hit 70½.

The rules governing withdrawals have also been loosened. The age requirements are still the same, but now the government will waive the 10 percent penalty for early withdrawals of up to $10,000 if the account holder can prove the funds were used to purchase a first home, emergency medical expenses, costs associated with unemployment, or "qualified" higher education expenses (like tuition) of the taxpayer, the taxpayer's spouse, or any child or grandchild of the taxpayer or taxpayer's spouse.

Roth IRA-Plus

This newfangled IRA was created under the 1997 tax bill and named in honor of Senator William Roth (R-Delaware), chairman of the Senate finance committee. Roth contributions are limited to $2,000 a year and the earnings grow tax-free, just like traditional IRAs. Roths are referred to as back-loaded, however, because while you cannot claim a tax deduction in the year you make your contribution, your retirement-year withdrawals are tax-free as long as you meet age and income requirements.

"A large group of people, easily 97 percent of the country, is now eligible to participate in an IRA, even if they're already contributing the maximum to their 401(k) plan," says Randy Hardock, a senior partner with the Washington, D.C., law firm Davis and Harman.

Which type of IRA is better? "If you're eligible for the deduction on a traditional IRA and a Roth IRA, it's a tough choice," admits Hardock. "In that case, you must calculate when the tax deduction will have more value—now or when you retire. You'll have to compare what your tax rate is today versus what you think it will be when you want to take the money out in the future."

Converting to a Roth

So you want to convert your tax-sheltered retirement account from the old-style IRA to the new Roth. What do you need to know?

- **You can't have earned more than $100,000 in adjusted gross income in the year you want to make the transition. This is true for both single and married couples filing jointly.**
- **You absolutely will have to pay taxes on the full amount of savings you've accumulated in your old IRA. That, after all, is the whole point: With Roth IRAs, you pay taxes on the contributions you make yearly into your plan, but your earnings grow tax-free. When it's time to retire and start withdrawing from a Roth IRA, you won't pay any taxes as long as you meet the requirements.**
- **Remember, yearly contributions to other tax-sheltered plans, be they 401(k)s or traditional IRAs, are tax-deferred, not tax-free. These plans allow you to take advantage of the time-value of money, letting interest compound tax-free for decades. But ultimately, Uncle Sam**

Education IRA

You may have heard of a third IRA account, the education IRA. But according to Hardock, this isn't an IRA at all. "It has nothing to do with retirement. It's a tax-sheltered custodial plan for kids. But Congress must have thought that tagging these as IRAs would be a good marketing move," he says.

The Ed IRA is limited to a $500 annual contribution for a designated beneficiary under the age of 18. The money grows tax-free, and withdrawals for higher education expenses are tax-free (much like a Roth IRA). After the child reaches 18, you can no longer make any additional contributions. All the money must be withdrawn by the time that person reaches age 30. Also, fund distributions for anything other than higher education expenses would be taxable and subject to a 10 percent penalty.

Learning to Do Rollovers

Another extended member of the IRA family is the Rollover IRA. Sometimes used as "conduit" IRAs, these are plans that protect your 401(k) plan when you leave your job. If you keep your 401(k) money in a separate IRA account (so that it does not combine with any preexisting IRA funds), you'll be able to transfer your 401(k) savings into the new plan at your next job.

wants his share. As a result, traditional IRAs have rules that make it mandatory to begin withdrawing a minimum amount of money from your IRA once you turn 70½. These withdrawals, unlike those made from Roth IRAs, are taxable.

• One last point to consider: Roth IRAs are more lenient on withdrawals than traditional IRAs. Specifically, you can take money out of your Roth IRA before the age of 59½ without a 10 percent penalty, provided it is either for a medical emergency or to buy a house if you are a first-time homeowner. Obviously, such a deduction would also be tax-free. So what's to prevent everybody from converting their traditional IRAs into Roth IRAs if they're desperate to raid their nest eggs without undue penalties? Well, Congress thought about this possibility. As a compromise between making it too easy to dip into your long-term savings and loosening the rules governing IRAs, they decided you couldn't withdraw any funds from a Roth IRA that hadn't been sitting there for four years. Now known as the "four-year holding rule," this little addendum means that you can convert your funds to a Roth IRA. But you better hope an emergency doesn't come up any time soon.

Be sure to have the old plan administrator transfer the money directly into the Rollover IRA. Otherwise, the IRS withholds 20 percent of your savings.

SEP-IRAs

SEP stands for simplified employee pensions. It allows small businesses to provide a plan for their employees. If you're self-employed, SEP-IRAs allow you to save considerably more than the $2,000 of a regular IRA. With SEPs, you can put away up to 15 percent of your salary, but no more than $22,500 per year. If you have employees in your business, you are required by law to contribute the same amount to their accounts as to your own. Furthermore, contributions to SEPs, unlike IRAs, are made by the employer, not by the individual employee.

SEPs are also front-loaded, just as traditional IRAs are. Lastly, you can change the amount of the contribution each year, which allows you to be generous during good times and frugal when business is slow.

SIMPLE IRAs

No, we didn't accidentally capitalize that first word. SIMPLE stands for savings incentive match plan for employees. These are regular IRAs that small businesses can open for their employees, assuming they have 100 people or fewer in the company. You're allowed to contribute up to $6,000 of your income and employers are required to match up to 3 percent of your salary. Unlike 401(k) plans, which have plan managers and administrative fees, SIMPLEs are in the hands of the employees. Also, you are 100 percent vested in your SIMPLE IRA, including your employer contribution, from day one.

Keogh Plans

In the old days, pension plans were the retirement savings vehicles for people at large corporations, IRAs were the savings option for lower-income people without access to corporate plans, and Keoghs, established in 1962 by Congressman Eugene Keogh (D-Brooklyn), were set up to be the qualified-savings plans for small businesses or self-employed people. You are able to put away up to $30,000 a year through a Keogh.

Keoghs are not IRAs and they are very complex to set up and administer. In fact, SEPs and SIMPLE IRAs were established to streamline the difficulties posed by Keoghs and offer simplified alternatives.

Withdrawals

How to Stretch Your Nest

It's time to look down the road to the eve of retirement. You've done the hard work: You've researched, you've strategized, you've scrimped on the $3 lattes, and you've made the automatic deposits to your various savings vehicles. It's the proverbial end of the rainbow and you've built up a pot of gold. What next? What is the best plan for withdrawing these funds (from what is sure to be a variety of sources) in such a way to ensure a worry-free retirement that could last up to 35 years?

The Basics

As you prepare for the day of withdrawal from professional life, so too must you start to marshal your forces in order to withdraw your fiscal resources from wherever they are. Here's what you need to do first.

Take an inventory of your assets. In the previous chapters in this section, we told you how to go about gathering estimates of what's coming to you from Social Security, pension payments, your 401(k) plan, and individual retirement accounts (IRAs). Tally them all up. Add in real estate holdings and nontax-sheltered investments including stocks, bonds, certificates of deposit, and/or traditional savings accounts.

Calculate your monthly needs. We'll assume you've worked out a monthly budget that takes into account your retirement lifestyle. "The rule of thumb that everyone hears is that you'll need 75 percent of your working income to retire comfortably," says Ralph Warner, author of *Get a Life: You Don't Need a Million to Retire Well.* "But it depends on the person or the couple. If people have deep bonds with their family and community, they often stay close to home and can live quite frugally."

Start to pay off your debts. As you get closer to retirement, it pays to pay down your liabilities. "The goal of retirement should be to minimize your expenses and maximize your income," says Suze Orman, president of Suze Orman Financial Group in Emeryville, California. "It does not make sense to have $10,000 in credit card debt that charges a nontax-deductible 18 percent interest when you have $10,000 sitting in a money market fund earning 8 percent interest. You are losing money."

Preparing for the Long Term

Now, you'll have some longer-term logistical questions to deal with. For example: As you approach retirement, your first decision will be what to do with your company-sponsored 401(k) plan. There's no question that you should keep it invested; however, should you leave it with the company or roll it over to an IRA?

Why leave your money in your former employer's 401(k) plan? It may make sense to do so if you are happy with your investments, you don't mind someone else managing your account, and you can accept a bit of inflexibility.

In addition, if you've retired early and you need emergency access to the principal in your 401(k) plan, a little-known IRS rule (known as "72T") allows employees who have stopped working to access income from their 401(k)s. You must be 55 years old the year that you retire in order to qualify for this benefit. It is usually used by those retiring prior to the age of 59½, says Malcolm A. Makin, a certified financial planner and president of Professional Planning Group in Westerly, Rhode Island. This rule does not apply to money in an IRA, however.

Why then move the money into an IRA? Primarily, because it gives you more control over how your money is invested. "The majority of people I see roll their 401(k) plans over to IRAs when they leave their companies," says Scott M. Kahan, a certified financial planner and president of Financial Asset Management Corporation in New York City.

The primary drawback of IRAs? The government created IRAs to be for retirement financing, and nothing else. So once you turn 70½, you *must* begin taking minimum withdrawals based on your life expectancy. If you don't, you'll get hit with a 50 percent penalty on the shortfall. On the flip side, if you take money out of an IRA before you turn 59½, you are subject to a 10 percent penalty, on top of regular income taxes.

"A lot of people think this is simple stuff, but it's not," says Kahan. Here are a few other things to bear in mind when planning your withdrawal strategies:

Minimum withdrawals are based on the life expectancy of you or you and your beneficiary. If you want the benefits of tax deferral to last as long as possible, your goal is to minimize the amount you must take out of an IRA each year. Minimum payouts can be calculated based on your own life expectancy, or the life expectancy of both you and your spouse. Many people choose the joint-life option, because it lowers the minimum payout. Why? Women on average live several years longer than men.

You must choose how often to calculate your life expectancy. You have two choices. You can use a fixed, or "term-certain," method that you calculate just once and then live by, year after year. Or you can choose a "recalc" method in which you recalculate your life expectancy each year. That gives you more flexibility and may even yield lower minimum payouts.

Remember the home sellers' tax break. When facing retirement, many people consider selling their homes and relocating to communities with lower costs of living. While there are a number of considerations you should face before selling your house, it is good to know that the bulk of the proceeds from the sale of your home are no longer subject to taxes. In 1997, Congress eliminated all capital gains taxes on proceeds up to $250,000 for individuals and $500,000 for couples.

Success is no longer penalized. Before the Tax Reform Act of 1997, Congress penalized the diligent savers whose tax-sheltered savings added up to substantial sums. What happened was that if your minimum annual withdrawal once you reached 70½ was greater than $155,000 (or if your lump-sum distribution was more than $775,000), you had to pay a 15 percent tax, also called a "success tax," on the excess amount. Before the act was passed in August 1997, many retirees were forced to start withdrawing funds from their IRAs earlier than they otherwise might have, in order to avoid the excise tax later on. Now, says Kyra Morris, a certified financial planner and registered investment advisor at Morris Financial Concepts in Mount Pleasant, South Carolina, "you have a lot more flexibility in terms of letting your money accrue in a tax-deferred account."

Which Piggy Bank Do You Open First?

In order to retire, you need to create a flow of money that will replace your monthly paycheck. Ideally, you do this by living off the interest of your investments, says Joseph Coyle, senior editor of *Money* magazine. This not only takes care of your financial needs but also provides a large inheritance for your children. But the fact is, estimating a conservative inflation rate of 4 percent a year, even people with sizable nest eggs will have to tap into their principal.

The goal is to do so prudently. Coyle suggests that you draw down no more than 5 percent of your principal in your first five years of retirement, then 6 percent in your sixties, 8 percent in your seventies, and 12 percent in your eighties.

Here are some other strategies you can follow.

Plan for inflation and longevity. When looking over your array of investments, the rule of thumb is to tap into your most liquid, lowest-yielding taxable assets first and your tax-sheltered retirement plans last.

"Inflation is going to eat away at the value of your investments, so you always have to invest for growth," advises Cynthia Oti, host of the San Francisco radio talk show *Financial Fitness: Your Weekend Workout.* "Plus, you're going to have to preserve your principal for a lot longer than your parents did, because you're probably going to live longer, too."

Look at your mutual fund families closely. You've been reallocating the percentages from 70 percent in growth stocks and 30 percent in income-producing investments such as bonds. As you approach retirement, you've probably reversed those percentages to 60 percent stock investments and 40 percent income-producing instruments. "The last investments you want to cash in are your growth investments," says Oti. "Remember that you still have a 15- to 30-year time frame, which is more than enough time to smooth out the risk of volatility."

Let the impact of taxation guide you. "Unless you're in a zero percent tax bracket, it's always better to go first for withdrawals to your taxable investments such as certificates of deposit or regular savings accounts," says Randy Hardock, a senior partner with the Washington, D.C., law firm Davis and Harman.

Even when choosing between two nontax-sheltered investments, such as selling individual shares of Microsoft stock versus tapping into a checking account, consider the potential for taxes. If you sell the stock, you're subject to capital gains taxes. If you turn first to your savings account, you will be lessening your reserves of liquid assets but saving money over the long run.

After savings, which should come first—your 401(k) plan or your IRA? If you have a Roth IRA, that may be the first account you'll want to tap, depending on how long you've had it and how old you are. In order for withdrawals to be tax-free, the Roth account must be at least 5 years old and you have to be at least 59½ years old. The taxes you'll pay on funds withdrawn from a traditional IRA and a 401(k) are "virtually identical," says Hardock. "At that point, it becomes an issue of administrative fees and asset allocation. What investments do you want to keep plugging along?"

Another issue: "Working part-time could change your marginal tax rate," says Hardock. "Social Security benefits could kick in, or you might receive a financial windfall one year. The loss of certain deductions might also change your tax status. But overall, the tax code has been compressed by constant tinkering by Congress. Most people are in the 28 percent tax bracket and stay there all their lives."

Grab your company's stock. If your 401(k) plan includes shares of company stock, don't blindly roll it over to an IRA. Instead, say advisors, consider the transfer of the money to an ordinary, taxable brokerage account. "You can delay the taxes on the gains until you sell the shares," explains Hardock, "and the appreciated value will be taxed at a lower, capital gains rate. In an IRA, the windfall would be taxed at the higher, income-tax rate."

Part Six

Real-Life Scenarios

Quest for the Best

They made their money the hard way—they earned it, and then some. Now, these money savants are going to tell you their secrets. And it won't cost you a cent.

You Can Do It!

These guys have come by their cash in different ways. But they've all learned how to make the most of their money—and their lives. Here are their stories.

Quest for the Best They made their money the hard way—they earned it, and then some. Now, these money savants are going to tell you their secrets. And it won't cost you a cent.

Andrew Tobias, Financial Expert and Best-Selling Author

Wit, Wisdom, and Financial Wellness

Andrew Tobias has spent half of the past 25 years working with money—getting it, spending it, and giving it away—and the other half writing about it. The writing part has gone well: he's done money columns for *Time* and *Esquire* and his best-selling *The Only Investment Guide You'll Ever Need* has been in print since 1978. He has some major trophies: the Gerald Loeb Award for Distinguished Business and Financial Journalism and the Consumer Federation of America Media Service Award.

The moneymaking hasn't gone too badly either, possibly because he at least partly follows his own stripped-down advice: Live beneath your means. Invest in no-load, low-expense stock market index funds (mutual funds that only buy stocks whose performance is tracked by a particular index, such as the Standard and Poor's 500). Pay off your credit cards. ("Not having to pay 18 or 20 percent interest is as good as earning 18 or 20 percent. Tax-free," he says). Maybe that's why he was able to title his latest book *My Vast Fortune*. Tobias claims, though, that the title is tongue-in-cheek, a joke really.

And that brings us to the next aspect of Andrew Tobias. He's a riot. Call his humor ironic or eccentric or whatever, it's a sure bet that he delivers more laughs and whimsy per page than anybody else in this solemn world of portfolios and prime rates. For instance:

- Though he understands many men's dreams of owning a Porsche, he doesn't share it: "I always wanted to be invisible and to fly."
- He observes that anticipating the nice things money buys can be as much fun as buying them, and words his advice thusly: "Ease the fingers of your aspiration up the inner thigh of your cupidity."
- After noting that Adolf Hitler always spoke of American automaker Henry Ford as his hero and role model, Tobias muses, "Gee, without Henry Ford, we might not have had the Mustang—or World War II."
- After telling us that most brands of vodka taste alike, he suggests that if status symbols are important we should "buy one bottle of Absolut and a 59-cent plastic funnel. It should last a lifetime."

Laughing All the Way to the Bank

Tobias traces the evolution of the humor in his work: "When you've lost as much money as I have, in as many ridiculous ways, you can only laugh at it. But I didn't decide, 'Instead of writing boring, I'm going to try to write funny.' It just came naturally. And I came quickly to see that people have a lot more fun reading something that has a little life to it."

The Tobias humor is there to work, though. Its job is to carry, like an elephant with a howdah on its back, the great Tobias message: If you want to enjoy the good things money can bring you—and boy, are they good—you have to watch it.

He did. When he was in his early twenties, Tobias had a fairly serious financial problem. "I didn't have a lot of money," he says. "But I lived frugally and I was enjoying it. I wasn't starving. I found you can live, in terms of basic food and shelter and clothes, for very little. I was making $15,000 a year. I took subways instead of cabs. I made my money stretch in the supermarket. And guess what? Instead of going a couple hundred dollars in debt, I wound up a couple thousand dollars in the black. That's when your money starts working for you. And a penny saved is like two pennies earned because you don't have to pay taxes on it."

Tobias doesn't like the word "discipline" applied to this sort of thinking, because discipline suggests to him that somebody else is making you behave a certain way. No, the key to all this is that you have to want to do this yourself. Tobias compares it to stopping smoking, noting that all the inducements don't work until the person really wants to stop.

"Similarly, if you take a moment or a weekend and have an epiphany and decide you want to be a person who gets from point A to point B financially—meaning maybe getting out of debt and becoming financially secure—and if you really want to get there, you will. The problem is that a lot of people don't take the time to think about it, or they just don't want it enough. Or they figure the future will take care of itself. It won't."

Simplicity, Sacrifice, and Satisfaction

His books repeat his conviction that there's nothing terribly complicated about success with money, and in conversation he hits the same note: "Live beneath your means. If it helps, read my books or this one, but somehow get to the point where you want to do this. It really is the only way."

He compares money management to exercise. "The first day you go jogging, it's *so* unpleasant. And the first time you sacrifice money—save it instead of spend it—you don't get much satisfaction. But as you become a good jogger and you get used to the rewards—endorphins and all that kind of stuff—it gets easier and you enjoy the progress. You're proud of yourself and you're still doing it and it's part of who you are. It's the same with saving."

"Discipline" isn't a word Tobias applies to his writing regimen either. To explain, he sets it up like a syllogism. He wants to be happy. Happiness to him means being "effective and successful. That in turn means I want to get those books written. So I have to sit down and write them."

There are obstacles he's had to overcome. Interestingly, he locates them within himself. He wishes he had a better memory and that he could read faster; he sees being a slow reader as a terrible handicap. He would like to not need so much sleep. He says he needs seven or eight hours a night to be happy and productive. "If I get less, I'm conscious of having an awful day until I can get to sleep again."

He speaks also of some unfinished business. One of his goals is to reform the auto insurance industry. He wrote a book about it, *Auto Insurance Alert!*, and he spent a quarter-million of his own money on a referendum in California that got nowhere. He wrote about it in *Time* and got two phone calls. "One was from my mother, but she always calls," he says.

"I still want to get the auto insurance industry fixed and to feel that I've helped save the country tens of billions of dollars a year," he says. "And mortality bothers me. I'd like to live forever. Other than that, I'm feeling kind of fortunate."

Nick Lowery, Veteran NFL Kicker

Fielding Financial Goals

Nick Lowery almost called it quits on his kicking career. He tried out 11 times with eight teams. He made a squad, at last, only to be released soon after. The Washington Redskins even cut him twice in one week. One well-respected sportswriter decried Lowery as "the worst kicker I have ever seen."

Lowery seemed ready to settle down to his steady, full-time job as an aide to the Commerce and Science Transportation Committee for the U.S. Senate, when the Kansas City Chiefs called. They asked him to give it one more shot. Lowery headed off in May 1980 to try one last time. Despite the string of failures, he had already developed a philosophy that he knew would eventually bring success in his football career and later in his financial endeavors: Look toward the long term, set specific goals, and surround yourself with supportive and knowledgeable people.

That strategy has served him well. Kansas City signed Lowery, and the player once called "the worst kicker ever" stayed in the game for 18 seasons—for the Chiefs, then for the New York Jets—earning a reputation as one of the best kickers in National Football League history. Lowery is the second all-time scoring leader in the NFL. He holds the records for highest field goal percentage and for the most seasons with 100 or more points. In 1996, he set the all-time record for most field goals.

Lowery's philosophy served him well off the field, too. Lowery turned himself into a savvy investor. Knowing that no matter how good he was, football wasn't going to last forever, Lowery set about building a fortune that would enable him to live well long after his kicking days were over. Now, his reputation as a smart businessman follows him around as much as his renown for putting the ball between the uprights.

Learning from Fumbles

Lowery wasn't always so concerned about money management. When he signed his first contract with the Kansas City Chiefs in 1980, he received a $2,500 bonus. "To me, that was huge. I bought a 1977 silver Scirocco," he says. He made $30,000 in his first year with the Chiefs.

But as he spent more time in the league, Lowery saw firsthand the importance of protecting his money. He watched fellow players getting taken in by fly-by-night investment schemes and others spending their money without thinking of the future. He even knew one teammate who picked up his check every Monday, walked over to the bank across the street, cashed it, and spent all the money by the next game. "When you are around the game, you see lots of horror stories," he says.

He especially understood the fine line he walked as a field goal kicker. While other football players get to show their stuff—and justify their paychecks—play after play, the field goal kicker only gets a couple chances per game. "I knew that I was always one or two kicks away from having my job be in jeopardy. That motivates you to be a little bit more responsible."

Lowery attributes part of his success on and off the field to the "angels" in his life. "These are the people who will help steer you in a positive direction," he says. They include coaches (like Dick Johnson, a volunteer high school coach and a retired stockbroker) who taught him the dynamics of kicking and friends who told him to keep going when the going got rough. Another of Lowery's angels was Supreme Court justice and former NFL star Byron "Whizzer" White, who lived next door to the Lowery family in McLean, Virginia.

Rather than follow the frivolous examples of some of his teammates, Lowery called a professional to handle his finances. He turned to a money manager, Fred Mitchell of Mitchell Capital Management in Kansas City. "I think that surrounding yourself with quality people who can give you advice, who have been there before in terms of investing, can only stimulate more thought and more evaluation and sophistication in your financial life," Lowery says.

But Lowery doesn't just seek the counsel of one financial mind. He decided to have more than one manager after noting the success the NFL Player's Association had when it expanded management of its pension fund from one money manager to three. After that switch, "the pension fund just exploded," Lowery recalls. The fund's success prompted Lowery to follow suit. He split up his investments between three different money managers. "Having competition between money managers is pretty critical. Competition and a diversity of strategies, whether it is in football or finances, is an incentive to do everything possible to be the best," Lowery says. His managers keep his assets in a mix of stocks, annuities, mutual funds, and other accounts. Although Lowery relies on his managers for advice and information, he keeps abreast of the markets and does a lot of his own research. For example, when one of his advisors suggested a particular company's mutual funds, Lowery personally met the fund managers and quizzed them about their strategies.

Lowery keeps aside 5 percent of his money to finance his more speculative investments, most of which he finds on his own. "I'll take some more risk and go in directions that my money managers might not think of," Lowery says. For instance, Lowery has recently studied a new technology that may render eyeglasses unnecessary. After researching the market and the company and going over it with his advisors, Lowery may invest in the venture. "But I never will invest in something that my money managers don't think is a good idea," he adds.

Kicking Back

Lowery's goal is to triple his worth in the next 10 years. By doing that, he'll be wealthy enough at age 50 to do whatever he wants for the rest of his life. The way Lowery sees it, financial security will allow him to spend his time doing what he loves—community service. "I want to see if I can make myself financially independent so I don't have to worry about money. I'd like to use my time and skill to make the world a much better place, especially for children. Any notion of success has to be tied into service to others," he says. Lowery got that idea from one of the three presidents he has worked for in national community service—George Bush.

After he meets his financial goal, he may run for government office or devote all his time to the programs and charities with which he currently works. With his fame as well as his money, he started the Nick Lowery Charitable Foundation in Kansas City to aid children who have any kind of disabling condition, whether emotional, physical, or environmental. Current programs include Kick with Nick, the longest-running fundraising program in the NFL; and Native Vision, a partnership between Johns Hopkins Center for American Indian Health and the NFL Players Association.

These days, Lowery divides his time watching his investments, working with his charities (he is the chairman of Kansas City's Alliance for Youth of America's Promise), giving motivational speeches, and writing a book using kicking as a metaphor for life. Whatever he does, he says he always thinks of the advice a friend gave him when he started out in the NFL: "It's not the decisions in life that are important, but the energy you throw into whatever you decide to do."

Ron Popeil, Entrepreneur and TV Pitchman

Savvy Salesmanship

You might not recognize the name Ron Popeil, but you'll recognize his products: the Veg-O-Matic, the Miracle Broom, the Dial-O-Matic, Mr. Microphone, the Pocket Fisherman—and don't forget GLH (Great Looking Hair) to cover your bald spots.

Popeil's commercials have literally set the standard for breathless, shameless, TV salesmanship. "Slices and dices and juliennes to perfection!" "Get one today, and receive this fabulous fork-tipped carving knife absolutely free!" "If you order right now, the price is not $29.95 but only two easy payments of $9.95!" "The only tears you'll shed when cutting onions will be tears of joy!"

A lot of people make fun of Ron Popeil (one of them was Dan Aykroyd, whose Popeil parody, the Bass-O-Matic '76, is regarded as a classic *Saturday Night Live* skit), but he's laughed all the way to the bank. He claims to have sold more than 11 million Veg-O-Matics alone and says he's been offered as much as $25 million for his company. Not bad for a poor kid with a lousy education who began his career literally selling products on the street.

The street in question was Maxwell Street in Chicago, a sort of open-air bazaar where anything and everything was for sale, most of it legal. It was there, as a teenager in the mid 1950s, that Popeil first discovered the joys of making money. Born in the Bronx, New York, in 1935, he was essentially abandoned by his parents. Popeil spent most of his childhood shuffling between boarding schools and uncaring relatives, living a sort of "peasant" life so grim he says he's blocked most of it out.

"Through sales, I could escape from poverty and the miserable existence I had," he writes in his autobiography, *The Salesman of the Century.* "I had lived for 16 years in homes without love, and now I had finally found a form of affection, and a human connection, through sales."

An Instinct for People

That hunger for sales soon earned Popeil a profitable spot pitching products at the giant Woolworth store in downtown Chicago, a job he calls his big break in life. Pitching to live customers at Woolworth (this was the heyday of the American five-and-dime) honed his instinct for salesmanship to a razor-sharp edge. And during the summer months, it wasn't uncommon for Popeil to spend 18 hours a day, 7 days a week, at state and county fairs, hawking his goods.

He's always had an instinct for what products people—masses of people, common folks—will find useful and what they'll be willing to pay for them. He's used that instinct to invent a variety of consumer products himself, always keeping the likes and dislikes of the masses in mind. "When you're used to dealing with live people, you have the benefit of a direct response," he says. "You can see by their movements, by the questions they ask, by how they're paying attention, whether they're really interested in your product."

Taking It to TV

Popeil's real breakthrough came in the late 1950s, when he married his talents as a pitchman to television. He made his first commercial for $550, selling the Ronco Spray Gun, a gun-shaped nozzle that washed cars, fertilized lawns, and killed weeds, among other things. He sold a million units in four years, and he was on his way.

Although he was one of the first independent entrepreneurs to grasp and exploit the potential of TV advertising, Popeil takes no credit for that discovery. "I was just lucky to be in the right place at the right time," he says. "In those days, you could advertise empty boxes on television and sell them. It was hard *not* to be successful."

Success brought riches, then problems. In 1969, Popeil and his partner took their company public and became instant multimillionaires. Popeil had a bout of bankruptcy with his company when the bank unexpectedly recalled their loan. He ended up personally buying the assets from the bank and making more millions. That painful experience helps explain why the Ronco of today is a privately held company with only 45 employees, most of them in sales and customer service. "Ask me how much money I owe banks today," Popeil says. "Zero. Maybe someday I'll have to borrow again but, at this point, I don't need banks controlling my destiny."

Popeil's personal investment strategy is similarly conservative. He counts on the earnings he gets from sales and puts his savings in tax-free municipal bonds. "That strategy works really well for me," he says. "How can you go wrong if you make 5½ percent on your money, tax-free, and it's guaranteed? I can make seven figures a year doing that."

He admits he probably could have made a lot more than 5½ percent by investing in the stock market, but he thinks the risk is far too great. "When I was an investor, I had a stock broker telling me what all these companies were going to earn," he says, "and one day he told me what *my* company was going to earn. Can you imagine someone telling you what your company is going to produce in earnings? He was talking to the guy who knows more about what's going on in my company than anyone else. So I learned a lesson from that. Playing the market is gambling, pure gambling. I have a lot of friends whose personal lives, their moods, are dictated by what happens with the market. That's not my style. I like to sleep comfortably at night."

A Penchant for the Product

One reason Popeil sleeps easy is his propensity for counting pennies. Like a lot of people who grew up poor, he doesn't see the sense in squandering money. He has a nice home in Beverly Hills and a boat (fishing is his passion), but he drives a five-year-old Lexus. His wife, by the way, would prefer a Bentley. "I can easily afford a Bentley or two," he says, "but the Lexus rides so good and it's so efficient. Who am I trying to impress?"

With regular spots on TV's shopping channels and new product ideas always in the works, Popeil describes himself today as a happy man. His great joy in life is derived simply from coming up with ideas for products and selling them himself. He's not the salesman of the century, he says, because he can't sell anything, anytime, anywhere. He says he has to truly believe in his products; when he does, there's nobody better.

He also takes pride in his ability to get his ideas into the marketplace, fast. After decades of listening to people tell him that they've developed the next big thing, he has learned that the sheer number of product ideas from the world's amateur inventors is "unfathomable." What counts is having the focus and the energy to actually get something from concept to reality, and the drive to always be looking for a way to take it to the next, higher level.

"My philosophy is when you snooze, you lose," he says. "If you have a great idea, do something with it. Don't let an idea remain an idea."

Humberto Cruz, Nationally Syndicated Financial Columnist

Self-Discipline Made Him a Million

He doesn't believe in budgets or saving a certain percentage of your income. Nor can he claim an Ivy League business degree. As a matter of fact, he majored in communications at the University of Miami. But Humberto Cruz's investment strategies have made him a wealthy man. The writer of such nationally syndicated columns as *The Savings Games*, *Mutual Fund Watch*, and *Ask Humberto*, Cruz paid cash for his newest house and makes more from his investment income than from his substantial writing salary. And he did it using simple techniques, like regular savings and self-discipline, that he says can help just about anyone gain financial freedom.

"By 1994, I had a $1 million just through not wasting, investing systematically, and letting compound interest do the magic," says Cruz.

Not bad for the son of a Cuban refugee whose family fled that country with about $300 to their name.

From Refugee to Financial Freedom

Cruz learned early that it was possible to get by with very little. After living in middle-class comfort in Cuba, his family had barely enough money to rent a small apartment when they came to the United States. For years, virtually every penny went for necessities, and young Humberto took jobs after school and during the summer to help out. Scholarships, with a little financial assistance from his parents, helped him attend and graduate from college.

A reporter for the *Kansas City Star* after graduation, Cruz decided to quit his job. Gathering all his money—$2,000—he fled to sunny South Florida. Within a few years, Cruz was married, and he and his wife began saving for their future. But it wasn't until the birth of his daughter that he really got serious about socking it away. "The expenses of having a child was a wake-up call for me," he recalls.

When he tried to purchase a home, the bank refused to give Cruz a mortgage unless he was willing to withdraw money from a tax-deferred annuity he had set aside. Cruz agreed, but it irked him. He vowed to pay off the mortgage as soon as possible.

This launched Cruz on what he calls "the two-year blitz": Every penny went toward eliminating that debt. "Instead of spending money on entertainment, we went to the library and checked out books, and took walks in the park. Instead of eating out, we packed lunches. My motivation was to be completely debt-free."

Meanwhile, Cruz made another discovery. A reporter in the news bureau that he helped supervise showed him a personal finance magazine that featured her brother-in-law on the cover. After barely glancing at the story, Cruz found himself studying the ads and features that focused on wise investing. Even though he'd been in journalism for decades, he'd never read anything quite like it. "There were ads for mutual funds, and I didn't even know what a mutual fund was." Cruz sent away for information and when the material arrived, would pore over each offer. Before long, he carefully selected some investments and, using "just enough money to get my feet wet," made a purchase.

When Cruz overheard a telephone conversation between a *Sun-Sentinel* freelance writer and a *Money* magazine editor regarding their search for a savvy amateur investor to profile, Cruz thought he fit the bill. The writer ended up interviewing Cruz, and the *Money* editors found Cruz's approach to financial management so compelling that they made it into a full-fledged story. Letters and phone calls poured in for more information, and Cruz suddenly felt compelled to write an investment column. That column was written biweekly in his spare time; he now cranks out three columns a week, writes a newsletter, and has time for little else.

How to Get Your Finances Humming

In some ways, a little bit of luck has helped Cruz's financial success, but it's the investment principles he's consistently followed that have essentially carried him through. Cruz's sound financial precepts will make you think twice about how you spend your money. For example, instead of budgeting, Cruz encourages everyone to carry a small notebook with them for three months and meticulously track every dollar spent. This record will then allow you to break down your spending into four categories: necessities, nice things to have, luxuries I can't afford now, and waste. "Waste could be money spent on soft drinks, vending machine snacks, magazines never read, CDs played once, and clothes worn once and then kept in the closet. You then eliminate the waste and put away the luxuries until you take care of the first column: necessities."

You have to determine your so-called necessities, but Cruz defines them this way: food, clothing, shelter and, of course, savings. "Food is a necessity, but is eating at a gourmet restaurant seven days a week? Obviously not." What about dining out once a week? "I would put that into nice things to do. I'm all for nice things to do—as long as you've taken care of the necessities." Cruz speaks from experience: Known to carry his lunch in the same plastic sack for weeks on end, Cruz recently took his wife and their daughter, son-in-law, and mother-in-law on a two-week Mediterranean cruise. "And because of our investment income, we had more money when we got back than when we left," he says.

Cruz's take on saving? "If you spend this much at the grocery store and pharmacy, this much for rent, and this much on clothes, how much is left? If there's $500 left, why not save the entire $500?"

Meanwhile, credit card debt has no place in Cruz's financial planning. "I use credit cards for convenience, to get a float from the money and rebates and then pay it off at the end of the month. And I have never incurred one penny of credit card interest. That compound interest works against you."

High insurance deductibles are another common financial pitfall. Cruz advocates having insurance in case of a catastrophe, but not using it for "day-to-day things that you need to take care of." He advises, "You should have an emergency fund of three to six months salary in reserve for things like that—like your fridge breaking down—whatever."

He also has a rule of thumb for larger investments. If you think you'll need the money in fewer than 5 years, stay out of the stock market. You're probably better off with a certificate of deposit or treasury note because the money might not be there when you need it, he says. If you won't need it for 10 years, "then few places make as much sense as the stock market. If it's somewhere between 5 and 10, you can go a number of ways: stock mutual funds or bond mutual funds or a combination of both."

The bottom line: "A slight difference in the interest rate can make a tremendous difference in your return. A savings account at 4 percent interest will take 18 years to double. If you can get a 10 percent return, it only takes 7 years to double. And in another 7, it will double again. It will quadruple in 14 years."

You Can Do It! These guys have come by their cash in different ways. But they've all learned how to make the most of their money—and their lives. Here are their stories.

Progressive Parsimony

Brad Lemley, Topsham, Maine

Date of birth: April 9, 1955

Profession: Staff writer, *This Old House* magazine

In the past eight years, on a middle-class income, my wife and I have socked away $70,000 in savings, paid off the mortgage on our home, wiped out all of our credit card debt, and begun saving 30 percent of our income. How? We didn't hit it big on Wall Street, win the lottery, or receive a visit from the Publishers Clearing House Prize Patrol. We simply began living a creatively frugal life.

We weren't always so smart about money. Back in 1978 when I finished college, I pulled down a meager salary as a reporter for a small television station. I wasn't irresponsible with money, but I never really seemed to have any either. By the time Laurie and I married in 1984, we had about $4,000 in credit card debt, a combined income of $35,000, and not an asset to our names. Yet we were careless about our spending; for example, we ate out at least twice a week. It was a time when we should have been putting money aside to buy a house or save so that one of us could quit work and stay home with children. You could say we were in the we're-young-and-in-love-and-don't-have-kids-so-let's-live-it-up stage. Too many newlyweds occupy this stage for too long.

In 1988, we moved to Maine to be closer to Laurie's family. Pursuing my lifelong dream of building a house, we took out a $60,000 loan and began construction. The loan ran out with only two-thirds of the house finished. To complete our home without assuming more debt, I abandoned freelance writing and its fiscal vagaries and became a staff features writer for the *Maine Sunday Telegram*. Financially, we remained afloat, but it was tough.

An Economic Epiphany

In October 1990, I was assigned to write a feature about Amy Dacyczyn, then publisher of *The Tightwad Gazette*, a newsletter that promoted frugal living. In the first issue, Amy explained that she, her husband, Jim, and their four kids had not only survived on Jim's salary of less than $30,000 a year, but had managed to save $49,000. I was skeptical, but curious.

During our interview, Amy explained that the critical factor in fiscal life isn't how much you make, but what you do with it. She drew a distinction between an investment purchase such as a home, which holds or even increases its value, and disposable purchases such as clothing. To get ahead financially, she said you must maximize the former sorts of purchases and minimize the latter.

But most striking to me was Amy's perspective. To her, the frugal life was fun, a game, a sport. She reveled in the challenge of seeing how inexpensively she could feed her family tasty, nutritious meals, or dress them as well or better than other kids in their school. Clearly, it was working. Frugality had purchased for them not only a huge home, but Amy's ability to stay at home with the kids.

I wrote a story about Amy for the *Telegram*, then for *Parade* magazine. *The Tightwad Gazette*'s circulation zoomed from

124 subscribers to more than 100,000. I was happy for Amy and her sudden success, but I was even more thrilled to finally have some strategies for extricating my family from our financial mess.

Bringing It Home

Laurie and I immediately began incorporating Amy's ideas into our life. First, as Jim and Amy had immediately after they married, Laurie and I had a serious talk about what we wanted out of our life. To our mutual shock, we discovered neither of us really coveted this large house we were building. We realized we would happily move to a smaller house in exchange for the freedom to become a one-earner family.

With the goal of finishing and selling the house firmly in mind, we began to incorporate several lifestyle changes. First, we frequented yard sales. I found that if you get in the habit of pulling yourself out of bed every Saturday morning and swinging by 15 or more yard sales, you'll find a few that have tons of great stuff.

We also sharply curtailed restaurant meals. We figured it this way: for the two of us to go out to eat, it cost about $40. At the time, it took me nearly half a day to earn that much take-home pay. So when the urge to eat out struck, I would mentally conjure up my worst day on the job. Was it worth half of that day to eat out? My wife and I both love to cook; we realized that the satisfaction we got from eating out just wasn't worth the sacrifice.

We expanded our garden. Today, our 2,000-square-foot vegetable garden is by far the largest in our neighborhood.

I'd always changed the oil and filters in my cars myself, but I learned to do other small maintenance tasks, too. My 1986 Toyota Tercel has 184,000 miles on it and runs like the day I bought it. I take fanatically good care of my cars, and expect them to last for many more years.

After about a year of happy, frugal living, Amy called and asked if I would help her to write the *Gazette*, as the strain of producing the newsletter and raising her brood (she now had six kids) was wearing her out. I agreed, and began working part-time for the newsletter for the next five years.

Around this time, Laurie and I reached our goal—we finished our house, sold it, and bought a smaller one. We also decided that Laurie would quit her full-time job to pursue her singing career and stay home with Alex. We've explained to him that fiscal life is multiple choice, and "all of the above" isn't on the form. The fact that we don't buy every plastic gadget on TV translates into Laurie's being able to stay home with him. From the time they can speak and understand, children should learn that fiscal life is a series of choices, and though you can't always get everything you want, you can fulfill your biggest desires if you are willing to work for them.

Within three years, we had paid off the mortgage on our new home.

The Frugal Philosophy

I don't advocate blindly chopping all pleasure from your life, but you have to decide what is important to you and identify your long-term financial goals. Many people continue spending unconsciously and then 10 years down the road wonder why they're still renting when all of their friends have purchased homes. Setting goals allows you to envision what it is you're trying to obtain so that you can then make the necessary changes.

Be creative—as we used to say at the *Gazette*, "Thrift without creativity is deprivation." Once you begin thinking thrift, you'll dream up many new ways to save money.

This culture is filled with people who lament the "fact" that they don't make enough money. Yet this is true only in rare cases.

You already make enough money. Think harder about how you spend it.

It's Never Too Late to Save

Gordon M. Bennett, Long Beach, California

Date of birth: January 8, 1949

Profession: Purchasing agent for Long Beach City College

I'm what you might call a late bloomer. I started saving for my retirement a few years ago, when I was in my mid-forties. That's when my wife, Patricia, became the live-in manager of a 44-unit subsidized housing complex for seniors in Long Beach. Living here, we get to see the seniors who didn't plan for their retirement. They're the ones who come in to apply for $450-a-month apartments, but they make $518, and you wonder how they're going to pay their electric bills. You see them trek over to the markets on the seedy side of town to get deals on groceries, and then wheel them back 10 blocks.

If we didn't provide low-income housing, they couldn't even afford to live here. Some of them qualify for a program where they pay only one-third of the rent and the rest of the money is theirs. But still, try to live on $400 a month in California. They can't have cars. They're slurping down ramen noodles and searching through trash cans for stuff to eat. We didn't really see this at the other buildings because we managed the apartments out of our living room. They came in and paid their rents and left. But here we see it every day.

So when Patricia started this job, that's when it hit me that I needed to start putting some money away. Before then I hadn't saved anything for my retirement. Not a cent.

Where the Money Goes

Before I came to this realization, my spending plan had been all spending and no planning. I admit it, I like my toys: computer equipment, electronics, and fast cars. I have a cellular phone, a state-of-the-art stereo system, and a 41-inch big-screen television. And then there are our most expensive toys—Patricia's '95 Ford Probe SE and my '93 Mercury Capri convertible. Our five pets cost us a pretty penny, too. We figure we don't have any kids, so why not? In all, we have three cats, a cockatiel, and an iguana. Our biggest cat, Rocky, who weighs in at 21 pounds, has been operated on twice, and that has set us back $2,555.

Credit card bills take the biggest chunk of money out of our pockets. I have 9 or 10 credit cards and two are Visas. Right now, I have $5,000 on one Visa and $3,000 on the other. We pay about $150 a month on them, and I'm realizing now how much money we're losing just paying interest on our credit card debt. I never used to think about interest rates, but when I see we're paying $80 to $90 a month in interest, it gives me some incentive to cut back on using the cards—or at least to try to pay the balance down faster. That realization has pretty much cured me of one bad spending habit I had: cash advances. I used to take out cash advances once a month or once every two months. I'd take out a few hundred bucks and it would be gone before I knew it. For me, getting a cash advance was like playing the slots in Las Vegas. You put the card in the machine and a bunch of money comes out. In the past, I've taken out a cash advance on one card to pay off another. I've also used a cash advance to cover a check. But the interest you pay on that money. . . . I see now how easy it is for people to get sucked into a hole of debt. I'll tell you, I haven't taken any cash advances in awhile.

Besides our credit card bills, we're also paying off a loan we took out for our two cars and the big-screen TV. Our car insurance runs us $3,200 a year, and we pay $382 a month on the mortgage for a vacation home we bought about 15 years ago. I guess we've had a lot of things to pay for in the past few years. And I've enjoyed the things we've bought with our money. But I want to enjoy our future, too, so that's why I started getting serious about watching my spending and building savings for our later years.

My Saving Grace

For now, our financial plan is simple, but it works. It's like exercising—you start out with slow and simple moves, and as you get better at it, you do the harder, more complicated stuff.

For starters, we've split up our earnings into two different pools. Patricia stashes her money in a savings account, which doubles as our emergency fund. As part of Patricia's working arrangements, we live in a $650 apartment for free, including the utilities. On top of that, Patricia gets paid $800 a month. My earnings go into investments for later. I'm building up the reserves for retirement and she's paying most of the day-to-day bills.

And we've gotten smarter about paying those daily expenses. Lately, we've been paying a little more than the minimum on the cards—we'll be paying off a lot less interest in the long run—and I've been trying to use cash instead of plastic whenever I buy something. I've even been paying cash to put gas in my car.

We made some improvements to the vacation home a few years back, which cost $800. Patricia and I saved $2,400 by doing the work ourselves. But now the place pays for itself. We realized we hadn't gone there for quite some time, so we started renting it out for $385 a month. That covers our mortgage payments, but it doesn't pay for the taxes or insurance. Still, it works out pretty well.

Seeing the Future

I make $2,751 a month as a purchasing agent for Long Beach City College, which I've been doing since 1994. I started putting $80 a month into a tax-sheltered annuity (TSA) a few years ago. Every year when I'd get a raise, I'd increase the deduction from my paycheck, and now I'm putting in $220 a month. Two years after I opened the TSA, I got into mutual funds, including one of the top performers. Right now, I have another $110 a month going into that. For me, the key to saving money now is to have it taken out of my check before I ever get my hands on it, because once it's in my hands, it's as good as spent. So far I have about $8,800 in the two mutual funds. It's not a lot, but it's a start. We're both in our late forties and we hope to retire by the time we're 65, although we'd like to retire sooner.

I figure we'll be pulling in about $3,000 a month when we retire, between my $1,700 pension and $800 in social security, plus whatever I've managed to make by then in the mutual funds. That's more than I'm making now a month. So I think we'll be okay.

We plan to buy a home in the low desert area of Hemet, California. Right now, a new 1,600-square-foot, two-bedroom, two-bathroom home on a big lot is selling for $94,000, which is a really good deal in California. Patricia and I hope to have saved enough to buy it outright and then pay the taxes and insurance with my pension and social security. So even though we started saving for our retirement later than many people do, we should still be able to make ends meet once we're out of the working world.

I even convinced four people at work who are a few years younger than me to start putting some money away. I told them not to be disappointed if they can only start with $25 or $50 a month. "Just keep plodding along and keep adding a little at a time and it will add up," I said. Well, after about a year, one of them has already upped her monthly savings from $25 to $100. She's on the right track. So are we.

Financial Fixer-Upper

John Shmilenko, Portland, Oregon

Date of birth: December 25, 1953

Profession: Roofer turned real estate investor

My father, Ivan, showed me that you don't have to settle for fate. Having survived a Nazi slave labor camp, and living on barely anything more than pig guts during the Stalin regime, my dad immigrated to America with my mother and sister in 1951. Determined to be the owner of a life free of fear, my dad did what it took, even if it meant working three jobs on the other side of the world.

My father's first job was at a Portland foundry, supplemented by selling eggs door-to-door nights and on weekends. Soon, he also began a successful roofing business. When I graduated high school, I joined my father as a full-time roofer. I guess you could say I was born into roofing.

We always had enough, but not much more for extra comforts. In fact, when my baseball mitt was stolen as a kid, I had to sit out of Little League for a season. Being poor can make a person powerless, dishonest, or resourceful. I opted for Ivan Shmilenko's value system and became resourceful.

While working on roofs, a guy has a lot of time to think. It often occurred to me: why should I be spending all my time fixing up other people's places? Actually, I had a fascination with owning property for as long as I can remember. I couldn't figure out why everybody didn't want to own rental property.

So when my roofing income started rolling in, I funneled it into real estate. The scoring I couldn't do that year in Little League I did later as a property owner, during the days spent looking at the junkiest property all over Portland. I soon learned to shrug off the red faces of agents cringing at my typical lowball offers. By age 40, I hit a home run, having accumulated $1.1 million worth of real estate.

My formal training in finance and real estate was really not much more than the Monopoly games I played as a kid. The secret, I found out, was to buy Baltic and Mediterranean (remember them?—the real cheapo properties), build hotels, then work your way into the midpriced property. (I think winning also had something to do with being the boat game piece. . . .) But seriously, this is basically the formula that still works for me—and I can honestly say I'm still having fun.

I buy lower-end property and breed capital. My first 12 houses in southwest Portland cost a total of $47,000 worth of down payments during the 1970s and 1980s. Don't think it wasn't a scramble to meet the down payments. The first four or five houses are always the hardest. I took extra roofing jobs. I even had to sell my rare guitar.

But once bought, rental houses should pay their own mortgages. Ideally, property appreciates, while income taxes depreciate. By 1995, I was able to sell my houses for $900,000 and reinvest in a midpriced apartment complex. The best part by far is that now I get an annual $60,000 return without doing anything. I could retire now. But my goal is to make a million more and still retire well before I'm 50.

A Roofer at Heart

You could say I've come a long way from the kid with the missing baseball mitt. But really, I'm just your average bear. I think the word *millionaire* is obnoxious—like it's assumed I'm interested in going to country clubs and buying overpriced watches. Not me. The people in my apartment buildings sometimes think I'm the maintenance man when I'm slumming around in my workboots and dirty jeans, painting and repairing units.

In a way, I'm still a roofer at heart. The difference, however, is that I never had the attitude that my life was about just going to work and getting by.

When I was younger, my father had been known to catch me fishing on the Willamette River for spring chinook salmon. Dad would make a big scene, standing by the bridge and hollering for me to reel in and get back to the roofing site. I tried to pretend I couldn't hear him down in the water, but soon enough he'd scare away the fish anyway, with all his Ukranian profanities. I decided right then and there that I was going to create a life that gave me Monday mornings to be alone with the water and the salmon. Far away from the traffic, and even farther away from anyone called boss. To me, my money is about buying myself freedom to have the time to do what I want.

I can hardly wait to get my hands on the next houses, though. Right now, I work for a real estate agency to generate income for my upcoming investments. My girlfriend, Patti, and I are going to put our pennies together. Our plan is to follow the same strategy as I did the first time. We'll buy 12 more houses—that's four a year for three years. These, however, will be at 1990s market prices, requiring a little more starting capital.

I'll probably have to put between $20,000 and $30,000 down this time for low-enders that cost between $70,000 and $80,000 (rather than some of those $8,700 steals in the old days!). We've already made our first two purchases. Patti and I expect to have strong equity again in six to eight years. The final step will be to purchase another multiplex and figure out where we want to travel (and fish) for the rest of our lives.

The Guts to Be Happy

Personally, I believe in fishing at least 100 days of the year. It seems like other guys who've made some money for themselves have the wrong idea. All they do is work, work, work to make even more money. For what? So they can mess up their health and not ever see the sun set outside of their offices?

The worst people with money are the ones who seem to think they're better than anybody else. Money has nothing to do with how good you are. In fact, I've discovered that a lot of those guys with the big image don't even have money. They slave away 60 hours a week at jobs they hate so they can be seen living in the ritzy part of town, making payments on expensive cars, but barely making it. I don't get it.

I don't think anyone on his death bed wishes he had worked more. He does wish he took more walks with his spouse, found out what people were like on the other side of the country, climbed mountains, worked out, and kept better health.

Life is weird. It seems like it takes guts to actually be happy. It definitely takes guts to be an investor. But not necessarily a lot of crazy risks. I like to think of myself as "aggressively conservative." Personally, I think it's risky *not* to invest. I mean, how secure is it to count on the money from your job alone?

All my money goes back into real estate, and I watch it grow. I only have $15,000 in personal debt. Rather than take out loans, I'd sooner score a big commission or take another roofing job to make a down payment.

Some investors do better with individual retirement accounts and stocks. But I personally do not touch the stock market. Why should I put money into something I don't understand? If I want to diversify, I'll spread out my purchases into different neighborhoods and regions. My next houses, for example, are going to be in southwest Washington state, an area showing good growth potential.

But really, I'm far from being any kind of sophisticated real estate hotshot. I have a great casting arm, a high school degree, a handyman's instincts, guts, and common sense. And I make a mean barbecued salmon. That's about it. If I can honestly buy my way to freedom, anybody can.

Building with Trust

Peter Simon, Chilmark, Massachusetts

Date of birth: January 26, 1947

Profession: Photographer and part-time record producer

I have always had a deep-rooted passion for photography and music—two art forms that require a lot of invested money and time. Fortunately, I had some money growing up, and my parents afforded me the opportunity to pursue my creative passions.

I admit that I come from a fairly opulent background. My father, Richard Simon, founded the publishing company Simon and Schuster. He built a successful business, and my family lived comfortably. My three sisters and I attended private schools. I suppose I was one of those fortunate silver-spooned kids. But as much as I was surrounded by money, it wasn't something my family ever emphasized. It was there, and it was at our disposal, but it was never really discussed in-depth.

My father invested all the money he received when he sold Simon and Schuster in 1952. He put a significant chunk of it in trust funds for my sisters and I, which would kick in when we turned 21.

At 21, I was studying at Boston University to get my degree in photography and broadcasting. All of a sudden, I was presented with this large sum of money, about $60,000. My father had also set it up so that I was given small increments of money each month from my trust fund. I guess he did that to ensure that I wouldn't blow the whole thing at once, and to give me some security with a regular income.

I wasn't raised to be very money conscious. My mother did teach me to be careful with what I had because it might not always be there, but I didn't quite know what to do with $60,000. On instinct, I put most of it away in a savings account while I finished my degree, and I used the living stipend to do just that: live.

Hippy Times

I was a product of the times: a hippy who lived a minimalist lifestyle. I consciously rejected material possessions and the quest for power and greed. When I graduated from Boston University, I decided to follow my hippy desires. It sounds pretty wild now, but at the time it wasn't so far-fetched. I needed a place to live, so a friend and I decided to buy a commune together. I took some of the money from my inheritance, and together we bought a rundown farmhouse up in Vermont. For two years, I lived on this commune in the woods with a dozen or so of my friends. It was a two-year experiment in living, a strangely unstructured, yet loving environment. When it was time to move on, I sold the commune, and actually made a small profit from the sale.

Since I was no longer part of communal living, I still needed a place to live. So I took the money from the sale of the commune, and I bought a small house on Martha's Vineyard. The rest of the money I socked away in savings. Ten years later, when I sold the little house to move into something more spacious, my original investment had quadrupled in value. Not bad for a first investment, although it was not my primary intent at the time.

Investing in Me

Once I was settled and I had a place to live, the next line of business was a job. With some of the money I had left over, I purchased photography equipment and built a darkroom in my house. I wasn't frivolous with the money I had, but instead invested on instinct. For me, where I spent my money was a no-brainer: I needed someplace to live, so I bought a house;

I wanted to be a photographer, so I bought equipment.

When I was just starting out in photography, I took a lot of photos of rock stars. What better way to combine my passions of rock music and photography than to take pictures of the icons? I started to build a name for myself, and pretty soon magazines and newspapers approached me for assignments. Today, I still make time for creative photography, but the lucrative side and—unfortunately, in my opinion—the not-so-creative side of it all, comes from taking portraits and weddings during the summer months here on the Vineyard. I also sell some of my landscape photos in galleries in the area. And all those shots I took of rock stars back in the day are serendipitously beginning to pay off. I still sell a lot of those images to stock houses for reprint use, and to individuals who love historical photographs of people like Bob Marley, Jerry Garcia, or Bob Dylan.

My trust fund money has also allowed me to take some risks and to branch out into other creative projects. For the most part, these projects have been successful, and I make my money back and then some. I put out a Vineyard calendar every year. I also publish posters, limited-edition prints, and I have had 10 photography books published on various subject matter, the last two of which I published myself. Had I never received my inheritance, I wouldn't have been able to fund this sort of venture. It turned out to be successful both creatively and monetarily.

When my mom passed away in 1985, I received the final payments of my trust fund in one lump sum, about $300,000. Most of the money went right into the stock market for my retirement years. But I did take some of the money to pursue my lifelong dream: music production. I scoured the streets of Martha's Vineyard to find good, raw, local talent. I mixed these local artists with nationally renowned artists who visit the island, such as Richie Havens, Jonathan Edwards, and one of my sisters, Carly Simon. So far, I have three CDs under my belt: *Vineyard Sound Vols. I, II, and III*, and I hope to continue music production on an off-season basis. In the music business, anything is possible.

I have to admit that I haven't made back the money I invested in these projects yet, but hopefully I will. It's been a lot of hard work, but it's also been a lot of fun. And now, at 50, I have acquired this brand-new skill through on-the-job training. I am talented at music production, and I have reached a point where people are hiring me to produce music for them. But again, without my inheritance, I probably wouldn't have been able to venture into the music world. I am very fortunate. The music business is fickle and unpredictable, so it's probably the biggest gamble I've taken so far.

Trusting Advice

One of the greatest benefits of this trust fund, of this financial infrastructure, is that I have had the freedom to pursue my creative endeavors without having to have a nine-to-five job. I have been able to afford the luxury of freelance photography and music producing on my own schedule.

While I doubt I'll ever be rich in the sense that my father was, I am basically happy with the lifestyle balance I have struck. I have more free time than most people I know, and I spend it sharing quality time with my wife, Ronni, and my son, Willie (something for which my own dad hardly had the opportunity)—playing sports, gardening, socializing, and simply enjoying the passage of time in general.

I would advise anyone who suddenly gets a lucky chunk of money to use it wisely. Use it toward building a foundation and future. Invest in what you find most enjoyable, with an eye toward making those passions pay off someday. I realize I hardly have all the answers, but this sort of philosophy has, fortunately, worked for me.

Credits

"Risk versus Reality" on page 76 was adapted from *Understanding and Managing Investment Risk* by Forum for Investor Advice (Bethesda, Maryland). Copyright © 1997 by Forum for Investor Advice. Reprinted by permission.

"Mutual Agreement" on page 81 was adapted from *Questions You Should Ask Before You Invest in a Mutual Fund* by Investment Company Institute, Washington, D.C. Reprinted by permission.

"The Cost of Improvement" chart on page 99 was reprinted from the November 1997 issue of *Remodeling* magazine. Copyright © 1997 by Hanley-Wood, Inc. Reprinted by permission.

"Are You in Trouble?" on page 125 was adapted from the Debt Test questionnaire by the National Foundation for Consumer Credit. Copyright © 1995 by Ken Scott. Reprinted by permission.

Index

Note: Underscored page references indicate boxed text.

Automated teller machine (ATM)
fees, 36, 37, 38
patterns in using, 14
questions about, 37
Automobile, buying, 116–20, 117, 118–19

Bonds
corporate, 82–83
risks of, 69–70
short-term, 65
Brokerage houses, 37
Budget, setting up, 24–25, 26–27

A

AAA (American Automobile Association), 51, 111
AAA (Area Agency on Aging), 129
AARP, 129
Accordion file, for organizing bills, 9
Accounting programs, computer, 9, 10, 11
Accounting tools, 5–7, 6–7
Adjustable-rate mortgages (ARMs), 94–95
Advisors, financial. *See* Financial planners
Affinity cards, pros and cons of, 40–41
American Association of Individual Investors, 69
American Association of Retired Persons (AARP), 129
American Automobile Association (AAA), 51, 111
American Express, 38
America Online, 57
Amortization tables, 6
Annuity, pension payments and, 135
Appraisals, property, 101
Area Agency on Aging (AAA), 129
ARMs, 94–95
Assets
allocation of, 68, 75
financial planners in managing, 28
invested, 18
use, 18
Associated Press, for investment data, 85

B

Banking
by telephone, 7, 34
checking accounts and, 37
electronic, 34–35
financial instutitions for, selecting, 36–37, 37
interest rates and, 34–35
online, 10–13, 11, 35
overdraft protection and, 35
savings accounts and, 65
traditional, 35
Bankruptcy. *See also* Debt
credit mismanagement and, 124
impact of, long-term, 32, 124, 126
increases in, recent, 38, 124
personal, determining, 125
reasons for, 124
types of, 124–26
Banks, 36, 37
Barron's National Business and Financial Weekly, for financial updates, 6
Bill-paying
approaches to, 9
automatic, 34
by telephone, 7
computer and, 9, 10, 11
credit cards and, 42–43
debtor tricks and, 44–45
electronic, 34–35
"float" and, 44–45
juggling, 45
timing of, 42–43
traditional, 35
utilities and, 43
"Blue Book," for car prices, 117, 118

C

Calculator, 5–6
Car
buying, 116–20, 117, 118–19
leasing, 120
Career-average pension payments, 132
Cash-balance pension plan, 132
Cash reserves, 24, 46, 70
CDs, 65
Central Registration Depository, 31
Certificates of deposit (CDs), 65
Certified financial planners (CFPs), 29
CFA, 3, 28, 30
CFCs, 29
CFPs, 29
Chapter 7 of U.S. Bankruptcy Code, 124–26
Chapter 11 of U.S. Bankruptcy Code, 124, 126
Chapter 13 of U.S. Bankruptcy Code, 124, 126
Charge cards, 38–39
Charities, donating to, 50, 89
Charles Schwab and Company, 13, 83
Chartered financial consultants (CFCs), 29
Checking accounts, 37
Clothing, savings tips for buying, 49–52
COBRA, 107
Cobranding, credit cards and, 41
Collection agencies, 123
College savings plans, 112–15, 114–15
Company credit cards, 40–41

Computer. *See also* Internet
  accounting programs, 9, 10, 11
  as accounting tool, 6
  bill-paying and, 9, 10, 11
  investing by, 83
  for money management, 10–13, 11
  shopping by, 56–57
Consolidated Omnibus Budget Reconciliation Act (COBRA) of 1985, 107
Consumer Credit Counseling Service, 32
Consumer Federation of America (CFA), 3, 28, 30
Consumer Price Index, 15
Consumer Reports, 6, 54, 56–57, 60, 120
Corporate bonds, 82–83
Coupons, store, 62
Credit agencies, 31, 123
Credit cards
  affinity cards, 40–41
  cobranding and, 41
  company, 40–41
  credit lines, 39–40
  debt, 23, 38–39
  fees, 38
  grace periods and, 39
  interest rates of, 19, 40
  lost or stolen, 105
  managing, 39–41
  paying, 42–43
  types of, 38–39
Credit ratings, 123
Credit unions, 36

D

Dallas Morning News, for investment data, 74
Debit cards, 39
Debt. *See also* Bankruptcy
  collection agencies and, 123
  counselors, 32
  credit card, 23, 38–39
  credit ratings and, 123
  credit repairmen and, 32
  managing, 121–23, 123
  in net worth measurement, 19
  paying off, 23, 42
  rights regarding, 123
Debtor tricks, 44–45
Defined benefit pension plans, 136
Defined contribution pension plans, 136
Dependents, tax deductions for, 90
Dining A La Card, 51
Dining out, savings tips for, 52
Discount brokers, 31–32

E

Earnings report releases, 15
Eating out, savings tips for, 52
EDGAR, for investment data, 13
Ed IRAs, 88–89, 142
Edmund's Automobile Buyer's Guides Web site, for car prices, 117, 117, 120
Education savings plans, 112–15, 114–15
  Ed IRAs, 88–89, 142
Electronic Data Gathering Analysis and Retrieval (EDGAR), for investment data, 13
Electronic banking, 34–35
Employee Stock Ownership Plan (ESOP), 140
Entertainment Publications, discount coupons from, 53
Entertainment, savings tips for, 53, 53
Equifax Incorporated, for credit ratings, 31, 123
Equity, home, 96
ESOP, 140
Expenses, controlling, 14–15, 16–17, 24–25
Experian, for credit ratings, 31, 123

F

Fair Debt Collection Protection Act, 123
Fannie Mae, 92
Fat Cat Web site, for investment data, 13
Federal Home Loan Mortgage Corporation (Freddie Mac), 92
Federal Insurance Contributions Act (FICA) taxes, 90–91, 139
Federal National Mortgage Association (Fannie Mae), 92
Federal Open Market Committee, 15
Federal Reserve System, 15
Fee-offset, financial planners and, 30
FICA taxes, 90–91, 139
Fidelity Investments, 83
Final-average payment of pension, 132
Financial aid officers, 114–15
Financial awareness, 3
Financial institutions, 36–37, 37
Financial plan, need for, 2–3
Financial planners
  in asset management, 28
  choosing, 28–32, 30–31
  fees for, 29–30, 83
  limitations of, 2
  in money management, 28–29, 29, 30–31, 32
  services provided by, 29
  successful, 32, 148–55
  types of, 29
"Float," bill-paying and, 44–45
Flood insurance, 101
Forbes, for financial updates, 6
Fortune, for financial updates, 6
Forum for Investor Advice, 69, 75
Foundation for Accountability, 109
401(k)s
  advantages of, 136
  choices regarding, 136–37

improving on company's, 138–39
income taxes and, 88
investments, 137–39
monitoring, 137
strategies, 137–39
Freddie Mac, 92

G

General Agreement on Tariffs and Trade (GATT) treaty, 135
Goal-setting, financial
changing and adapting to goals, 23
defining goals, 4
issues in, 22–23
in money management, 22–23, 23
steps in, 4, 22–23
Grace periods, credit cards and, 39
Growth funds, 138

H

Health Association of America, 109
Health insurance, 104–9, 107, 108–9
Health maintenance organizations (HMOs), 105–8, 108–9
Hedge programs, investments and, 76
HMOs, 105–8, 108–9
HO-1 property insurance, 100
HO-2 property insurance, 100
HO-3 property insurance, 101
HO-4 property insurance, 104
Home. *See also* Mortgages
equity, 96
flood insurance for, 101
improvements, 97–99, 99
investing in, 97–99, 99
investments versus, 18, 96
moving and, 97
possessions in, inventory of, 102–3
property insurance and, 100–103, 101, 102–3
replacement value and, 101–2
sale of, 89–90
Home office
income taxes and, 90
insurance and, 104
organizing, for money management, 8
Hope Scholarship, tax savings and, 114

I

IAs, 29
Ibbotson Associates, 72, 75
IBM Corporation, 15
Inc., for financial updates, 6
Income taxes, 88–91, 89, 91
Individual retirement accounts. *See* IRAs
Inflation, 23, 113
tables, 6
Institute of Certified Financial Planners, 65
Insurance
buying, by telephone, 7
flood, 101
health, 104–9, 107, 108–9
life, 110–11, 111
long-term, 25, 129
in net worth measurements, 18–19
private mortgage, 95
property, 100–103, 101, 102–3
renters, 104
Interest rates
banking and, 34–35
compound, 23
of credit cards, 19, 40
Federal Reserve System and, 15
importance of, 15
Internal Revenue Service (IRS), 88, 89, 135
International Business Machine (IBM) Corporation, 15
Internet. *See also* Computer; *specific Web sites*
researching investments on, 12–13
sales tax and, 59
shopping on, 56–57
Inventory, making personal, 3–4
Invested assets, net worth and, 18
Investments. *See also* Savings; *specific types*
balancing, 70–71, 70–71
bonds
corporate, 82–83
risks of, 69–70
short-term, 65
buying, 82–83
by computer, 83
choices, 74–79, 75, 76–77, 78
diversifying, 71
401(k), 137–39
hedge programs and, 76
home improvements as, 97–99, 99
home purchase versus, 18, 96
Internet in researching, 12–13
knowledge about, 84, 85, 86
long-term strategies for, 86
maintaining, 84, 85, 86
mutual funds
no-load, 82
prospectus for, questions about, 81
researching, 74–75
retirement and, 146
variety of, 71
personality types and, 75–77, 78
price movements and, 86
prospectuses for, reading, 80–81, 81
risks versus reality of, 76–77
stocks
buying and selling, 7, 79
fad, 73
growth, 69
large-cap, 69
mid-cap, 69
prices of, 69
pump-and-dump, 70

Investments *(continued)*
stocks *(continued)*
small-cap, 69
value, 69
variety of, 68–69
timing of, 72–73, 73
Investment advisors (IAs), 29
Investment clubs, 31
Investment Company Institute, 81
IRAs
Education (Ed), 88–89, 142
Keogh plans, 143
rollover, 133, 135, 142–43
Roth IRA-Plus, 142, 142–43
SEP-IRAs, 143
simple, 143
traditional, 141
"I" rate, for mutual funds, 82
IRS, 88, 89, 135
IRS rule 72T, 401(k) and, 144–45

K

Kelley Blue Book Used Car Guide, for car prices, 117, 118
Keogh plans, 143
Kiplinger's Personal Finance Magazine, for financial updates, 7

L

Layoffs, 64, 107
Lease, for car, 120
Liabilities, 19. *See also* Debt
Life expectancy, determining, 145
Life insurance, 110–11, 111
Lifestyle Funds, 71
Lifetime Learning Credit, tax savings and, 114
Line of credit, 35
Loans. *See* Debt
Long-term insurance, 25, 129
Lump-sum pension payments, 135

M

Manufacturer's suggested retail price (MSRP), for cars, 117
Microsoft Money software, 9, 10, 11
Mission statement, personal, 4
Money, for financial updates, 7
Money management
budget for, 24–25, 26–27
computer in, 10–13, 11
financial planners in, 28–29, 29, 30–31, 32
goal-setting in, 22–23, 23
mindset for, 2–4
net worth and, measuring, 18–19, 20–21
organizational tasks for, 8–9
real-life scenarios, 148–63
spending habits, controlling, 14–15, 16–17, 24–25
telphone in, 6–7
tools for, accounting, 5–7, 6–7
Money market accounts, 65
Moody's ratings, of bonds, 70
Morningstar ratings, of mutual funds, 13, 74
Morningstar Web site, for investment data, 13
Mortgages
adjustable-rate, 94–95
importance of, 92
as liability, 19
paying off, 43, 93
points and, lender, 92–93
private insurance for, 95
reverse, 96–97
tables for, 95
tips for better deals on, 92–94
Motley Fool Web site, for investment data, 13
MSRP, for cars, 117
Mutual funds
Internet and, 13
no-load, 82
prospectus for, questions about, 81
researching, 74–75
retirement and, 146
variety of, 71

N

NADA Web site, for car prices, 117
NASDAQ index, 15, 83
NASD Regulation Web site, for broker information, 13
National Association of Home Builders, 96
National Association of Independent Insurers, 101
National Association of Securities Dealers, 81
National Association of Securities Dealers Automated Quotation System (NASDAQ) index, 15, 83
National Automobile Dealers Association (NADA) Web site, for car prices, 117
National Center for Retirement Benefits, 133
National Committee for Quality Assurance (NCQA), 108–9
National Flood Insurance Program, 101
National Foundation for Consumer Credit, 125
National Practitioner Database, 109
NationsBank, 3
NAV, 85
NCQA, 108–9
Negotiating prices, 60–62, 61
Net asset value (NAV), 85
Net worth, measuring, 18–19, 20–21
Newsweek, for HMO rankings, 109
New York Stock Exchange, 83
New York Times, for investment data, 74
No-load mutual funds, 82
No-load options, 82

O

Office supplies, 6
Online banking, 10–13, 11, 35
Orange County Register, for investment data, 74
Overdraft protection, 35

P

Paperwork, 8–9. *See also* Bill-paying
PCPs, 106
Pension Benefit Guaranty Corporation, 133
Pension plans, 132–35, 133
Pension Rights Center, 133
Pension and Welfare Benefits Administration, 137
Personal financial specialists (PFSs), 29
PFPs, 29
PFSs, 29
PMI, 95
Point of service (POS) plans, 105–6, 109
Points, lender, 92–93
POS plans, 105–6, 109
Preferred provider organizations (PPOs), 105, 108–9
Price movements, interpreting, 86
Primary care physicians (PCPs), 106
Private health insurance plans, 109
Private mortgage insurance (PMI), 95
Producer Price Index, 15
Product complaints, 49
Professional financial planners (PFPs), 29
Property insurance, 100–103, 101, 102–3
Prospectuses, reading, 80–81, 81

Q

Quicken software, 9, 10, 11

R

Recalc method for life expectancy, IRAs and, 145
Record-keeping, 8–9. *See also* Bill-paying
Registered investment advisors (RIAs or IAs), 29
Renters insurance, 104
Replacement value of home, 101–2
Reserve credit, 35
Reserves, cash, 24, 46, 70
Restaurant savings tips, 52
Retirement
  401(k)s
    advantages of, 136
    choices regarding, 136–37
    improving company's, 138–39
    income taxes and, 88
    investments, 137–39
    monitoring, 137
    strategies for, 137–39
  IRAs
    Education (Ed), 88–89, 142
    Keogh plans, 143
    rollover, 133, 135, 142–43
    Roth IRA-Plus, 142, 142–43
    SEP-IRAs, 143
    simple, 143
    traditional, 141
  long-term insurance and, 129
  mutual funds and, 146
  pension plans and, 132–35, 133
  planning for, 128–29, 129
  saving for, 25
  Social Security and, 130–31, 131
  withdrawals and, 144–46
Reverse mortgages, 96–97
RIAs, 29
Rollover IRAs, 133, 135, 142–43
Roth IRA-Plus, 142, 142–43

S

Sales schemes, 61
Sales tax, 58–59, 59
Savings, 66–67
  investing versus, 66–67
  reasons for, 64–65
Savings accounts, 65
Schedule C tax form, 89
SEC. *See* Securities and Exchange Commission
Secured credit cards, 39
Securities and Exchange Commission (SEC), 30, 31, 81
  Web site, 13
Securities Insurance Protection Corporation, 32
SEP-IRAs, 143
Shopping
  for big-ticket purchases, 64–65
  coupons and, 62
  on Internet, 56–57
  maximizing time spent on, 54–57, 55, 57
  negotiating prices and, 60–62, 61
  sales schemes and, 61
  sales tax and, 58–59, 59
  savings tips for, 48–52
Simple IRAs, 143
Simplified employee pension IRAs, 143
Single-company cards, 39
SmartMoney, for financial updates, 7
Social Security, 130–31, 131
Social Security Administration, 131
Spending
  frugal
    for clothing, 49–52
    complaints about products and, 49
    for entertainment, 53
    mindset for, 48–49
    organizations aiding in, 51
    at restaurants, 52
    for travel, 52–53
  habits, controlling, 14–15, 16–17, 24–25
  splurging, times for, 53
Standard and Poor's 500 index, for investment data, 70, 77

Stocks
buying and selling, 7, 79
fad, 73
growth, 69
large-cap, 69
mid-cap, 69
prices of, 69
pump-and-dump, 70
small-cap, 69
value, 69
variety of, 68–69
Stockbrokers, 13, 31–32
Stock indexes, 15
Straight bankruptcy, 125

T

Tax(es)
Federal Insurance Contributions Act, 90–91, 139
income, 88–91, 89, 91
sales, 58–59, 59
withdrawals of financial resources and, 146
withholding, 90–91
Taxpayer Relief Act of 1997, 88, 91
Telephone, in money management, 6–7
Term-certain method for life expectancy, IRAs and, 145
Term life insurance, 110–11
Thriftiness, 48–53, 49, 51, 53
Tools for money management, 5–7, 6–7
Trans Union Corporation, for credit ratings, 31, 123
Travel, savings tips for, 52–53
Treasury bills, short-term, 65
Truth in Lending Statement, 93
Tuition plans, 112–15, 114–15

U

UGMA, 114
Unemployment, 64, 107
rates, 15
Uniform Gift to Minors Act (UGMA), 114
Uniform Transfers to Minors Act (UTMA), 114
U.S. Bankruptcy Code, 124–26
U.S. Department of Labor, 140
U.S. government bonds, 83
U.S. News and World Report, for HMO rankings, 109
U.S. Public Interest Research Group, 12
Use assets, net worth and, 18
Used car, buying, 118–19
Utility bills, paying, 43
UTMA, 114

V

Vacation, splurging on, 53
Value funds, 138

W

Wallet, organizing, 46–47, 47
Wall Street Insurance Group, 110
Wall Street Journal, for investment data, 7, 74
Whole life insurance, 111
Withdrawals of financial resources, guidelines for, 144–46
Withholding taxes, 90–91
Worksheets
budget, 26–27
expenses, 16–17
net worth measurement, 20–21
World Wide Web. *See* Internet
Worth, for financial updates, 7